Warriors and Kings

Warriors and Kings

The 1500-Year Battle for Celtic Britain

MARTIN WALL

AMBERLEY

In loving memory of Elsie and Andrew

First published 2017

Amberley Publishing
The Hill, Stroud
Gloucestershire, GL5 4EP

www.amberley-books.com

British Library Cataloguing in Publication Data.
A catalogue record for this book is available from the British Library.

ISBN 978 1 4456 5843 8 (print)
ISBN 978 1 4456 5844 5 (ebook)

Typesetting and Origination by Amberley Publishing.
Printed in the UK.

Contents

Introduction

The idea of a 'Celtic' civilisation has been, and remains, controversial, and like many other subjugated cultures and peoples, such as the Native Americans, it has proven easy to romanticise them in retrospect. That we wish to do so tells us something about our own guilty secrets, and our own fallen times. We seek noble savages, courageous heroes, gallant knights of old and the fabled towers of Camelot as psychological refuges from the vapid, aimless march of consumerism, with its beguiling electronic hallucinations. The collapse of the Church and its possible extinction has left a spiritual void, and nature abhors a vacuum. A resistance fighter, a hero, destined to transfigure the world and initiate an age of gallantry, romance, and redemption, even if he is a mere phantasm of a senescent mythology, is sorely needed. Celtic traditions have bequeathed us the supreme folk-hero in the shape of 'King Arthur', and this myth has retained its miraculous potency even in the computer age. But King Arthur, while he is the supreme exemplar of the traditions of the Celts, does not stand alone. Over two thousand years of history a long line of Celtic warriors and kings have shown their resistance to all comers – Romans, Saxons, Vikings and Normans.

The Celts were almost physically intermeshed with the land, with deep spiritual connections to it, hallowed by centuries of ritual and embodied in the shape of their kings. Their heroic defence of this inheritance lasted for almost 1,500 years, an epic testament to their resilience, comradeship, loyalty, and sense of honour.

1

Their adversaries included some of the most fearsome military powers in history. Undaunted, the 'Brythons' or Britons, as they originally called themselves, fought to the last, and even today their descendants are stirring once more, acutely aware of their noble predecessors and their sacrifice. Today, only the Republic of Ireland has political independence, while the subjugated Celtic nations are dependencies of Britain and France. The struggles for Irish independence are beyond the scope of this book, and it is only proper that they should be commemorated by a historian from that island. Irish, Scottish and Breton affairs will impinge on my story only insofar as they influenced events in Britain as a whole. Nevertheless, the same fanatical belief in their destiny, their right to be free, to speak their own tongue, and worship their God that inspired the Irish revolutionaries, can be seen time and again in the pages that follow. The complex mythology that underpinned Celtic religious belief has given the Celts a reputation for being irrational, almost suicidal, always prey to their own dreams and visions. But their impractical and often doomed schemes were not ultimately futile, and their heroism, endurance and self-sacrifice ensured the survival of their precious culture and languages, and gave the world stories to inspire the downtrodden and despised, the 'wretched of the earth', which will still be told in a thousand years, tales that became the underpinning lore of the greatest empire in history. But they gave us something more than that, the desperate hope that one day the golden days will return, and 'all wrong will be made right'.

Martin Wall

1

An Ancient Land

The liminal region between England and Wales; these borderlands exemplify peace and calm and timeless beauty, but beneath the surface lies a past. The verdant pastures are a thin integument, cloaking events of great violence and high drama down the ages, indeed in many places the ruins of castles and forts still protrude through the thin screen of modernity, shattered monuments lowering over the landscape like rotten teeth. There is one line marked in the landscape that defines the Welsh borderlands, the incredible work called Offa's Dyke. The 149-mile-long linear earthwork was attributed to the King of Mercia, Offa (reigned AD 757–96), by Asser, the Welsh scholar who wrote a life of King Alfred of Wessex. Asser said the dyke ran from 'sea to sea', from the Dee Estuary to the Severn Estuary, the Môr Hafren or 'Severn Sea' as the Welsh call it. There is considerable dispute about whether it was in fact the work of the mighty Mercian king, even though the Welsh themselves call it 'Clawdd Offa' to this day. If he did order its construction in the 780s it was one of the supreme engineering projects of the early Middle Ages, but some think it may be the lost 'Wall of Severus', supposed to have been built hundreds of years before by the African Roman Emperor, Septimius Severus. A hearth was discovered beneath Wat's Dyke (a companion earthwork to Offa's Dyke), which was covered over in the construction in the late fifth century. Steve Blake and Scott Lloyd in *The Keys to Avalon* (Shaftesbury, 2000) cite the sixth-century historian Procopius of Caesarea, who says that a tradition existed that 'the souls of the departed were conducted to that place'. Whoever built it, and whenever they did it, the structure has remained as an enduring boundary between two cultures, languages, and nations – the English and the Welsh – for at least 1,200 years. Naturally intertwined with the slopes and ridges in some parts, such as Clun Forest, in others it imposes itself on the lowlands, where it would have been a continuous palisade atop an embankment many metres high with a 4-metre-wide ditch in front of it. If it were to be undertaken today it would be a major strategic project that would require thousands of men to complete. Even with what seems a simple and straightforward historical 'fact' such as Offa's Dyke, we find we are immediately confronted by contention and controversy, and that is why these borderlands retain their mystery and magic. There is almost too much history to take in. But if we are to make a start, we must go back way beyond Offa of Mercia, before the Romans and the Celts, and try to conceive of the area as it was when the first people that we would recognise as similar to ourselves arrived.

During the Stone Age, isolated bands of itinerant hunters roamed around in a seasonal cycle. We find the simple tools they used, stone axe heads, flint arrowheads and the like, all over the British Isles. The very earliest pioneers were so few in number that it has been supposed artefacts found in Kent's Cavern in Devon and Creswell Crags in Derbyshire were left behind by the same small group, so similar are they (see *Stone Age Britain* by Nicholas Barton, London, 1997). Sir Winston Churchill in his *A History of the English Speaking Peoples* (London, 1956) thought that there may have been only a handful of original clans of this type in the whole of Britain; humankind was rare, almost an endangered species. In the early nineteenth century a skeleton was found in a cave in west Wales. It was originally thought to have been the remains of a woman and was dubbed the 'Red Lady' because it had been stained with ochre and grave goods included mammoth-ivory bracelets and periwinkle shells. By the prejudices of the time this indicated a female, but in fact the 'Red Lady of Paviland' was a young man, buried with high honour over 20,000 years ago. Perhaps it was a sense of their own rarity that caused these early humans to honour their dead with such ceremony. Not long after the young man was buried, the glaciers began to encroach south again. People left what is now Britain and took refuge for thousands of years in Spain, particularly around the Basque region. But as soon as the ice sheets retreated they returned, as the rich quarry of game extended their range north again. These were a people whose entire life depended upon the hunt, for meat, and skins, as well as bones from which they made utilitarian items and the kind of personal adornments buried in the Paviland cave. Yet they too were hunted. The wolf, the bear and the wild cat prowled near their encampments, watched from concealment the fire-glow outside the cave entrance in the cold night. Mammoths lumbered over the bleak, forbidding landscape. It is too easy to imagine such scenes and then dismiss our ancestors as benighted savages and indeed until quite recent times this was our conception of them. The increase in the number of humans and the complexity of their social organisation arose, in part, from climatic change. Around 13,000 years ago an interstadial, that is drier and warmer, period commenced. There was a corresponding expansion of forest, and the woods were teeming with game, deer, bears, even aurochs (giant cattle), but 11,000 years ago the ice began to encroach again. Suddenly, maybe in the space of a few generations, it retreated once more. Britain was covered in dense woods of birch oak and ash. Then, 8,000 years ago came a colossal event: Britain was suddenly sundered from the European mainland and became an island, as sea levels rose to engulf what had been a broad plain under what is now the North Sea. The final inundation may have taken place within one day. If we think of this as a catastrophe, cutting the island folk off from the rest of the world, we would be mistaken. British-based bronze metalworkers were trading overseas 4,500 years ago; for those near the coasts the sea was not a barrier, rather it facilitated wider contacts, whereas those deep inland remained in relative cultural isolation. There were specific zones of maritime contact with the outside world, the east, approximately East Anglia, Lincolnshire and Humberside, and the south-east, Kent and Sussex, facing northern France. In a narrow strip, stretching along the western littoral (strangely, along a line drawn approximately where Celtic languages survive today), west Wales, Brittany, Man, and west Scotland and the

Hebrides, there was a thriving culture of sea-faring. These western, Atlantic-facing areas were also in contact with Ireland. What must be understood is that from the very earliest times western Britain has been influenced by the sea. From Brittany, past Cornwall, Wales, the Mevanian Islands of Anglesey and Man, on to the Hebrides and the Orkneys and Shetlands, a highway for trade and cultural exchange existed. The inhabitants of the west had more in common with folk dwelling along this western seaboard than with their insular, eastern neighbours. This sense of a cultural unity of these peoples at what we would now describe disparagingly as 'the Celtic margins', was so deep-rooted that it survived right through the Roman imperial period, and indeed has not quite been extinguished today. The people eventually came to know themselves as 'Britons', but Britons existed in an arc from central Scotland to the Loire. Pytheas of Massalia, a Greek traveller, had called the islanders *Pretanike*, meaning 'the Painted People', or 'People of the Designs', because of the crazy whirling shapes warriors wore on their skin. This morphed into Britannia, but Britannia (more anciently Albionon), the main island, was not the only 'Britain'. The early Welsh persisted in calling that country 'Britannia', but there was another, Britannia Minor (what we call Brittany today), and in north-west Spain there was a British enclave called 'Britonia' who were refugees from the Anglo-Saxons, before it was overwhelmed by continental barbarian invasions (see *Wales and The Britons, 350–1064* by Thomas Charles-Edwards, Oxford, 2012). The Roman province called 'Britannia Prima', the whole of south-west Britain, contained the region upon which this book mainly concentrates, which was for many centuries situated within this western-focused culture.

This divide between east and west was striking, even to the Roman writer Tacitus, who noted the resemblance of the Silures tribe of south Wales to the Spaniards with their dark features and curly black hair. Ultimately it is worthwhile to consider just how deep a divide this really represents. The folk of the southern and eastern lowlands were probably almost all descended from fair-headed, fair-skinned, blue-eyed immigrants from the European mainland, but in the west migration had come from Iberia and the Atlantic seaboard, people whose movements probably commenced in North Africa, originally. Perhaps here we have the origins of the 'little dark Welshman' of the English imagination? What political arrangements prevailed we do not know, but the population at the time was tiny, probably under 1 million for the whole of Great Britain. Sometime around 3,200 years ago this ancient society underwent a change, as significant as the Industrial Revolution was to our culture, perhaps even more profound than that. Coalitions or congeries of clans must have come together and distributed the land among themselves, and instead of tiny scattered communities, large villages were built and tribal zones marked out by dykes, fosses and similar earthworks. Field systems were laid out, which are still clearly visible from the air today. Ditched enclosures and hill forts began to appear, which may have had a dual function as grounds for fairs and feasting centres, as well as refuges in time of conflict. Just as in the Industrial Revolution later, Britain was at the forefront of technical development. The ubiquitous metal of that time, bronze, was an alloy of copper and tin, and western Britain had abundant quantities of both ores. This made the island wealthy and powerful. A dominant elite must have existed, whose chieftains or kings were capable of organising the huge outlay of labour entailed in erecting the megalithic monuments. Before long the entire area corresponding to the Welsh border was thickly dotted with hill forts, attesting to the wealth and status of the communities they served. It would appear that about 3,000 years ago this wealthy and outward looking culture in the west became temporarily pre-eminent. During a relative lull in immigration across the North Sea and the English Channel, there was a sudden upsurge in longer distance Atlantic maritime trade. Phoenician colonies at Gades (modern Cadiz) and elsewhere along the Lusitanian coast had begun regular large-scale trade with Britain for tin, copper, and finished bronze. They brought with them new, longer swords and burnished bronze shields, which soon caught on among the British tribal elites. At this time Britain first entered into the imagination of the classical world, and it is no accident that it was just about then that the megalithic monument building probably reached its zenith. In 1833 an astonishing discovery was made near Mold in Flintshire. It was a 'cape' of sheet-gold, of exquisite workmanship and design. It was likely part of the ritual dress of one of the priests or priestesses of the local tribe, people whose wealth derived from trade in precious copper and salt. Now in the British Museum, it shows just how sophisticated this culture must have been. What is perhaps more extraordinary, was that the place was called Bryn-yr-Ellyllon, 'the hill of the fairies', and local people avoided the place at night, lest they see the ghostly shade of a man dressed in a golden gown, 'the king of the hill'. If these stories are true, then it is possible that they preserved folk-memories going back over 3,500 years. But, just as this rich and ancient culture was opening like a flower, a new danger was emerging. Immigrants from the Continent began to arrive in the south-east. They had perfected the technology for smelting iron, and this superior technology doomed the Bronze Age folk to obsolescence, changing the socio-economic, military and power relations of the times. The Iron Age had arrived. It seems clear that the transition was gradual, but thorough. It must have left a marked psychical impression on the folk-memory, and it is just possible that we may be able to reconstruct something of what went on from folk-mythic sources.

Until quite recently it was fashionable to conceive of the peopling of Britain as if it had taken place according to a fixed schedule, various folks arriving in waves, and asserting themselves by military superiority, in a chronological succession. It is not hard to see the reasoning behind such a perspective, and it may yet prove correct, but doubt has now been cast. Naturally, early experts in history at the elite universities saw that the Normans had come, before them the Vikings, before them the Anglo-Saxons, still further back the Romans, and in the remotest times they could then imagine, the 'Celts'. This prejudice meant that as even earlier waves of settlement were identified, the same principle was applied. Until the early twentieth century, the biblical account of human development was sacrosanct, and it too portrayed history as an orderly series of events. The *Leabar Gabhala Eireann* or 'Book of Invasions', a twelfth-century Irish text, purports to record the waves of migration into that island from prehistoric times, and may contain important factual evidence derived from folk traditions. But because it had to comport itself to the Christian and therefore biblical model of a fixed schedule of settlement, it too is suspect as a strictly historical document. So we are in a dilemma. Much of what we used to take for granted is now doubted, and the claims of experts in the field made only a few years ago are contested. It is only right that this should happen. It was an 'expert' of his time who created the myth of the 'Red Lady of Paviland'. But on the other hand, archaeology should not be allowed simply to overturn all our folk-traditions, because too often they contain a kernel of truth, as we will see time and again in the forthcoming pages. It seems to me though, that some sophisticated culture existed in Britain in the late Neolithic and Bronze Age that had oversight of the construction of the megaliths, and that the decline of that civilisation coincided with the coming of the Iron Age.

We think of the Anglo-Saxon and Viking invasions as two different events involving two distinct peoples. This is true, they came some hundreds of years apart, but the two folk were not very different: they came from the same original geographical area, and their languages were almost the same. The thing that differentiated the Normans was their language – Norman-French. But essentially they were all three the same type of people, arriving over centuries. Yet this is not how we imagine things, for we immediately conjure up pictures of all three peoples and their distinctive appearance, dress and military accoutrements. This is, I suggest, how we should think of the Celts. They came in at least three waves hundreds of years apart, all of them speaking Celtic languages, with some variations and inflexions. Their religion and their dress and their laws and their military methods were basically the same. But to each other and to outsiders it was clear that they were different peoples, with their own distinctive customs and territories. This throws up a very interesting question: were the people who preceded the Celts in Britain really so different from them? An Oxford scholar, Sir Barry Cunliffe, has even suggested that the Celtic diffusion began in the British Isles, spreading gradually eastward, and this would throw all we think we know on its head. The main evidence for separate 'waves' of Celtic immigration into Britain was long cited as the divergence in their languages between Goidelic (so-called 'Q-Celtic') and Brythonic (so-called 'P-Celtic') dialects. It was assumed that the Goidels or Gaels of the north and west of Britain and Ireland had been the 'first wave' of Celtic speakers. They sounded the letter 'Q' as something like '*cu*' or '*qu*', whereas Brythonic speakers sounded it as '*p*' or '*b*'. It was assumed that some struggles between the two groups, analogous to the Anglo-Viking wars had taken place, and that in the south-east the Brythons or Britons, had prevailed, driving the Goidels gradually west and north into the more desolate regions. Finally, a few hundred years before the Roman invasions, a third Celtic folk, the Belgae or 'boastful ones' arrived from France and Belgium, before they in turn were displaced by the Romans. It may be though, that these differences were overstated or misunderstood, for the 'Iberians' or pre-Celtic people may well have spoken a similar proto-Celtic language, derived from PIE (Proto-Indo-European), which we now think was the bedrock of most European speech. Jean Markale, a Breton scholar has made a study of this transition in his *The Celts* (Paris, 1976), in which he postulates that a tribe called the Cimbri may prove to be the 'missing link' between the Celts and the megalith builders.

In 113 BC, a massive tidal wave destroyed the homelands of the Cimbri in Jutland. They left as a folk entity and wandered around central Europe until they were repulsed by Bohemian tribes. They then made incursions into the lands of the Taurisci, who were allies of Rome. The Romans demanded that the Cimbri go elsewhere, but these poor desolated people were analogous to the refugees wandering through the Balkans in our own times. They insisted that Rome find them somewhere to go. Eventually they conjoined with the Teutones and Helvetii, two very numerous and powerful tribes, and in vast columns, perhaps 300,000 in total, they moved westwards. In their time the name of the Cimbri inspired sheer terror among the peoples of Western Europe (as the Huns were to do later), they overwhelmed armies sent against them and roamed around Germany, Gaul and Spain at will. Eventually they set their sights on Rome itself and crossed the Alps, but as soon as they reached Italy, vacillated and waited for their allies the Teutones who, unbeknown to them, had been annihilated by the Romans. They were in their turn annihilated. For a while all of Europe had dreaded these mysterious folk, but who were they? It was assumed for a long time that they must have been Celtic or Germanic. They came from areas of Germanic settlement and spoke a Celtic language, but what Markale suggests is that they were in fact the last remnants of the populations whose ancestors had constructed the megaliths centuries before. Driven to despair by gradual encroachment on their territory and culture by the Celts, and then finally undone by natural disasters, they made a final perambulation of the regions where their ancestors had once held sway, before being destroyed. Robert Graves, in his *The White Goddess* (London, 1948), proposed that an ancient Welsh poem '*Cad Goddeu*' or the 'Battle of the Trees' concerns a poetic or magical contest between the devotees of the gods Bran and Beli. This seems like a similar folk-memory of a struggle between the Celtic/Brythonic people and the earlier indigenous folk, and according to the (admittedly controversial) theory, the Brythons seized control of the national necropolis on Salisbury Plain – Stonehenge and its related monuments. A folk legend claims that 71,000 of the devotees of Bran were slaughtered in battle. If Graves was right in his hunch that Stonehenge was the centre of some ancient struggle in the fourth century BC, a claim partly based upon an extract from Geoffrey of Monmouth's *History of the Kings of Britain*, perhaps this may shed some light on the importance of these religious monuments to the Bronze Age people.

The Dissolution of the Monasteries took place in the sixteenth century, but Christianity, though much diminished thereby, still clings on, and Christian churches are still among our national treasures. I believe some such process must have happened with the megaliths. Their 'golden age' was long past, but there was still veneration and respect for them hundreds of years later. The people still made an attempt at devotional activity and tried to remember the sacred traditions. But the new culture was ascendant, theirs was in decline and, by the time the Romans arrived, the whole edifice, grandeur and wonder of the ancient world lay in ruins, largely as we see it today. The monuments became mysterious, even sinister – the haunts of ancient gods and demons, spirits of the dead.

It is just possible that in remote regions the predecessors of the Celts held out, like the Attacotti or 'ancient ones' of western Scotland. In the mountains of what is now Wales people stuck to their valleys; they did not move too far, and may have remained almost unaffected by the successive invasions. If, as seems likely, they spoke a Celtic-related language, over time they would have been subsumed by the new tribal cultures. In the next chapter we will examine this transformation into a 'Celtic' tribal society, but we must not forget that it overlaid an almost unimaginably ancient culture that had gone before – a time when it seemed like gods and giants had lived on earth. The spiritual infrastructure of the megalith builders still stood around them, evoking thoughts of magical beings and wizards of olden times. Such beings and spirits needed to be appeased, and this was one of the functions of a new priestly class: the Druids.

We have seen how one late-Roman historian, Procopius, had mentioned a 'wall' in Britain running north to south, which has suggested to Blake and Lloyd in *The Keys to Avalon* that the 'Wall of Severus' may have been in situ centuries before King Offa of Mercia, and that the dyke has been misattributed to him. They also mention the legend that the 'souls of the departed' were conducted to that place, and that living men could not cross this interface between the land of the living and the abodes of the dead. Now, while I am not a supporter of the 'Wall of Severus' theory, it is a fact that among the Iron Age folk of Britain and Ireland there *was* a long-standing superstition that the western lands were indeed the abode of the dead. To have 'gone west' still means that someone has 'passed over', and even today Gaelic speaking people in the West of Ireland still associate the western facing doorway of the house with the setting of the sun. The setting sun symbolised death, for reasons we will examine, and a complex superstition prevailed that the deceased souls of the dead were irresistibly drawn westwards, and that they foregathered around the offshore islands to the west of Ireland before disappearing from this world forever. In the first century AD, a sailor, Demetrius of Tarsus, reported to Plutarch that certain islands to the west of Britain were inhabited exclusively by holy men who conducted the souls of gods and heroes into the far west, where the 'mighty ones' departed, and that five days sailing beyond these islands, the god Chronos was confined. These tales are too numerous and well-attested to be mere accidents, and must recall some reciprocal relationship between the Celtic and pre-Celtic peoples of the Atlantic seaboard and the vast ocean into which the sun sank each evening. The psychical consequences of these notions for the Celts will become clearer as we proceed.

At last we have reached a point where strictly historical accounts exist that tell us a little bit about Britain, or at least Belerium, as the Atlantic tin-traders called Cornwall. On an offshore island tin ingots were exchanged, a place called Ictis, possibly St Michael's Mount near Marazion. On cliff promontories 'castles' were built, looking out to sea and defended by embankments. Souterrains, underground tunnels for storage, are often found in Cornwall, locally called 'fogous' and these features are also found in Brittany, suggesting close contact between the Atlantic peninsulas. The mariners must have penetrated even further than this – into south Wales, the Severn Estuary, south-western Ireland, and probably the copper mines of north Wales – but evidence of these contacts is limited and of an archaeological, rather than documentary, nature. This contact with sophisticated outsiders seems to have concentrated the minds of the ruling elites, who were determined to project their status and power by means of constructing massive hill forts, much bigger and more complex than their Bronze Age predecessors. In fact, even though defence against aggressors was one of their purposes, a more important aspect was likely the expression of power, community organisation and wealth they conveyed. During this period, from about 800 BC onwards, large-scale forest clearance was gathering pace, probably thanks to the iron axe. Large open fields and pastures surrounded the hill forts, and the timber required to smelt iron in large quantities contributed to the ongoing deforestation; it has been estimated that to produce each kilo of iron, 1 tonne of timber would have been required. As large buildings, imposing gateways and vast circuits of timber palisades were built, the countryside was denuded of its ancient woodland in areas in close proximity to larger settlements. It is possible that timber was used in large quantities to lay causeways across boggy areas, and these have been excavated in Ireland where the peatbogs have preserved them virtually intact.

The landscape was radically changed by all this activity, and the population probably expanded at a rapid rate. Alongside this growth came a stronger focus on ethnic and kinship relationships, in other words the emergence of a distinctive tribal culture. As we have seen, the word 'Celtic' conceals as much as it reveals about the diverse patchwork of tribal groupings. It was probably only comparatively late on in the Iron Age that defined folk-groupings we can identify emerged. Even then, the commonality of culture we think of as 'Celtic' was probably mediated by a ruling elite who predominated in the area between the Danube and the Atlantic littoral, those who could afford to commission the kind of superior metalworkers represented by the art of La Tene in Switzerland, where a huge cache of such objects was discovered in the nineteenth century. It seems that ironworkers were highly regarded, their skills seen as a kind of magic, and these smith-wizards would have enjoyed the protection of the tribal chieftain and his retinue. Specialists of this type were essential for the success and credibility of the tribal leadership, whose heroic military traditions were underpinned by the access to elite military gear, such as swords. In short, the world had become more complex, relationships more strictly defined and regulated, and the hill forts were intended to 'show off' this sophistication to the outside world, in just the same way as skyscrapers do in our day.

The area around the upper Severn and its tributaries became a nexus for these huge and labour-intensive structures. There had been hill forts in the Bronze Age throughout the Welsh borderlands and the western Midlands. Some of these were refurbished and their defences enhanced during the Iron Age, and it is only recently that their origins have been redesignated as Bronze Age. A recent survey utilising Lidar, a laser imaging technique, has revealed that the promontory hill fort at Kinver, Staffordshire, once thought to be Iron Age, is in fact considerably more ancient. It has been noted that more Celtic place names survive in Staffordshire than in Shropshire, and Kinver is one of them, possibly derived (according to the archaeologist Stephen J. Yeates) from the Celtic root words '*Cuno-Breigr*', translating as 'the fort of Cunomaglos' or the 'Hound Lord', a local god of the hunt. Dogs and horses were especially revered totem animals. More often, however, earlier forts were abandoned in favour of new structures. Proximity to the Severn was especially desirable and there were practical as well as 'ritual' reasons for this. Valuable commodities were traded downriver, such as copper and iron ingots and salt, but the Severn was considered a sacred waterway from the earliest times. The phenomenon of the Severn Bore, the second largest tidal surge in the world, causes spring tides to be funnelled into the estuary with a tidal range of 50 feet as it washes upriver. It is very probable that the astronomer-priests of the Druidic classes could predict these events and they took on magical overtones. Forts such as Old Oswestry, Breiddin, Fridd Faldwyn, Llwyn Bryn-Dinas, and many more, were all designed to be seen from a considerable distance, but other smaller forts like Kinver or Burf Castle at Mose, Shropshire, nearby the Severn, were less distinguished, probably because their functionality was oriented to quite local requirements. Not all hill forts are on hills. Some, such as Wall Camp in Shropshire, seem to have been 'marsh-forts' located in fens, which acted as a defence for the settlement without the need for a massive conscription of labourers. We may surmise that this need for defence was the overriding concern of the communities, and where the advantages of height and a clear view were not to be had, palisaded islets in boggy areas or surrounded by rivers or streams would do equally well. King Alfred the Great famously resorted to such an 'Isle', Athelney, as late as the ninth century. The siege of even a small hill fort would have been an extremely dangerous affair. The deep ditches surrounding the approaches to the gateways were designed as 'ankle-breakers' and the author can attest their effectiveness even after a lapse of several thousand years, when they have become shallower and are undefended. Any approaching hostile force would have been greeted by a hail of sling-stones. Thousands of such stones have been found ready to use at many hill forts; they were cheap and easy to use for men, women and even children, and were very deadly. The penetrative power was effective even against state-of-the-art Roman armour, and even if the attackers somehow survived the volleys raining down upon them in the deep ditch, they would then have to clamber up the steep embankments, storm the heavily defended palisades and gateways, before finally engaging in grim hand-to-hand combat. Few tribes, no matter how powerful, could afford to sustain the heavy losses which were the inevitable consequence of such an enterprise.

Once again it was geography that was influencing the developmental trajectory of tribal formations. The sea trade was the key to obtaining rare and valuable commodities, as we have seen. People in what is now the Welsh Marches would have avoided a long and dangerous journey round Cornwall by utilising the river system to trade down to the south coast in Hampshire and Dorset. A hugely influential political event took place around 200 BC. Rome defeated its antagonist Carthage and its famous general, Hannibal. The Carthaginians had inherited a large Celt-Iberian colonial settlement in modern-day Spain and Portugal; the areas became increasingly Romanised, and a huge wine trade began. The Celts had a tradition of lavish, almost never-ending ritual feasting, and the Gauls and Britons began to import vast quantities in exchange for slaves, dogs, gold, and furs. The focus of commerce began to shift away from the Cornish peninsula to the Solent and the central-south coast. Even further east, Kent became another key area for foreign entry and commercial exchange, and as Strabo wrote in the first century BC, at this point ships could easily cross within a day in good conditions. The overall effect of these changes was probably a relative decline in the prosperity of the western regions, and this may have gone alongside a diminution in their political status and influence, but in general terms their way of life was secure and no really great upheaval supervened until the Roman invasions. People still lived in their thatched roundhouses, many within the defences of massive hill forts like Maiden Castle or medium-sized ones like Croft Ambrey, right down to 'forts', which were just little defended farmsteads or customs posts like Solcum Fort in north Worcestershire. Almost 4,000 such sites have been identified in Britain.

The geopolitical shifts outlined above culminated in the arrival of a new wave of Celtic-speaking immigration, probably presaged by military intimidation. A tribe called the Belgae or 'boastful ones' arrived in the south-east. They carved out a tribal region for themselves, and the tribes of the interior came to terms with them, since they now controlled the landing places for overseas trade, in particular Hengistbury Head, Dorset, the main entrepot. There was also another aspect. The new influx alerted the tribes to the danger of full-scale invasion from overseas, which probably led to a hardening of martial loyalties and resorting to reliable tribal kin-bonds. At around this time the Celtic tribal chiefs must have become dimly aware of an even more daunting threat: Rome. The two cultures and peoples had 'a history' as they say, and there was a deep divide between the warm countries of the Mediterranean with their arid and scorched pastures, long cleared of forest, and the colder, wetter regions of the north, still densely wooded, despite the deforestation we have noted. To the classical mind the people who dwelt in these dark impenetrable woodlands were 'savages', from the Latin *silva* which literally means 'a wood'. The archetypal barbarian was a Gaulish or British savage, painted, naked or nearly so, ferociously warlike, perverted (the Romans calumniated the Celts as sodomites), drunken and/or mad, and finally in thrall to demonic deities to which they routinely made human sacrifices. This hysterical propaganda has unfortunately permeated our subsequent cultural stereotypes to such an extent that it is only in recent times that a more balanced overview has emerged, so much so that a new danger presents itself. For, while it is true that Julius Caesar was a genocidal maniac, and that the Romans imposed themselves on the Celts with the same brutality and disdain for 'human rights' as the European settlers in the Americas in more recent times, we should not treat all that they recorded about the Celts as suspect. Indeed without their testimony we would be left with very little in the way of genuine historical evidence about them at all. The clash between the two mighty peoples, when it came, was a war to the death, fought with a bitter hatred on both sides, and one of the most epic encounters was to take place in the Welsh borderlands.

2

The Tribes

It is time to look at the tribes of the region we are considering and their relationships with each other just prior to the Roman invasions. Celtic peoples were fanatical about war. Indeed, the Romans thought them 'war mad'. They believed that heroism was hereditary, and the extreme veneration of the ancestor spirits encouraged them to display their military capabilities as an almost religious duty. Only one class of people stood above this cult of violence and aggression, the Druids, and it is said that even in the midst of furious battle the opposing sides would lay down their arms when a Druid crossed the battlefield. Only Druids, pedlars or smiths were exempted from the prohibition on crossing tribal boundaries, and their schools and sanctuaries interpenetrated the whole island, but even their influence was insufficient to control the martial eagerness of the tribes. A particularly gruesome aspect of Celtic culture was the practice of head-hunting. At Bredon hill fort in Worcestershire excavations revealed a row of skulls set over the gateway to the fort, and at tribal boundaries 'ghost-fences' were erected, similarly bedecked with severed heads and impaled skulls. The spirit of a man was thought to reside principally in the skull, and so a fallen adversary's power to do harm in the otherworld, encouraged the practice of embalming the skulls of fallen enemies in cedar oil to keep their mischief in check. A chieftain would consider it a particular honour to offer alcoholic beverages to visitors served from the skull of some fallen adversary. The Greeks and Romans were particularly shocked by the practice of suspending severed heads of enemies from their horses' necks. Normal political and strategic considerations, alliances and cooperation in the face of a common foe hardly ever entered into the minds of the tribal leaders, but local feuds and hostile traditions were paramount. Only when the Roman incursions became an existential threat did they combine, probably through the influence of the Druids, in a spasmodic rebellion.

In north Wales, the most remote and mountainous terrain, lived the Ordovices, 'the Hammer-Wielders', perhaps named for their national weapon, a stone hammer or axe. This may indicate that they were a relatively primitive folk, but more likely referred to some specialised use of the weapon, perhaps the ability to throw it with deadly accuracy. In the mountain passes such guerrilla tactics would prove effective for many centuries, as we will see. In the territory of the Deceangli was the island of Ynys Mon, *Mona* or Anglesey. This was the breadbasket of the tribe, as well as being the main centre for the Druidic cult. It was also a crucial hub for trade and communications by sea, especially with Ireland. The Gangani or (in Irish) Concani seem to have occupied the Lleyn peninsula in westernmost Gwynedd from Ireland not long before the Roman onslaught. Another branch of the tribe (their name means 'People of the Branch') migrated to the Clwyd area where they built strong hill forts. Tre'r Ceiri 'the home of the giants' in Lleyn contains ruins of over 150 stone huts of very solid construction, probably one of their hill forts. Although they came from Ireland they probably originally emigrated there from Britain, but had failed to maintain their foothold in the face of opposition from numerous Celtic tribes that had preceded them there. So, from the earliest times, a concourse between Ireland and Britain existed with a hub on Anglesey, and this still remains the case even today. In what is now Shropshire, Staffordshire and parts of Cheshire a powerful tribe, the Cornovii, controlled the upper Severn, the salt pans of Cheshire, and the arboreal wildernesses of the western Midlands. Their name probably means 'People of the Horn'. There are several theories about what this implies, one being that it is a reference to their devotion to a horned god, such as *Cernunnos* or Herne, the god of the hunt. At Abbots Bromley in Staffordshire a 'Horn Dance' is still ritually performed to this day every September, and may be a survival of ancient cult practices associated with the tribe. The Cornovii have been seen as an underdeveloped or primitive folk, based mainly on the lack of evidence for indigenous manufacture of pottery, and that they did not use coins. They did import pots, however, from manufactories at Madresfield near Malvern, and other places. They seem to have been a pastoral people, for whom luxury items were to some extent an encumbrance. They may have used tough rigid leather for drinking vessels, for instance, which have not survived in the archaeological record. They certainly knew how to make exquisite swords, and these have been discovered in some numbers. John Morris and others have suggested that they may have had a particularly ferocious military tradition, surrounded as they were by other hostile tribes. They became the only British tribe to supply auxiliaries to the Roman legions. If this is true, this may explain the large concentration of hill forts in their territory. Their main enemy was the Ordovician realm, but in practice they would have been hostile to all their neighbours.

South of these fierce people lived another tribe, in the area approximating to Worcestershire, Gloucestershire and parts of Herefordshire and Somerset. By contrast they were peaceful farmers, as one would expect from their location in the rich soils of the lower Severn Valley. The origins of their name are contentious. Cassius Dio, a Roman historian called them the 'Bodunni', which would mean 'the Victorious Ones', but a new theory by the archaeologist Stephen J. Yeates has been suggested, which is fascinating. Yeates, in his *The Tribe of Witches* (Oxford, 2008) and subsequent works, makes the tantalising suggestion that the Dobunni worshipped a goddess named Cuda, after which the Cotswolds area is named. When the Dobunni were conquered by an Anglo-Saxon tribe, the Hwicce, they continued in these ancient devotions – a complex nature religion. The basin of the lower Severn and Avon, enclosed by the Cotswolds on the east and the Malvern Hills to the west, is dish or cup shaped, and Yeates thinks the tribal name alludes to this, making them 'the People of the Cup'. Professor Patrick Sims-Williams observes that the name of the Hwicce tribe, pronounced 'witch-a', may mean something like a 'meal-ark', similarly deriving from the dish-shaped topography. We will look at these theories in due course, but there is a general impression of a prosperous tribe with many hill forts such as Maes Knoll, Blaise Castle, Bredon and of course British Camp on the Herefordshire Beacon in the Malvern Hills, from whose commanding heights it is possible to imagine the idea behind 'the People of the Cup' or dish with a special poignancy. Perhaps some evidence for the continuity Yeates suggests between the Dobunni and the Hwicce is to be found in the place name of the mysterious Wychbury hill fort near Stourbridge. This may well have been at the extreme northern frontier of their territory, and means 'the fortress of the Hwicce'. They had large defended *oppida* at Cirencester and Gloucester, which eventually developed into Roman towns and cult centres such as the devotional shrine at Sulis Minerva, modern Bath.

In south Wales lived the most ferocious tribe of all, the Silures. We have already seen how Tacitus thought these people, with their dark features and curly black hair, seemed to resemble the Celt-Iberian tribes of Spain. Their totem animal was the elusive, unpredictable wild cat, and they were masters of irregular guerrilla warfare, as the Romans were to discover to their cost. Like the Cornovii they were underdeveloped, with no coinage or *oppida* (sizeable defended villages). As pastoralists they lived a tough existence in the barren mountains of the Brecon Beacons and the steep wooded valleys, and could suddenly appear by stealth in night attacks on enemy positions, disappearing just as quickly. They were capable of more coordinated action, however, and were impetuous enough to assault a full Roman legion in open battle and put it to flight. They were so resilient and brave that it was to take many years for the full might of Rome to finally defeat them, so much so that experienced Roman generals were reduced to broken men as a result of their tenacious resistance. These then, formed the principal tribal agglomerations in the area just prior to Caesar's expeditions, but the Celtic tribal system extended across Britain, a proud, warlike, tenacious people determined to fight for their way of life, their religion, and the honour of their esteemed ancestors.

For an entire millennium the hill forts dominated these tribal societies. They were a deliberate statement of community solidarity, and the kind of ritualistic warfare we read about in old Irish legends served to bind the local people together against the outsiders. Their proliferation was not just to do with an increasing population. A peculiar feature of Celtic society was the principle of partition of the paternal inheritance among all male heirs, including illegitimate sons. This practice fatally weakened the Celtic resistance to their oppressors, whether Roman, Saxon or Norman. Each son was given a domain to rule in his own right and so hill forts were constructed in close proximity to each other as offshoots of an original centre. Many of the centres would have served as feasting centres and fair-grounds, where the ritual observances that marked the passing of the year were held. In fact the hill forts' main function may have originally been as a centre for annual agricultural shows and metalworking. Few smithies have been found from this period, but iron was plentiful, so we must suspect that smiths were itinerant, processing from one centre to the next. Within the enclosures the magical process of forging iron was carried out, and it would be a mistake to think of them as mere redoubts in times of emergency. They were also holy places, containing shrines.

At Old Oswestry in Shropshire a figure of a horse has been discovered, which was probably once the focus of the hill-fort shrine, perhaps the goddess Epona, the patron of horse rearing. There was something deep in the race-consciousness about these places. When the Roman Empire collapsed and new enemies, the Anglo-Saxons, arrived, the Celts immediately resorted to the old hill forts that had been largely abandoned for 400 years. One possibility is the survival in the lowlands of a compliant Celtic aristocracy that had adapted itself to Roman ways. Many Roman villas were constructed inside the old hill-fort defences. If there was this kind of continuity, the civilised Latin-speaking, but still Celtic, magnates would have known their ancient tribal traditions. Within a century of the Roman departure powerful overlords were overseeing the refurbishment of massive and sophisticated defences, such as that excavated at South Cadbury Castle hill fort, which some people think may have been ordered by no less a person than King Arthur himself. In fact in remoter regions, such as Braich-y-Ddinas, Caernarfonshire, the old way of life went on well into the Roman era. The Romans reused the forts themselves, usually as marching camps, but sometimes utilising more substantial structures. A fort near Bravonium (modern Leintwardine) called Brandon Camp was reused, as was a crucial fort at Forden Gaer near Montgomery, the so-called 'key to Wales'. The Anglo-Saxon construction of the earthwork known as Wat's Dyke, a prototype for Offa's Dyke, incorporated such ancient strongholds as Old Oswestry hill fort, now sadly threatened by a housing development. This was one of the largest hill forts in western Britain, four times the size of the average construction, indicating how important a centre this was for trade in breeding stock, horses and cattle, the effective currency of the day. The canny Normans, always on the lookout for promising defensive sites, constructed many later castles on top of ancient hill forts, such as at Dudley in the West Midlands. William the Conqueror arranged a great conference at Old Sarum, one of the oldest and most impressive hill forts in Wessex, and built a new town inside the ramparts, complete with a cathedral. Nevertheless, by the end of the first century the hill fort culture was in a state of general decline in the south. They were being replaced by new communities, called *oppida* (the Roman name for them), which were still enclosed by a bank and ditch, but lying lower in the landscape near rivers. Because the Romans adapted many of these 'towns' to their own uses, and many modern towns developed on top of the Roman centres, we are still unsure as to why this change had taken place. Almost certainly though, the fact that hill forts were first supplanted by them in the south-east gives us a clue.

It was in the south that the consequences of Caesar's wars in Gaul were felt first, and we should recall that the British and the Gauls were closely related, some tribes having territory on both sides of the Channel. The Gauls had introduced coinage to the southern British tribes, and this change in the medium of exchange led on to an emulation of other continental innovations. The gallant resistance put up by the Gaulish leader Vercingetorix, who was finally beaten in a titanic struggle at Alesia in Burgundy in 52 BC, showed that in a time of supreme national emergency the Celts were capable of uniting under one king. More than a quarter of a million Gauls fought a considerably smaller Roman force, but the genius, and ruthlessness, of Julius Caesar overcame them. One million Gauls died in the Roman occupation, and a million more were dragged off to become slaves. The importance of powerful kings, who could deploy armies composed not only of men of their own tribe, but levies from dependant peoples, was not lost on the British. A leader from a tribe called the Catuvellauni, Cunobelinus, united his tribe with the neighbouring Trinovantes, and this new bloc in what is now Hertfordshire soon expanded until large tracts of southern Britain were under his sway. Shakespeare used him as the prototype for his play *Cymbeline* and the story is based on ancient legends purporting to derive from the corpus of myth known as 'the Matter of Britain'. Such a man was no mere tribal leader, but a king, as we understand that term. He may, like his counterparts in Ireland, have been a 'high king', able to direct an incipient 'national' policy. The Catuvellauni were famous warriors, their name means 'battle-experts'. This domination by more powerful kings, who could exact increasingly more lucrative tribute in the form of slaves, beasts, and raw materials, gave rise to a thriving cross-Channel trade with Gallic tribes under Roman influence or domination. It was soon clear to the Romans that Britain had abundant surpluses of things vital to their economy, and elites who had the wherewithal to purchase vast quantities of their exports, like wine. British warriors, eager for fame, had joined rebellious or recalcitrant Gallic tribes in their struggle against the Romans. Caesar immediately saw this as an excuse to invade, a decision that he may well have regretted. It was to take another century before a full-scale Roman invasion succeeded in gaining a secure foothold, and by then the 'battle-experts' of the Catuvellauni and its rulers formed the nucleus for British national resistance.

Finally, we should not neglect another aspect of the hill fort mentality, one which is all too obvious when we explore them today. They were elevated, set like beacons atop the most prominent, dominating features in the landscape – 'high places' as the Celts knew them. The Druids were especially interested in the patterns they observed in nature, the flight patterns of birds, especially ravens – they appeared to foregather at battlefields *before* conflicts commenced. The Morrigna were three Celtic war goddesses. They were seers who could predict the outcome of battles, and when battle was joined they took the form of ravens. When the slaughter was complete, the severed heads of defeated enemies would be offered up to the 'Battle Crows' so that they could feast on the eyes. The concept of 'shape-shifting' was a corollary of the belief in the transmigration of the human and animal soul into other bodies. The Celts had inherited a very ancient cult of ritual veneration of birds and other sacred animals. Nodens, or Nudd, could take on the form of a dog, but other sacred beasts included the ram, snake, wild boar, swan, owl, goose, duck or the wolf. It is imperative to understand that this was not a purely totemistic 'religion'. There was no separate system of religious congregation, no corporate 'worship' as such, but there were sacrifices and consultations with masters or mistresses of divination. Superstition and religion permeated every aspect of daily life and, until recent times, the conflation of the two, so typical of the rural people of the west of Ireland, preserved a distant echo of the original Celtic cult practices, shrouded in Christian form. The shifting clouds of the British Isles suggested possibilities immanent in nature, in the realm of the sky-father above, and to dwell in a 'high place' brought one closer to the elemental forces. This reverence for elevated locations may even have been the motive force that selected them for settlement in the first instance, with purely practical considerations following on. The magicians of the Druidic orders, analogous to the sadhus of ancient and modern India, operated at two basic levels, one of which was invocation, calling upon sky spirits to descend on the mediator of the divine so that he or she could transmit sacred knowledge to the clan. The other method, evocation, called forth the chthonic spirits of the earth, denizens of the underworld, a most dangerous enterprise, even for a skilled practitioner.

This brings us neatly on to what we might call the 'psychology' of the Celts, and this is a subject of profound importance if we are to understand their, to some minds, queer belief system. Any coherent social system relies on a commonly held set of values, conformity to which is an essential prerequisite for ethnic or tribal membership. In our day this is provided by the educational system, the mass media and, precariously, religious institutions, which mediate the mores of the culture, so that they operate at a deep subconscious level. In a pre-literate culture, which relied exclusively on the transmission of sacred knowledge from mouth to ear, this function was provided by myth. These myths, according to the famous anthropologist Adolf Bastian (1826–1905) are universal, but their variations are particular – what he called *Volkergedanken*, or 'folk-ideas'. These sacred stories were inculcated by the immediate kin in the first instance, but also by a class of people called by the Celts *bards*, or in Greek, *bardoi*. They seem to have been an outer order of the Druids but their main function was to memorise the tribal history in extended poems, which they sang before the tribal chieftain and his retinue, and at larger communal gatherings at the crucial celebrations that marked the passing of the seasons. This oral tradition, in Welsh *Cyfarwddyd*, survived well into the late Middle Ages, and fortunately is resurgent today – the word means 'he who has the (sacred) knowledge'. The passage of time was of paramount importance to the Celts. Time was short, people did not live long, and a man or woman of fifty would have been exceedingly venerable. The passage of time seemed to them to reveal mysteries inherent in nature. Rivers, with their headwaters, representing youth, middle-section (middle age), and their mouths representing senility and union with the greater scheme, were sacred symbols of time and the medium of water was considered holy.

The year began, curiously to our modern minds, on the first day of November, or *Samhain*. At this time the whole tribe, both the living and the dead, united to perform rituals connected with the commencement of the dark half of the year. The main activity of the whole community, agriculture, was held in abeyance, and the best breeding stock separated from those beasts destined for slaughter, so that the community could survive the challenges of the cold winter ahead. The concept of a dark and light half of the year suggested a primordial dualism between dark and light, perhaps along similar lines to Manichaeism or Zoroastrianism. Nature ordained that some days, months, or seasons, were unpropitious and others fortunate, and this was an ineluctable fact of life. Thus, interpretation of omens, divination, and the visionary powers of seers in trance states called *Awenydion* by specialised intermediaries known as *Dyn Hysbys* became essential, so that people could navigate the winding pathways of life and their attendant dangers. The next crucial ritual time was *Imbolc*, the first day of February.

As pastoralists, the Celts noted that sheep and goats began to lactate at this time, a promise of hope and life at the bleakest time of winter; *Imbolc* means 'first milk'. At last, at *Beltane* on the first day of May, came *atenoux* 'the return of the light', marked by beacon fires atop the 'high places', fire calling to light. Beltane means 'fire of Beli' – Beli was a Celtic Apollo, the sun god. The whole community combined to bring forth the fruits of the earth during the propitious summer months until the final community gathering, *Lughnasadh* when grain and other fruits of the earth were almost ready for harvesting. The rituals were performed not in a spirit of thankfulness and praise, as at a Christian harvest festival, but as sacrifices, designed to appease the god Lugh, called in Welsh Lleu, or Gallic Lugos. He was analogous to Mercury, and according to Caesar this was the chief god of the British tribes, a master of skills and competence. These deep-seated elemental rituals permeated the psyche of the entire people, a revelation of primordial truths. A measure of the supreme importance of story and myth in Celtic culture, and of their tenacious power over the imagination, is that Celtic myths are still right at the heart of our modern consciousness. The Arthurian myth cycle still exerts its power today, and interest in the rich myths and tales of ancient Ireland, Wales and Scotland is resurgent. We will look at these folk-stories and their significance later on, but an important point to bear in mind is that for the Celts these sacred stories were inextricably linked to their conception of who they were, both individually and collectively. As the scholar Mircea Eliade said, they, 'narrate an event which took place in the earliest times, the fabulous times of our beginnings'. This has remained an attitude of mind among the Celts, not only the Irish and the Welsh and Scots, but also the English, for the adoption and adaptation of the Arthurian myths and the 'Matter of Britain' by the Normans in the medieval period, recycled them, projecting them in new forms. So in some sense, history and legend are entwined, the ancient mysteries still potent, too deep to be entirely eradicated, even if this were possible. The Iron Age Celts and the Druidic religion of Britain and Gaul were both in decline before the Romans arrived. While the Druids remained at liberty in Britain the Gauls were in constant danger of contamination by their doctrines, which to the Romans were not only barbaric but politically subversive.

This was one among many reasons why Britain became a target for Rome. On 23 August 55 BC, Julius Caesar, with two legions, set sail for the mysterious island. The Roman onslaught had begun.

A ship had been scouting the south coast for some days, under the command of Tribune Gaius Volusenus. He had been sent by Caesar to seek out the landing beaches and harbours, but was spotted by British warriors on the clifftops. This was reported to the British chieftains of the south-east immediately. They had already tried to dissuade Caesar from his invasion plans by crossing the Channel to meet with him (they had been tipped-off about his plans by cross-Channel merchants) but he was already resolved to carry out the raid, for political reasons. His excuse was that the chieftains of the interior were not among the delegation, but they would have had no time to set out anyway. Caesar demanded that the chieftains return to Britain, and compel a complete surrender, and sent one of his Gallic allies, Commius, a member of the Atrebates tribe, which had territory on both sides of the Channel, as his intermediary. This was merely a ruse, and the British leaders knew it. Caesar needed to avoid being recalled to Rome at this time and the mysterious unknown island of Britain was about as far away as you could get. He claimed later that his main mission was to stop fighters and supplies reaching the Gauls from Britain, and while it is true that the warlike British probably did supply troops this would not have been a political policy as such, rather the boyish enthusiasms of eager Celtic warriors. The British had always traded with the Gauls. Suffice to say that nothing was going to stop the mighty general now. The fleet came in sight of the cliffs of Dover, which were swarming with British warriors who tracked the ships as they sought out a beach near Walmer where the legions would not be so heavily exposed as they disembarked. The Roman warships could not put in to the shallows, and so the water was waist-deep and the legionaries were in grave danger of drowning, weighed down by their cumbersome armour. The British cavalry were cavorting in the spume, shouting out fearsome war cries. Little wonder then that the Romans hesitated, but the standard-bearer of the tenth legion leaped into the sea, holding aloft the sacred eagle. He shouted to the men that he would not dishonour the eagle, Rome, or Caesar, even if they would, and immediately the thousands of soldiers followed his example. The fighting as the legions pushed onto the beach was savage, but ship-borne artillery hurled missiles among the British warriors and they were beaten back. They were still full of fight, however, and as dusk fell Caesar's beachhead was small. Fortifications were thrown up and during the following days the British sent messengers offering a negotiated peace. Caesar's immediate response was to demand the release of Commius, his negotiator, whom the British had taken as hostage. In his turn Caesar demanded hostages and the British returned to arrange their delivery. For all Caesar's accomplishments, he could not control the British weather. His cavalry reinforcements were blown off course in a storm and this constrained the Roman general's ability to drive further inland. Shortly afterwards, a more severe gale smashed Caesar's essential transports and supply vessels after they had been cast adrift in heavy swells. The British now sensed victory, because if it were possible to isolate the Roman force in the island until spring the 20,000-strong Roman army would perish for want of food. The British attacked the Roman fortified position but were repulsed. The food situation was already precarious and Caesar immediately saw the danger. He sent out one of his legions to gather in anything which could be found close at hand, while the other legion guarded the camp. The British, who specialised in attacking enemy units as they deployed outside their defended positions, harried the Romans so severely that Caesar had to intervene to recall the foraging parties. The British then tried another large-scale assault, possibly under cover of darkness, but were confronted by much more robust and disciplined opposition. The tribal leaders sued for peace again, to be admonished by Caesar, who increased his demands for tribute and hostages. Caesar was bluffing. The risks with the fleet were simply too great, so he cut his losses and asked for the hostages to be delivered to him on his return to Gaul. Shortly afterwards the Romans withdrew and the raid was over – for the time being. Although it had been good for his political image the campaign had failed, but a man like Julius Caesar would not give up so easily. His attempt the next year was to be on a much larger scale,

800 ships and five legions, the largest amphibious landing until 'Operation Husky', the invasion of Sicily in 1943.

The Britons could not hope to oppose such a landing and so the vast Roman force disembarked. Caesar was in the vanguard and wasted no time, forming up a large reconnaissance-in-force and setting off inland immediately, in the general direction of the River Stour, his first major natural obstacle. The Britons were waiting for him there and were attacked and driven into the woods, where they regrouped. The legions assaulted them again and routed them, and with a good knowledge of the local geography Caesar was in a position to secure his enclave, and push on to the Thames, where Cassivellaunus, the British supreme commander, could be brought to battle and destroyed. But once again the British weather foiled Caesar's plans. A sudden and devastating storm destroyed forty ships of the fleet and it was necessary to suspend further offensive operations for ten crucial days. Cassivellaunus saw his opportunity and called in levies from all the tribes, who acknowledged his status as overall field commander. A huge army of mobile charioteers was deployed, which cut Roman foraging parties to pieces. Caesar received more bad news. The Gauls, realising how exposed he was in Britain, began to become restless, and the Romans were threatened in their rear. Resolved to conclude the campaign as quickly as possible Caesar drove inland to ford the Thames, possibly at Cowey Stakes or Brentford. The Britons had driven sharpened stakes underwater and their side of the riverbank was similarly bristling with stakes. Perhaps 20,000 British warriors were massed opposite Caesar, but even such a mighty force as this was would not be sufficient to stop him. Using an armoured war-elephant, an animal the Britons had never imagined in their wildest dreams, the river was forded and the British line broken after savage fighting. Cassivellaunus withdrew to his own tribal capital, but this was betrayed to Caesar by the Trinovantes. The vast Roman force marched towards the territory of the Catuvellauni. In desperation Cassivellaunus sent word to his allies in Kent to attack the Roman fortified base, but this effort was too desultory to distract the main Roman force. If it had not been so late in the year, Britain may well have come under Roman sway a century earlier than it actually did. The British chiefs, including Cassivellaunus, offered Caesar vast numbers of hostages and tribute, and the British commander-in-chief relinquished his claim on the territory of the Trinovantes. Cassivellaunus had killed Imanuentius, king of the Trinovantes, and Caesar demanded the installation of his son, Mandubracius, as the rightful ruler. This was conceded and so Caesar could portray the campaign as a glorious victory, undertaken in a mysterious island 'beyond the inhabited world' – as the Romans imagined it. With trouble brewing in Gaul, the great commander withdrew his entire force before the equinoctial storms commenced. In essence the second invasion was merely the first repeated on a more serious scale. But the intention was clearly not to invade the whole island and, although the British had been defeated in battle, they still remained at liberty. Before long they resumed their intertribal struggles, with the Catuvellauni still solidly in control of much of the south. The Roman achievements were not forgotten, however, and successive emperors tried to revive the plan for an invasion and conquest of Britain during the next century.

It is important to bear in mind that Caesar's business in Gaul had not yet been concluded at the time of the British expeditions. Commius, his ally, defected and joined the combined Gallic rebellion led by Vercingetorix, but was defeated and had to seek refuge in Britain. If Caesar had had effective control of Gaul, and had not been constantly enmeshed in political stratagems and intrigues, he would most likely have been able to establish some sort of permanent enclave in Kent at least, or compel its compliance. The fact that this did not happen perhaps made the British tribes complacent, even reckless. It is not known for how long the delivery of tribute and hostages was kept up, but it probably had already ceased by the time of Caesar's untimely death. The mad emperor Caligula promoted a self-glorifying scheme for another invasion, but instead set his men to the task of gathering up seashells on the beaches and never actually set sail. His uncle, Claudius, who replaced Caligula following his assassination, although he was weakly and disabled, had studied accounts of the British adventures, including Caesar's *Gallic Wars*. In an attempt to forestall intrigues against him he revived a plan for the complete subjugation of Britain, so as to win public support by the demonstration of an emphatic victory, surpassing even Caesar's achievements (he was by now deified). In fact the expedition was planned and executed not by Claudius, but by Senator Aulus Plautius, one of Rome's best military minds. Following Caligula's example he assembled a gigantic fleet at Boulogne, and an army of 40,000 crack Roman legionaries. The invasion of AD 43 was not just a raid, but was intended to subdue or to compel the alliance of all the tribes of the south-east. Like Caesar, Claudius had a political demand, the installation of his ally Verica as king of the Atrebates tribe, but this was just political sophistry, so as to portray the submission to the demand as an indisputable victory to the senate. The Britons were now in a war for their very survival and, as their great-grandfathers had done, they combined to resist the common enemy.

The political situation in southern Britain was extremely complex at this time. As we have seen, the most powerful tribe in the South were the Catuvellauni, who had expanded their territory around Hertfordshire and Essex under one of Cassivellaunus's sons, Tasciovanus. His son, Cunobelinus, who became the model for Shakespeare's *Cymbeline*, had imposed his rule over the neighbouring Trinovantes tribe, and soon he was so powerful that the Romans described him as 'King of the Britons'. Cunobelinus tried not to antagonise the Romans, but two of his sons, Togodumnus and Caratacus (in fact his British name would have been Caratacos, but I use the more familiar, though flawed, version in this book) took a more militant stance. If they were to expand their territories and intimidate their neighbours, it was inevitable that the kingdom, which Caesar's former ally Commius had established around Calleva Atrebatum (modern Silchester), now ruled by his son, Verica, would lose territory. Verica was an ally of Rome, and when Verica's small kingdom was overrun, he fled to Rome to appeal for help from the mad emperor Caligula. The emperor's madcap scheme to invade in AD 40 ended in farce as we saw, and this emboldened the Catuvellaunian brothers. But there was a third brother, the youngest, Adminius, who ruled over the Cantiaci tribe of Kent. In AD 41 Cunobelinus died. Togodumnus and Caratacus divided the kingdom between themselves, excluding Adminius who, like

Verica, now appealed to the new Roman emperor, Claudius. This was all the excuse the emperor needed. Of the two more independent-minded brothers, Caratacus seems to have been the most aggressive towards his British neighbours, and soon he had conquered the area around modern Sussex and imposed a virtual vassal status on the Dobunni of the south-west. A coin depicts him as a British Hercules on the obverse, with an eagle swooping on a snake on the reverse, and this was a man who thought much of himself. When Verica fled into exile, Caratacus even demanded his extradition, and threatened the Romans with economic sanctions. It was into this hornets' nest that Aulus Plautius and his four legions were pitched as soon as they made landfall, and there can have been little doubt in the Romans' minds that they were in for a tough and bitter contest with a very dangerous and resourceful enemy.

The Roman landing had taken place in the summer of 43 AD but the legionaries were reticent about going 'beyond the limits of the known world' and the whole business of embarkation had dragged on for weeks. In the event the landing was unopposed, because, as the historian Dio Cassius said, 'The Britons ... did not expect the Romans to come, and had not even assembled an army. Even when they did muster they did not attack the Romans openly, but lurked in the marshes and woods, hoping to wear down the invaders.' Plautius brought both Togodumnus and Caratacus to battle and defeated their forces in detail, but they survived to fight another day. At this point the Dobunni, who had been reduced to the status of vassals by Caratacus, submitted to the Romans, and to prevent further defections and collaboration with the enemy Togodumnus and Caratacus decided to make a stand on the River Medway, probably near modern Rochester. We have noted the superstitions about sacred rivers among the British people before, and they were confident that the sacrifices to the river goddess would preclude a successful attack across the sacred waters. They were also completely convinced that such a crossing would be physically impossible, but they were in for a nasty surprise. Rhenish auxiliaries serving in the Roman army specialised in swimming rivers while wearing their full armour, an extraordinary feat. The Batavians, whom Cassius Dio called 'Celts', swam the river and began to hurl their *pila*, barbed heavily-weighted javelins, among the horses, which drew the British charioteers, the British weapon the Romans most feared. The chaos this caused proved a sufficient distraction for a general attack, led by Flavius Vespasian who later became emperor. The British were forced to withdraw but came on again the following day. The Romans were sorely pressed but rallied and, thanks to the gallantry of an officer named Gnaeus Hosidius, Caratacus was repulsed.

This was one of the most important battles in British history, and the two day-long struggle indicates that the British army must have been very large in numbers and of high fighting quality. It was also clearly led by a brave and determined man, Caratacus (Togodumnus may have been killed or fatally wounded shortly after the battle). He escaped across the Thames, with the amphibious Batavians hot in pursuit, and prepared to make a last-dich defence of Camulodunum, modern-day Colchester in Essex. The entire operation up to this point had been under the supervision of Plautius, but now that a final victory was in sight, the emperor himself was summoned to Britain to lead his triumphant legions into the Catuvellaunian capital. Claudius brought with him elephants, just as Caesar had done, and spent a little over two weeks in Britain – or 'Britannia' as we should now call it. The siege and assault on the squalid, primitive timber-palisaded settlement, was strictly 'show-business' and Claudius was never in any danger of seeing any real fighting. A humiliating submission of eleven Celtic tribal chieftains was similarly entirely stage-managed. Claudius arranged for the 'town', if we can call it that, to be rebuilt as a Roman colony, named in the emperor's honour, Colonia Claudia Victricensis. A huge temple was to be built as the centre of this colony, a symbol of the new order, dedicated to Claudius himself. When he returned to Rome he was hailed as *Britannicus* and honoured with a triumph. Leaving orders for the 'remaining districts' to be subjugated Claudius left the delicate business of conquering the country to Plautius. The subjugation of the 'districts' amounted to an initial occupation of a line from the Exe, to the lower Severn, along a line of the Ouse and Welland – roughly all of modern England south-east of the Fosse Way, Exeter to Lincoln. This was to be the first Roman frontier in Britain, but hard fighting still lay ahead before even this comparatively 'civilised' zone was pacified. As well as this, the war was far from over; Caratacus had escaped, but where was he? He had somehow slipped away, to the wildernesses of the western lands. Probably he retained only a core of his own personal warriors, and would have extricated his vast wealth in gold. His family were with him as he wandered, not a defeated fugitive, but a god-like hero, the epitome of the Celtic warrior elite, dearly loved by the people for his patriotic struggle against the invaders. His name means 'the beloved one'. One of the greatest guerrilla fighters in history was born, a man whose exploits are equal to those of Geronimo in nineteenth-century North America. He was the first warrior-hero of the British Celts, and was to become a legend in his own lifetime – Caratacus.

3

The First Hero

The man known to history as 'Caratacus' conjures up pictures of a wild outlaw leader ambushing detachments of Roman troops, the classic image of a guerrilla fighter, but to understand who he truly was we must try to envisage the power of a Celtic high king, the embodiment of the Celtic warrior traditions. Suetonius, a Roman historian described Cunobelinus as *Rex Britannicus* 'King of the Britons', and his son was revered by the Britons in the same way. In the last chapter we saw how the most important duty was loyalty to the tribe and its kings, but at a more profound level there was a concept of the whole people of Britain under an over-king, or *brenin*, whose legendary seat lay at Caer Lundein, or London. This supreme royal status was rarely invoked, but the Roman invasions had the effect of uniting the tribes behind the most powerful king of the most powerful tribe, which had been the Catuvellauni. But if we conceive of this in purely practical and military terms we would be underestimating the immense kudos that went with the title, for its origins were originally religious and went far beyond merely mortal considerations. The spirit of the homeland, known as *Clas Myrddin* 'Myrddin's' (or Merlin's) enclosure', was represented in the form of a goddess. D. A Binchy in *Celtic and Anglo-Saxon Kingship* (Oxford, 1970), thought that the goddess of the northern tribe called the Brigantes may have been connected linguistically to the concept of the *brenin* and that a variant of the goddess personified the island people. The over-king thus became a consort of the goddess, and in a spiritual sense the king was literally the husband of his country, and the land itself was his bride, a motif sometimes known as 'the Sovereignty of the Land'. It is extremely ironic, as we will see later, that devotion to this goddess of the Brigantes, Brigantia (or Brigit) was what secured the patriotic loyalty of the free Britons for Caratacus. He was to them what Winston Churchill was to the British Empire in 1940. Every true Briton was prepared to die rather than submit to an oppression that was as brutal and cruel as the Nazi regime, if not worse. There were 'quislings' of course, and a large part of southern Britain was occupied (though not without hard fighting, as the last-ditch defence of Maiden Castle in Dorset attests). This 'Sovereignty' had other implications. There was a deep folk-belief in the primacy of the British race in the island. They were the true heirs to the stewardship of the sacred territories and the *nemetons*, or sacred groves, which served as open-air places of worship, where hallowed ceremonies were performed that possibly did entail human sacrifices. It may be that Brigantia morphed into a goddess that the Romans depicted as the personification of the newly won colony, literally named Britannia, who still appears on our modern coins. If so, she was now in mortal danger, and the high king, if he was to defend her, needed to recuperate from the defeat he had recently suffered and rebuild from scratch. It was also necessary to intimidate and punish traitors and collaborators. So, ironically, the first task confronting Caratacus was to devastate the lands of the Dobunni, who had gone over to the Romans, and it is in their lands, around the Cotswolds, that we think he retired to lick his wounds.

He almost certainly established a base at Minchinhampton, near Stroud in Gloucestershire. This was ideally placed so as to serve as a sally-fort from which he could devastate the treacherous Dobunni, but it was also near a crucial Severn crossing should he need to make a sudden escape into what is now South Wales. Although his war-band was small, perhaps only a few hundred men and their families, he would have enjoyed the crucial support of the Druids; the more primitive and warlike tribes of the west and north were still actively belligerent towards Rome. The Dobunni were not alone in trying to come to terms, and the

Iceni of modern East Anglia, and the Brigantes confederation of northern Britain chose to become client states of Rome (though there was vocal dissent among hardliners). The Cornovii of the western Midlands seem to have chosen submission too and Caratacus fought many battles to reassert his authority, and proved so ferocious and ruthless that he seems to have succeeded in this aim. His power grew slowly but surely, as more and more renegades arrived to swell his ranks, but if he was to confront the enemy in open battle again he would need the backing of entire tribes, who would agree to put their armies at his disposal. The Dobunnic kingdom was divided into two, with sub-kings ruling each portion. The southern Dobunni in Gloucestershire and north Somerset were allies of the Durotriges people of Wiltshire, Dorset and parts of Somerset. They clashed with the Romans, and so the southern portion of the Dobunni, in the area where Caratacus had his base, now returned to the British cause; the northern section of the Dobunni, in what is now Worcestershire, remained as Roman allies. The people to the north of them, the Cornovii, had also made pledges to Rome and so a large bloc in the West Midlands along the Severn Valley was amenable to Roman influence.

With such divided loyalties as this even within tribes, the complexities of the intertribal politics and diplomacy may be imagined, and the Romans exploited this. As Tacitus, our most reliable source for this period, comments, 'It is a policy long since adopted by Rome to make use of the influence even of kings in order to enslave people.' Some kings and queens did collaborate, but now that Caratacus had larger forces he wasted the lands of any who had betrayed him. Moreover, the common people, while they were constantly in fear of both sides, would have been under powerful influences from the Druids whose unswerving loyalty to Caratacus was born out of a desire to keep the Romans well away from their chief religious centre on Ynys Mon or Anglesey. Although the Roman forces were huge as a mass, when they were spread out over the country, their lines were thinly manned, and they had not as yet fanned out into the hinterland. As soon as they deployed forwards to confront him, they would inevitably become dispersed, they would have to construct new bases, and their lines of communication would be broken up by rough country, woods and marshes and mountains – and with their forces so dissipated they would be in danger of renewed British rebellions in their rear areas, which had been denuded of troops for the offensive campaigns. All this was known to Caratacus, and all that was needed was for the Romans to make some political or military error, to tip the balance in his favour. In the summer of AD 47, the Romans began a massive three-pronged advance that put them in control of virtually the whole of the lowland zone. Caratacus was forced to move into south Wales, where he was accepted as the tribal war leader of the Silures. Among the mountains and valleys thousands of British renegades and patriots came to join him, until at last he was strong enough to attack.

In fact Caratacus was now in a position to exploit a fresh opportunity. In AD 47 Plautius had been recalled to Rome to be replaced as governor by Publius Ostorius. It was politic to change commanders in the field, along with their legions, every few years lest the bonds forged in combat develop into loyalties that may threaten the emperor. It was a classic moment to foment rebellion and disorder, as Tacitus describes:

> The governor Publius Ostorius was greeted by chaos in Britain. The enemy, not believing that a new commander would take the field against them with an unfamiliar army and with winter already begun, had burst violently into the territory of our allies. But Ostorius, knowing that it is initial results that produce fear or confidence, rushed forward his light troops at once, cutting down those who resisted and chasing off the broken fugitives. Then, to avoid a new rally by the enemy or a precarious and resentful truce which would allow no rest to the general or his army, he prepared to disarm all suspects and subdue the whole area on (the south-east) side of the Rivers Trent and Severn.

This was the mistake Caratacus had been waiting for. The green Roman troops, vicious, arrogant and ruthless, held the British in contempt. In an effort to find hidden caches of arms the entire lowland area was ransacked and villages ruined. Many innocent folk were forced to flee into hiding from the ravages of the Roman army. The area specified included the territory of the Iceni, who were not actually a subjugated people, but allies of Rome. Celtic warriors guarded their weapons with a religious zeal, and to surrender one's arms was to relinquish one's entire status as a free man. The Iceni immediately rebelled and took on a Roman army at one of their hill forts but were defeated. A few token executions followed but the Romans could not afford to antagonise this powerful tribe and seem to have let the matter drop. A similar uprising took place in the north-west, among client-clans of the Brigantes, but their queen, Cartimandua ('sleek pony') reined in the rebels. She was a staunch ally of the Romans. This enabled Ostorius to turn his attentions on the Deceangli tribe of Flintshire and parts of Cheshire. His object was to block communications between the Brigantes, who were on the verge of total rebellion against Rome, and Caratacus with his forces in the highlands of Wales. The depredations of the Romans had hardened British attitudes against them and so Caratacus counter-attacked and raided over the frontier, carrying off vast booty, burning Roman fortlets, and taking prisoners whose grim fate may be imagined – human sacrifices to the gods in times of war were very real. Tacitus tells us that the Silures 'upon whom neither harshness nor clemency had any effect' had broken through the new Roman frontier. The Roman effort to contain and repel this major thrust cost Ostorius many casualties, and blooded his fresh troops. He began to make preparations for a campaign to destroy Caratacus in AD 49. The Twentieth Legion was redeployed from Colchester to the area directly opposite Caratacus, at Kingsholm, outside Gloucester. To prevent insurgency in the east, a colony of Roman veterans was established at Colchester, a sort of 'Dad's Army' of men too old or weakly to withstand the demands of offensive operations. In the friendly areas of the northern Dobunni and the Cornovii, along the Severn Valley and into Staffordshire and Shropshire, a line of powerful forts and bases were established, at Penkridge, Metchley near Birmingham, Wall-by-Lichfield, and at Greensforge just south of Wolverhampton. These complex bases were clearly designed to provide the springboard for further operations to the west, but their strong defensive positions demonstrate that not even the mighty River Severn was considered an obstacle so great as to prevent incursions by Caratacus. The long and savage war was becoming legendary throughout the empire, and the name of Caratacus and his daring exploits was on the lips of people in Rome itself.

The Roman military deployments had now changed. The Twentieth Legion was at Kingsholm, and the Fourteenth was concentrating around Wroxeter in Shropshire. With a corresponding complement of auxiliaries, approximately half the Roman army in Britain was now facing Caratacus – around 20,000 men at a minimum. In addition there was now a Roman fleet operating in the Bristol Channel, and the Romans had enlisted the aid of the Demetae of modern Dyfed so as to block Caratacus in in his rear. Ostorius threatened to exterminate the Silures, as had been done before to many Germanic and Gallic enemies of Rome. A savage and brutal war commenced, whose stated aim was genocide. Small wonder that patriots sought out the veteran British commander and laid their swords at his feet, but the hard core of the British force were the Silurian warriors, 'a naturally ferocious people' as Tacitus calls them. Their army cannot have been very large in numbers, for the entire tribal population was tiny by our standards. Perhaps a maximum of 10,000 warriors would be reasonably accurate, with half as many again of various malcontents from other tribes. It was not their numbers but their reputation that worried the Roman soldiers. Pausanius says that Celtic warriors

> ...rushed upon their enemies with the unreasoning fury and passion of wild beasts. They had no kind of reasoning at all. They slashed with axe or sword and blind fury never left them until they were killed.

Just as the Berserkars and Ulfhednir warriors of Scandinavia imitated the savagery of bears and wolves in battle, so the Celts became possessed by totem animal spirits and ferocious god-forms. They were utterly careless of their lives, for reasons we will examine shortly, and completely reckless of danger. They would wear no body armour but relied instead on designs painted on their bodies as protective charms and on amulets. There was no need to protect oneself in any case, for in battle there could only be two outcomes: victory or death. There would have been no mercy for Roman soldiers and no quarter was given or expected. The chieftains did have distinguishing military accoutrements to symbolise their status. They wore helmets and bore brightly decorated shields, some may have worn chain mail and they would have carried long swords for slashing their enemies. The basic weapon was the spear or javelin, but bows, slings and axes were common too. The *covinus*, or war chariot, was a fearsome addition to the British arsenal. The historian Diodorus Siculus wrote down a succinct description of what these were capable of:

> Two-horsed chariots carry the charioteer and the warrior. When they meet with cavalry in war, they throw their javelins at the enemy, and, dismounting from their chariots, they join the battle with their swords.

In joint attacks with squadrons of cavalry (the British were exemplary horsemen), these chariots could break formations of legionaries and cut to pieces troops that had become detached. Caesar himself had admitted his troops had panicked at the sight and noise of a massed British chariot attack. All these finely-honed military skills and the almost fanatical mindset of the British warriors were undermined by their tendency to individual flamboyance and the concentration on aggression and personal valour. It caused them to overestimate their own strength and to underestimate the methodical, disciplined machine that was the Roman army. The Romans were proto-fascistic, indeed the *fasces*, or bundle of rods, around a single axe adopted by the twentieth-century fascists, was originally the symbol of Roman jurisdiction. By contrast, the Celts were individualists, libertarians, anarchistic in their world view. The two systems could not live side by side, and now the vast resources of the whole Roman Empire were brought to bear on the hills and valleys of south Wales.

We cannot know precisely what plan Ostorius followed, but his overall strategy was clear enough. Supported by the fleet the Twentieth Legion would have marched into the Silurian heartland, exposed to constant ambush, 'bandit wars' against the 'obstinate' Silures, who had little choice but to defend their own hearths and homes. The Fourteenth Legion perhaps marched down the Wye Valley in support, hoping to encircle Caratacus, but they were too late. He had extricated his main forces and had easily evaded the Romans, basing himself in the territory of the Ordovices, the 'hammer-wielders' of north Wales. The Druids must have panicked at this point and the Ordovices also acknowledged Caratacus as their war leader. The wily British commander had humiliated the Roman governor and gained the support of a new army of tough Celtic hill-men. Tacitus pays tribute to Caratacus and his cunning, his intimate knowledge of the country and his ability to defy a more numerous Roman army. Moreover, if he were hard-pressed he could easily flee into northern Britain and foment rebellion there. Ostorius had presided over a botched campaign, and was personally humiliated to such an extent that his health began to deteriorate. The Roman colonial venture in Britain now depended upon the destruction of Caratacus. The scene was set for one of the most epic confrontations in all British history – but where did it take place?

Although Tacitus describes the battlefield in detail, drawing on written accounts from veterans of the epic struggle, he does not tell us the precise location. This is frustrating, and thanks to the heroic legends that attached themselves to the name of Caratacus, many sites have been postulated. An ancient association is with the British camp on the Herefordshire Beacon in the Malvern Hills, but the topography does not seem to match the description Tacitus gives us. Graham Webster in his *Rome against Caratacus* (1981) interpreted the reference to a 'stream' in the description given by Tacitus, which ran below the fortified high ground where the British were mustered, as the River Severn. But there are numerous 'streams' and rivers in the Welsh borderlands, and a contest on the Severn is perhaps a little too far west, out of Ordovician territory, in its middle and lower reaches at least. Some possible candidates do exist within Ordovicia itself, such as Llanymynech in Powys or Cefn Carnedd hill fort, also in Powys, which lies on a spur of land that projects into the Caersws Basin. Caersws became a major Roman base and a concentration there would have been easy, using the ancient Kerry Ridgeway route. The rough country between Caersws and Trefeglwys near Llanidloes is dominated by this large hill fort, and we know that Caratacus had left his family within the protection of a hill fort before battle commenced. A 'stream' does run below the ramparts, but there are no steep 'almost vertical' cliffs to be found. 'Caer Caradoc', the great hill fort in Church Stretton, Shropshire which still bears his name, may well be the actual battlefield, but of all the candidates the one which seems to me most plausible is the site postulated by Charles Kightly in his *Folk Heroes of Britain* (London, 1982). This is the tiny settlement called Stowe near Knighton on the border of Powys. It is a place I have visited often, trying to imagine the action there as it is described in Tacitus, and it does comport to it in every respect. This is especially true if, as I suspect, Caratacus had decided to bring about a showdown between himself and Ostorius. The Celtic warlord had been on the run for years now, living a dangerous hand-to-mouth existence, constantly in fear of betrayal, with a wife and children in tow, including youngsters who may not even have remembered their Catuvellaunian homeland. He was advancing in years, probably in his fifties, and it would be impossible to evade the Romans forever. If, however, he could inflict such severe casualties on the Romans that they were handicapped, and their commander humiliated – or, even better, if he could inflict a defeat – the emperor would almost certainly have to replace his governor, and the whole colony would rise in arms. Caratacus staked everything, the entire future of Britain, on this battle. There may well have been pressure too from the Druids, desperate to prevent a Roman breakthrough into Gwynedd and the sacred groves of holy Ynys Mon. Tacitus sets the scene as follows:

> The site was so chosen that approaches, escape routes, and everything else were unfavourable to us and most advantageous to his own men. On one side rose steep hills, and wherever there was an easy ascent the enemy had piled up boulders into a kind of rampart. In front of this position flowed a stream with an unsure

ford, and all the defences were bristling with warriors. The British chieftains, meanwhile, went around encouraging their tribal warriors, uplifting their spirits by making light of fear, inflaming them with hope and otherwise inciting them to battle. Caratacus himself, flying about from one position to another, proclaimed that this day and this battle would mark the beginning either of the recovery of their liberty or of a perpetual slavery. He also invoked the ancestors, those who had driven out Julius Caesar the dictator: only their valour had kept them free of the axes of Roman executioners and the demands of Roman tax-gatherers, and had preserved the bodies of their womenfolk and children from defilement. The warriors roared their approval and swore that they would never relent or give way. Their passion for battle was such that the Roman general was dismayed, he was already apprehensive about fording the river, then scaling the ramparts and overhanging cliffs and the crowds of savage defenders who thronged everywhere. But his soldiers demanded a battle, crying out that no strong position was proof against their courage, while their officers, using the same arguments, spurred them on to still greater zeal. Then Ostorius, having carefully examined the enemy lines to seek out weak points, led his eager troops forward. They crossed the river without difficulty, but when they ascended the ramparts they came under a hail of missiles, and the Romans had decidedly the worst of it, and many were killed. So, after they had locked their shields together in a protective 'testudo', they pulled down the crude and ill-built heaps of stones: then hand-to-hand fighting ensued, on equal terms and the barbarians were forced back onto the hill-tops. Even there they were pursued by light auxiliary troops and heavy legionary infantry, the former skirmishing with their spears while the latter advanced shoulder-to-shoulder. The British, lacking any protection from breast-plates or helmets were thrown into chaos, if they resisted the auxiliaries they were laid low by the javelins and stabbing swords of the legionaries, and if they turned to face them they were confronted by the lances and slashing swords of the auxiliaries. It was a famous victory, and Caratacus' wife, daughter and brothers were captured after offering to surrender.

Caratacus had failed in his gamble and paid with the loss of his family, but not his life. As soon as it became clear that all was lost, and the formidable position had been stormed, and his army broken, Caratacus fled into the wilderness, perhaps over the Black Hill into the Clun Forest, a hunted fugitive again. Today, if Mr Kightly was correct, this furious battle scene is a tiny cluster of farm settlements in a bucolic valley beside the River Teme. His reasoning, with which I concur, is that in order to concentrate the maximum forces of both tribes, a site was chosen close to the junction of the tribal borders between the Silures and Ordovices, but also accessible to 'all those who hated Roman rule', itinerant war-bands who were driven before the Roman advance, from various tribes. Caratacus had one advantage. Only he could know where he was going to concentrate. It is just possible that a folk legend preserved the memory of the battlefield. In the early 1560s the Welsh antiquary Humphrey Llwyd heard tales from local shepherds which held that the hill fort above Chapel Lawn was the very same where Caratacus's family had been taken, and that '...the place was called Caer Caradoc, that is the city of Caradoc, and that formerly a great battle had been fought there against a certain king called Caratactacus [*sic*] who was at last taken by his enemies'. Tacitus had not yet been published in Britain at the time this garbled story was recorded, so it is unlikely that rural shepherds in the Welsh borders obtained the tale from that source, even supposing that they could read. Everything about the location fits. The Roman fort at Leintwardine (Bravonium) was very close, and as soon as auxiliary Roman scouts ran into the British skirmishers and probes the message would have gone out to concentrate at this midway point between the bases of the Fourteenth and Twentieth Legions. The Teme is a substantial stream with an 'unsure' crossing below the concave valley, which ends in a horseshoe shape surmounted by 'almost vertical cliffs' called Holloway Rocks. The gradient as one climbs to the top of the narrow valley is extremely steep and it would have been easy to fortify it with stone-built ramparts, as described by Tacitus. The hill fort of Caer Caradoc lies directly behind the redoubt, on a plateau of high ground. Of course, every antiquarian will have their own favourite candidate for the battlefield, this first 'Battle of Britain' but the result is what mattered. It was a catastrophic defeat and ultimately proved decisive, but Caratacus did not know that. He had probably planned a quick retreat using relays of swift ponies well beforehand, and some months later he turned up again. His new plan was to try to convince the Brigantes to rebel.

The consort of the Queen of Brigantia, Venutius, was a known sympathiser of the resistance, and if he could be convinced to switch his allegiance to Caratacus the fight could go on. Queen Cartimandua was very fearful of the consequences for herself and her people if they let their hearts rule their heads. She must have known of Caratacus's arrival and must have sent guarantees for his safe passage into her lands, but as soon as he was in Brigantian territory he was taken and clapped in shackles, before being handed over to the Romans at Rigodunum, now known as Castleshaw in Greater Manchester. It was a sickening betrayal of the British cause. Welsh literature remembers Cartimandua as *Aregwedd Voeddawg* – 'the stinking one' a 'mistress of seduction, trickery and scheming'. Her treachery is one of the 'three secret betrayals of the Island of Britain' in Welsh tradition. This was the lowest point in the heroic British leader's fortunes, and now he was swiftly conveyed to the south coast. For such a famous enemy as he was could expect nothing less than to be transported to Rome, where he would be paraded in chains before the baying mobs, humiliated and forced to his knees in front of the raised dais of the emperor himself. In the parade ground of the Praetorian Guard he would be cruelly reunited with his wife, children and kinsmen, before grovelling in the dust they would be ritually strangled, one by one, with Caratacus the last of all. This was the fate Vercingetorix had endured before him, the lesson all enemies of Rome must learn. But at this moment, as the executioners were making ready, Caratacus walked out of human history – and into legend.

Tacitus gives us a great build-up to this classic moment, the subject for artists over many centuries:

His fame had spread from the islands of Britain into the neighbouring provinces, and he was even well-known in Italy itself: everyone was desperate to see the man who had scorned our might for so many years. Even in Rome the name of Caratacus was not without honour, and the emperor, seeking to enhance his own splendour, only made him seem more glorious in defeat. For the people were summoned as if for some magnificent spectacle, while the Praetorian Guard stood to arms on the parade ground before their camp. There, while Caratacus's lesser retainers were herded past, the neck-rings and other trophies he had won from other British tribes were displayed: next his brothers, his wife and his daughter were put on show, and finally the king himself appeared. Fear made the rest of the prisoners degrade themselves by appeals for pity, but Caratacus sought mercy neither by words or downcast looks. Coming before the emperor's dais he spoke in this manner:

'If my high birth and good fortune had been matched with moderation at the hour of success, I would have come to this city as a friend, not as a captive: nor would you have rejected an alliance with a man of such noble ancestry, the ruler of many nations. But as it turned out, I was humbled, while you are glorified. Once I was the owner of many fine horses, master of many warriors, fine weapons and great treasures. Do you wonder that I tried so hard to keep them? Just because you Romans want to rule the world, does it follow that everyone else wants to be a slave? If I had been dragged here before you after surrendering without a blow being struck, neither my misfortune nor your triumph would be remembered by posterity. If you execute me, we will both soon be forgotten. Spare my life then, to be an everlasting memorial to your mercy'.

This early example of Celtic eloquence, if it was not stage-managed by the emperor (which it may well have been), brought its just reward. As he was marched away to his new residence, a palace on the Palatine Hill where he remained for the rest of his days under house arrest, he was said to have gazed around him at the forum and the magnificent temples and public buildings, and asked 'Why, when you have all this do you envy us our poor huts?' So at least our hero survived, a prisoner in a gilded cage in Rome, but his countrymen never forgot him. He became a figure of enduring legend. It was said that in his palace-prison Caratacus gave refuge to the priests of a notorious radical sect, the Christians, and that he gave shelter to Linus, one of the first Roman bishops. Other traditions state that he converted to Christianity himself and fathered a line of saints. These stories are probably later interpolations, but are not completely implausible. What better amusement for a privileged prisoner than to mock the authorities by colluding with subversive elements? His daughter Gladys was said to have been renamed Claudia in the Roman style and married a Roman cavalry officer, who was sent to Britain. Claudia returned to her homeland and became one of the first British Christians. We simply cannot know whether there is any truth in these legends, and other later stories, recorded by Iolo Morganwg (Edward Williams) in the eighteenth century, are either so suspect or contaminated that they give us little by way of reliable historical evidence. This, however, is not the point, because such tales convey a character we would regard as a 'super-hero', a man worthy of respect, veneration, and a subject for British pride. In this respect at least, his courageous nine-year-long struggle had not been in vain. He had stood up to the mightiest empire in history and fought them to a finish. He had not disgraced himself or his people, and ultimately even his enemies saluted him and spared him.

Caratacus was gone, but the Silures were still full of fight. The tribe Ostorius had condemned to death repaid him with an implacable resistance. A legion sent into their territory to construct forts was ambushed and almost annihilated before being rescued. Many Roman soldiers were taken prisoner and parcelled out as slaves among the Silurian clans. Ostorius 'worn out by anxieties and cares' Tacitus tells us, died a broken man shortly afterwards. Even as Caratacus was pleading for his life in Rome, the Silures were taking the fight to the Romans. There is a hint in Tacitus that the betrayal of Caratacus had the effect of redoubling the struggle against Rome, in tribute to the lost British hero. The whole Silurian adult male population must have been in arms by now, and in AD 52 they attacked the Second Legion and defeated it in open battle. Even when the Romans counter-attacked, they merely fell back into the forests and marshes from which they waged a pitiless guerrilla war. By their heroic struggle, the Silures kept alive the hopes for liberty and encouraged other tribes to join in the fight. What was more, the war had revealed the true scope of Roman ambitions. Their objective was nothing less than conquest of the entire island and the elimination of the Druidic cult. There could be no compromise with the Romans, and the miserable ease of a 'civilised' way of life in their new towns was small compensation for slave-status and the loss of sacred religious traditions. The war would continue, for Rome had still only occupied the lowlands. The more resolute and hardy highland folk began to look to their weapons.

The new governor, Aulus Didius, arrived in a divided island. The business of opening up the colony in the south for trade and commercial activity was proceeding at a frantic pace, and a large trading centre, Londinium (London) on the Thames had grown up. It was a 'boom-town' and expanded rapidly until by AD 60 it had a population of 20,000 or so. Within a century it was to increase to a population of over 50,000 and had the largest public buildings of any provincial city in the empire. There was big money to be made in Britannia and people arrived from all over the Roman Empire to set up in business, including people from Rome itself, as dental testing on recently excavated skeletons has discovered. This bustling, energetic population of risk-takers mixed with British collaborators and men on the make, keen to learn the ways of the new order. The Romans thought that it was part of the divine dispensation of the god Jupiter, or Jove, that Rome spread the good news of its way of life to all humanity, so that they too could enjoy the comforts and conveniences, as well as all the refinements and etiquette of the Roman regime. Education and literacy were promoted among the wealthy classes, and the common linguistic medium of Latin encouraged. Greek tutors were employed to teach Latin and Greek to male children of elite households. Scientifically and technologically the Romans were in a different league to the Britons, who did not even know how to lay masonry with mortar. All these advantages – and they were very real – were supplemented by the total security the Roman army and navy provided, a military machine with no equal anywhere on earth. But everything has its price, and the cost of conspicuous consumption and decent roads, and luxuriance in the public bathhouses and saunas – was slavery. It may be reasonably objected that such opulence as that discovered at Fishbourne in Sussex, a building larger than Buckingham Palace, complete with formal gardens, fountains, exquisite mosaics, hypocausts for the central heating, the largest building outside Italy itself in the empire – was the kind of slavery we would all accede to. Of course, these palaces and villas were only for the privileged elite, those whom the Romans targeted for the new imperial deal. Ultimately though, the 'good life' was predicated on absolute submission to Rome and its emperor. Although the Romans were very tolerant about local deities, sometimes renaming them in the Roman manner, the strange and fearful practices of the Druids they utterly abhorred. Londinium was not the only town, of course. There were new towns springing up all over the south-east, and the forts that had housed the legions as they fanned out and expanded northwards and westwards were often the template for later towns. But in the unoccupied territories the Druids were still at large, and even within the Roman zone of influence, deep in the woods and marshes, Druids lurked. They were the implacable enemy of everything Rome stood for. So long as they survived and their network of schools continued to operate the Romans could never be safe. They were to the Roman state what extremist terrorism is to the Pentagon today, hostile, elusive, mysterious, cunning, impenetrable, fanatical, and promoting a cult of suicidal resistance to the 'civilising' influences of foreign interlopers, whose 'unclean' way of life threatened spiritual pollution and degradation.

It should not be supposed that any of the advantages the Roman Empire brought to Britain were evenly spread out across the general population. Indeed, it may not have been clear to the poor folk in remoter regions that they had been conquered. The task of constructing the new towns fell to slave labourers, and one of the reasons the urban population expanded so rapidly was that huge numbers of slaves were imported or created. There were two main sources for local slaves: fathers had a legal right to sell their children, and if they were poor they often did so; and debtors who had failed in business of some kind were regarded as the property of their creditor or creditors, who were permitted to sell their children as slaves. Their labour underpinned the urban economy. As a road network was gradually built it became possible to travel easily across the country from one town to another, but the countryside was another story; life went on there in the traditional way for many generations, people still lived in their large thatched roundhouses in intimate villages with their animal pens and stockades. Outside the Roman-occupied area life went on in exactly the same way as before, except that the aristocracy probably enjoyed a wider variety of luxury food, wine and olive oil for their lamps.

One such beneficiary was undoubtedly Queen Cartimandua, the Roman client-queen of the Brigantes. Her betrayal of Caratacus had impressed the Romans but had hardened attitudes against her among her own people. Her political disputes with her husband, Venutius, seem to have become personal. She seems to have taken Venutius' armour-bearer as her lover and when Venutius rebelled she seized his brother and his parents and threatened them. The Romans quickly sent troops to support the queen.

For the time being the north could be left to look after itself, but now, ten years after the invasion, a thorough policy of Romanization began in earnest. Roman law, language and religion were imposed with a new rigour. During the consulship of Cesonius Petus and Petronius Turpilianus, the new Roman commander-in-chief in Britain, Gaius Suetonius Paulinus decided to act decisively. The chief sanctuary of the Druids was on Ynys Mon, the island of Anglesey in Gwynedd. Here the most sacred groves and most august schools were located, presided over by an Arch-Druid, whose edicts and pronouncements were faithfully obeyed and conveyed around the country by a vast network of priests, in three separate religious orders, whose influence with the people was absolutely sacrosanct. Their magical powers were to be treated with respect. To offend them was dangerous – they might cast a 'madman's wisp' by uttering incantations into a blade of straw or grass, driving the victim insane. Their curses could poison wells or cause sickness among beasts or children. Druidism was not maintained by these means, but through its primordial connections to the folk-psyche, the sacred places, and the ancestor spirits. It was this 'barbaric' religious practice that could no longer be tolerated by the empire, and which Suetonius Paulinus was determined to extirpate. Tacitus says that the holy island had become a refuge for exiles and British refugees and guerrilla fighters. It was the Roman expedition against the Druids on Anglesey that provoked the bloodiest rebellion in British history, led by the legendary warrior queen, Boudicca. In the next chapter we will examine the controversial doctrines of Druidism, to try to divine what it was about the faith that touched off this most horrific paroxysm, an insurrection as serious for the Roman Empire as the so-called 'Indian Mutiny' of 1857 was for the British imperial scheme.

4

Rebellion

Despite the powerful hold they have over our imaginations and our idealised depictions of them, we actually know very little about the Druids. What is more, what we do know is largely derived from Greek or Roman sources that have tended to distort the facts, either demonising them as bloodthirsty wizards in league with dark forces, or lionizing them as philosopher-mystics, guardians of a sacred esoteric knowledge. Professor Stuart Piggott's *The Druids* (London, 1968) remains one of the best scholarly attempts to steer a middle course between these two extremes; his study is as much an attempt to debunk pseudo-historical and romanticised portrayals of the Druids propagated by neo-Druidism as it is straightforward historical scholarship. For our purposes, we are concerned mainly with the rationale for Suetonius's campaign in north Wales and the rebellion that followed; such a major effort indicates what a dangerous threat they represented to Roman rule. The extirpation of the cult was somewhat analogous to the British imperial suppression of the Thuggee brigands in India. The Roman revulsion was not just a matter of political expediency, but emerged from deep-seated fears of barbaric anarchy, chaos, and the psychical projection onto the Druids of all that was cruel, perverse, sinister – in short, all those forces that lay beyond their control. The symbols of this barbarism were the groves, hidden among the forests and hills – we have already observed how the Romans were an urban culture, and that they projected their fantasies of untamed beastliness onto 'savages', those who lived in the deep woods.

But to the native tribes, the Druids were the revered intermediaries between themselves and the ancestor spirits, embodying all that was holy, the guardians of the sacred knowledge. In their offices they combined many functions, as law-makers, judges, medicine-men, poets, historians, astrologers, diviners, and interpreters of omens. Their privileges included exemption from military service and paying taxes, and they were free to travel throughout the land without hindrance. It is a strange thing, but the Romans, who were quite tolerant of the religions which they encountered throughout their vast empire, made an exception when it came to the Celtic Druids. I believe that the reason for this was simple. The Druidic faith was at its heart diametrically opposed to the Roman imperial project, not at a simple political level, but because of its aim, which was to tame nature, to impose itself by force. This profound psychological divide was unbridgeable. But what do we actually know about the underpinning philosophy of the Druids? Strangely, some of the best evidence is to be gleaned from Caesar's memoirs of his Gallic wars:

> The cardinal doctrine which they seek to inculcate is that souls do not die, but after death pass from one body to another and they discourse upon the stellar movements, the size of the universe, and of the measurement of the earth, the order of nature and the potency and power of the immortal gods.

So, that the Druids were interested in metempsychosis, astrology, geodesy, physics, and theology is clear. But they had a more sinister side too. The most famous depiction of their alleged depravities comes from Lucan's *Pharsalia*:

> Here, barbarous rites are practised in honour of the gods and the altars are sprinkled with human blood ... the people never venture very near it, but leave it to the gods ... the priest himself dreads to approach fearing to come upon the lord of the grove.

The seeming dichotomy between these two extremes is perhaps what lies behind the polarised attitudes towards the Druids ever since they were eradicated. On the one hand they were wise philosopher-priests, an ancient theocracy overseeing a natural religion in harmony with elemental energies. On the other hand they were callous detached witnesses of ritual murders by clubbing, stabbing, and strangling at the edge of swamps, studying the writhing agonies and death throes for signs and portents. A body preserved in a peatbog at Lindow Moss in Cheshire in 1984 (known by the ironic nickname of 'Pete Marsh') is one among dozens that have been found in Britain, Ireland and Denmark. He was subjected to the 'triple-death' by the methods indicated, and was certainly a 'human sacrifice'. It may also be true that humans and animals were immolated in giant wickerwork structures as Roman sources attest. Human sacrifice did take place and perhaps cannibalism too. A cave near Severn Beach contained gnawed bones of dogs, a totem animal of the god Nodens, or Nudd, but among the dog bones were the bones of a lame young girl (a virgin no doubt) who had been cooked and eaten, including the bone marrow. How are we to reconcile these two contrasting aspects of the Druidic contribution to Celtic culture?

The belief in the survival of the human essence beyond death was sacrosanct. The soul was reincarnated endlessly and the new form it took would depend entirely upon the ethical, moral and spiritual conduct of the individual in its present incarnation. To ensure a propitious mortal incarnation a strict regime of devotion, study, fasting, and self-mortifications was necessary, and it was profoundly to be wished for the aspirant to seek out a Druidic school, where he or she would be tutored – Caesar says for up to twenty years – and rigorously examined by superiors in their ability to retain vast quantities of sacred information, by means of mnemonic prosody, the precise recital of verses, histories, legal statutes and the likes. Writing, though known to the Druids (they understood Greek and Latin) was prohibited. It introduced the possibility that the sacred doctrines may become contaminated by profane or hostile influences, and was a medium which could be used by persons unlicensed to convey sacred doctrine, not under the direction of the divine or discarnate entities. Many Indo-European peoples – the Celts were one branch – also believed in the concept of reincarnation, and indeed they still do so. The Romans did such a thorough job of destroying the Druids in Britain that we have to look to Ireland, where the cult remained until it was later displaced by Christianity (the first Irish bishops were former Druids), to get some idea of how the Celtic afterlife was envisaged in the popular imagination. Also, studies of comparative folk beliefs among the Celtic people, notably *The Fairy-Faith in Celtic Countries* by W. Y. Evans-Wentz (London, 1911) provides us with a fairly comprehensive picture. Fundamentally the doctrine was one of constant reciprocity between life and death. Like Einstein, the Druids seemed to think that energy could not be destroyed and that the spiritual life force, once it had shed its physical body, departed to an otherworld, believed to be in the west over the great ocean. There it would repose until the time came for it to be physically remanifested in this world again. It was not a world very dissimilar to this one, and Valerius Maximus, a Roman observer, wrote that it was common practice for people to arrange loans, which they promised to repay in the next world. It was a normal everyday manner of life, starkly different to the stale dank underworld with its eternal darkness, aridity and decay, which characterised the Roman afterlife.

The bard Llewellyn Sion set down some of the complex processes by which the human soul was reborn in a document called *Barddas* in the mid-sixteenth century, when a more intrusive and dogmatic Christianity had placed prohibitions on the wandering bards. The bards were one of the three orders of the Druids and, because their functions were specific and they operated in every community, they survived in a bowdlerised form right into the early modern era. Sion thus relinquished his oath never to record the doctrines in writing, in a bid to preserve them for posterity. He says that three 'circles' of existence were envisaged. First the circle of infinity or *Ceugant*, which is infinite unmanifest space; then the circle of *Abred*, where the dead have dominion over the living, the circle of rebirth; and then the circle of *Gwynvyd*, the 'white circle', where life becomes stronger than death, this earthly life, which alone offers the aspirant the chance to attain absolute knowledge by 'having borne and suffered every condition and incident', remembering them all faithfully. Life then was a dramatic lesson, whose joys and vicissitudes were to be endured with unflinching devotion to the 'truth' – but, as Pilate said, 'What is truth?'

For the Druids, this was the supreme question. There seems to be an ancient folk connection for many Indo-European people between the words for 'tree' and 'true'. In Old English *treow* meant both things. The Druids venerated trees and the sacrifices to the gods were made among sanctified groves or enclosures called *nemetons*. The trees they especially revered were the oak and the ash. Oaks are particularly prone to lightning strikes, which marked them out as the favoured receptacle of the divine energies. Pliny and Strabo were of the opinion that the word 'Druid' derived from the Greek *drus*, meaning 'oak' (Irish – *dair*, and British – *dar*), thus the Irish city of Derry means literally 'place of oaks'. A *Derwydd* (Druid) means literally an 'oak-seer' or 'oak-knower' (*Gwyd, Videre*, and *Uid* in British, Latin and Irish respectively mean 'to see', with the connotation of 'to know'). The oak was venerable and immovable, deep-rooted in the underworld but also reaching its mighty boughs into the realm of the sky-father in heaven. The 'truth' was similarly changeless and timeless, above and below – and the aspirant to the divine wisdom needed to steel himself to stand rooted and undaunted, exposed to the elemental forces, marshalling his powers for expansion and growth. This innate capacity was a divine dispensation, to attain the knowledge of 'the land of truth', the source of all, was every person's natural birth right. There was no predestination, no 'fate' – every individual was responsible for their own condition. If they were 'true' they would honour justice, right action and be brave and faithful until, through successive incarnations, they would achieve union with the divine. This formidable religion, incorporating three orders of officers called Druids, Vates, and Bards had its origins, according to Caesar, in Britain, and he says 'those who wish to make a profound study of their doctrines go there to be instructed'. The headquarters of the religion was on Holy Island off Anglesey, accessible by sea from all the Celtic realms. So long as novitiates continued to travel there for instruction the potential for a holy war being proclaimed was a constant threat. In spring AD 61 Suetonius set out to destroy the headquarters of the cult. A tough old veteran of many years campaigning against the Moors in North Africa, his experience of mountain warfare was second to none. A sexagenarian, his was the world view of a grizzled old general. The barbarians were concentrated on Ynys Mon and it was from that island that the rich grain supplies that kept the resistance fed were coming in abundance. He was not perturbed or intimidated by these savages with their wizards and wild women and prepared an assault on the holy island. Tacitus gives us a vivid account:

> Drawn up on the seashore was a dense mass of armed warriors. Among them, bearing flaming torches, women ran in funereal robes, with dishevelled hair like furies, and the Druids, raising their hands to heaven and calling down the most dreadful curses. This weird spectacle temporarily unnerved the Romans, but they advanced with their standards, and cut down all who stood against them, pushing the enemy back onto their own fires. Afterwards they destroyed the sacred groves, where the Druids practised their cruel superstitions, where they dictated that altars must smoke with the blood of prisoners and the will of the gods be discovered by examining the entrails of men. At this moment news reached Suetonius of a sudden and unexpected uprising...

This cannot have been an accident. With the Roman army far away in Wales, the long-suffering lowland tribes only needed some provocation to start an insurrection. The common 'clergy' of the Druids must surely have been agitating against the occupying forces at such a sensitive time and now the Roman authorities made a catastrophic mistake. The curses called down on the Romans as the Druids perished in the flames on Anglesey were to visit a grim revenge, in fire and blood and anguish, on those who had desecrated the sacred sanctuaries.

The proximate cause, however, was another desecration, which had occurred in the territory of the Iceni in what is now East Anglia. This was the humiliation of the queen-dowager of the tribe, Boudicca, by subjecting her to the lash, followed by the public rape of her two daughters, then only in their early teens, by men in the employ of the Roman imperial agent, Catus Decianus. The short-lived rebellion of the Iceni a few years before had not been forgotten by either side. The Romans had probably installed Prasutagus, a compliant Roman ally, as king of the tribe, on the strict understanding that all males would surrender their weapons. Boudicca was Prasutagus' wife and queen, mother of his two daughters, but in AD 60, or early in AD 61, the king died, Tacitus says, 'After a life of long and renowned prosperity'. This prosperity derived from two main sources. The first was the rich culture of horse-rearing, which is still a feature of the area to this day. The horse was a sacred animal. The goddess Epona was the patroness of horses and horsemanship, and it is difficult to imagine, in this age of the internal combustion engine, just how crucial the industry then was. The finest horse was a status symbol for the owner, just as luxury sports cars are in our day. The other reason for the good fortune of the Iceni was that they had always been keen allies of Rome, all the way back to Caesar's time. They feared Catuvellaunian power and took no steps to assist Caratacus. Even the brief rebellion under Ostorius had been an aberration, caused by his absurd decision to try to disarm the tribe, who were not Roman subjects. This arrogant strategy was just one aspect of Roman misrule. The veterans' colony at Colchester had degenerated into corruption, venality and oppression by the Romans redolent of the treatment of Native Americans in the nineteenth century by white settlers. The old 'grunts' who had served on the frontiers of empire for all their adult lives began to seize lands, to which they were not strictly entitled, around Colchester, which lay in the middle of the territory of the Trinovantes. Many British slaves sweated on the construction of the mighty temple of Claudius (the Emperor Nero had deified Claudius) and fine marbles and building materials were shipped in from Italy, North Africa, and Greece to decorate the massive and elaborate building, the largest structure in all Britain. As Roman villas were built on land in the countryside and the former owners displaced, the Trinovantes became more and more disgruntled.

Prasutagus had been a beneficiary of what we would call today 'overseas aid'. The Roman conquest was not just military, but economic. This was the second source of Prasutagus's wealth. Huge gifts of monies were made to tribal leaders so as to 'buy up' Britain for the empire. The Britons were already taxed up to the hilt – with corn-duties, customs levies and taxes for the maintenance of roads – but now came another unpleasant surprise. The Roman procurator redesignated the imperial gifts as loans at interest and demanded that they be paid in full. This was a trick of the degenerate Emperor Nero, whose chief advisor, Seneca, was also one of the leading moneylenders in Rome. He lent out 40,000,000 sesterces to the British and then called in his loans at a hugely inflated interest rate. The British, unused to the ways of usury, were shocked when the armed bailiffs arrived to sequester their estates and seize their beasts – including some of the best horseflesh in the empire. Nero, like Caligula before him, was a sadistic maniac, completely unmoved by the miseries his corrupt officials were inflicting on the Britons. Prasutagus, who correctly divined the danger inherent in displeasing Nero, made him the co-heir to his kingdom and left him half of his personal wealth in gold in his will – the other half to his wife and daughters. Tacitus traces all the troubles that followed back to this, seemingly generous, settlement:

> King Prasutagus ... long renowned for his wealth, had died leaving the emperor as joint heir with his own daughters: he believed that such an act of submission would secure both his kingdom and his family fortune from harm. Just the opposite happened, for both his realm and his household were plundered as if they were spoils of war by the procurator's slaves. First of all Boudicca was flogged, and her daughters cruelly raped. Then the Icenian chiefs were stripped of their ancestral lands – as though the Romans had been made a present of the whole country – while the late king's relations were treated as slaves. Faced with these outrages, and fearing worse to come once they had been absorbed into the Roman province, the Iceni reached for their weapons. They also incited the Trinovantes to rebel, and other tribes, who, still unbroken by subjection, had secretly plotted together to regain their freedom.

This remarkably honest account was probably written down after Tacitus had listened to the war stories of Agricola, Tacitus's father-in-law, who fought in the campaign as a young officer. It conveys the sense of deep injustice and sickening brutality, and is obviously sympathetic; but, if a Roman writer could be so outraged, we may imagine how the bleeding, half-naked Boudicca must have felt, as she tried to comfort her violated children. What was more, the

Roman army was hundreds of miles away, and the steady drip of Druidic agitation was now heard and acted upon. The royal person of the queen was thought to be an apotheosis of the war goddess, Andrasta, and her name, Boudicca, means 'the Victorious One'. This was no ordinary woman, but a force of nature, and in her fury she resolved to destroy all Romans in Britain, and to slaughter all those who gave them aid. The most horrific war in British history had begun.

In recent years Boudicca's ill-starred insurrection has eclipsed the achievements of Caratacus, partly because of the modern feminist movement, who see in her an exemplar of their gender, striving to resist the brutal and abusive – and male-oriented – Roman regime. It is true that the Romans held the idea of female military leadership in contempt; it was considered a misfortune to have daughters, so much so that baby girls were often deliberately exposed to the elements so that they died. It was a patriarchal, male-dominated society. Tacitus tells us by contrast that 'the Britons were accustomed to female war-leaders, but she did not come forward as one of noble descent, fighting for her kingdom and her wealth: rather she presented herself as an ordinary woman, striving to avenge her lost liberty, her lash-tortured body, and the violated honour of her daughters. Another historian, Cassius Dio, is clear that the Romans were ashamed that all the trouble had been initiated and sustained by a woman and, to lessen this embarrassment, he notes that 'she was, however, possessed of greater intelligence than usually belongs to women'. The patriarchal ideology that permeated Roman attitudes was simply incapable of understanding how a mere woman could possibly have been responsible for so much chaos. What they could not comprehend was that women in Celtic society often took the lead in political matters. Some tribal dynasties may have been matrilinear, with the 'king' (Prasutagus) being no more than a consort of the queen, as was the case with Cartimandua and the Brigantes. The queen was the focus of the tribal entity, and her precious daughters were the repository of the dynastic succession. Paternity was, after all, a suspect qualification for rule. But it was not so much her royal status or her gender that rallied so many tribes to her, but rather natural human empathy with a defenceless woman and her children. The violation of the latter incensed the Britons with a bitter hatred – paedophilia is not too strong a term for the Roman abuses. Fortified by the prayers and invocations of Druids, who now emerged from their concealment, the warriors sought out their hidden weapons and the smiths made themselves busy forging spearheads, axes, and swords. Messengers were sent out to the Trinovantes, who immediately swore oaths of allegiance to Boudicca. Within weeks she had gathered an army (or rather a *levée en masse*) of people from both tribes, probably numbered in the tens of thousands. Alongside the fighting men, women and children came as camp followers, for every Briton was enraged and this was a holy war. One by one the villas in the countryside were burned and their inhabitants cruelly slaughtered until the rapacious horde arrived outside the hated colony of Colchester, with its ostentatious temple. The puny force of retired Roman troops there would have had no time to prepare a defence, instead hurrying for refuge to the great temple itself with its gilded statue of the hated Roman emperor, Claudius. The holocaust that followed was awful, and there can have been no survivors. Boudicca was no longer a mere woman, but an avenging goddess, Andrasta, 'the Invincible One' – and her vengeance terrible to behold.

The hapless Romans and their British quislings and slaves knew what was coming. Women ran around in the streets shrieking in anguish and tearing their clothes, bloody spume washed up at the seashore, and terrible cries disturbed the emergency meeting at the town council. A motley reinforcement of just 200 troops was sent from Londinium to assist, a puny contribution; as the British horsemen and chariots rolled into the city, it was immolated and ransacked, any poor souls who had not found refuge in the temple were cut down without mercy. Some brave veterans tried to resist but were swept aside by the thousands of enraged British warriors. Inside the temple, the defenders cowered in dread as the British rammed the doors and clambered onto the roof to tear off the tiles. After two days the besiegers burst in and massacred all inside, before putting the building to the torch. Even the Roman cemeteries were violated, and their remains exhumed. The tombstone of a former cavalryman named Longinus, from what is now Bulgaria, was smashed with especial venom. It depicted the great man on horseback, about to slay a cowering British warrior. Longinus's face was erased, and all similar evidences of Roman cultural imperialism were effaced, including the statue of the hated Emperor Claudius, whose head was hacked off, before being thrown into the nearby river. The symbol of Roman authority, the imperial colony itself, had been completely destroyed, but in truth it was a small city and easy meat. With an army that had no shortage of horses, the cavalry and chariots of the Iceni and Trinovantes could move on to a much bigger target, and one that was similarly completely undefended – Londinium.

The elderly but energetic Suetonius had ridden hard with a small bodyguard all the way from Anglesey in an attempt to prepare the city for a defence, but he immediately realised it was too late. London was a magnet for British hostility, the headquarters of the hated Catus Decianus, whose rapacity was responsible for the uprising. He, seeing which way the wind blew, immediately took ship and fled to Gaul for his own safety, but 20,000 less fortunate Londoners were left behind, in an undefended town – the Roman city walls were a later innovation. By now the rising had spread all over the country, spontaneous mobs roaming around, roads blocked, entire legions blockaded in their fortresses. There was nothing to be done, despite the pleading and tears of the inhabitants. Suetonius prepared to evacuate those with the means to follow him northwards where, he hoped, he could conjoin with his two legions who were marching day and night to join him somewhere in the English Midlands. The British mood was jubilant, and if the Roman investment at Londinium could be eradicated and the Roman army surrounded and wiped out, all Britain might be freed. In his biography of his father-in-law Tacitus describes empathetically the mindset of the despised British people:

In war it was the stronger party who gained the spoils. But now it was the cowards and stay-at-homes who were seizing British property, kidnapping their children, and conscripting their dear ones into the Roman army – where not knowing how to die for their own country they would die for another's. What a contemptible number of soldiers the invaders had brought over, compared to their own numbers! The British would be fighting for their homes, wives and families, but the Romans had only greed and luxury to inspire them: they would be made to run home, like Caesar had run – if only the Britons were worthy of the struggles of their ancestors. Now, at last, the gods had taken pity on the Britons, causing the Roman commander to be exiled in another land...

Boudicca, if the historian Cassius Dio was not exaggerating for mere effect, had become the goddess incarnate, someone much more awe-inspiring than the avenging suffragette portrayed in some modern cinematic depictions. In Celtic society warriors had a curious relationship with women. Aspirants to a martial career were required to seek out magical womenfolk whose task was to instruct them in the use of conventional weaponry, but also in psychic self-defence. These goddesses were artful and protective, but also vengeful and possessed of a primeval fury. The personification of such a deity was not merely a 'political' figure, as we understand that term, but a representation of a deep-seated archetype, the violation of which caused an outpouring of fanatical extremism and violence. For the assembled Celtic warriors she was literally a divine being:

> She was very tall, and her aspect was terrifying, for her eyes flashed fiercely and her voice was harsh. A mass of red hair fell down to her hips, around her neck a twisted golden torc: over a tunic of many colours she wore a thick mantle fastened with a brooch – this was her invariable attire. Now she clutched a spear to help her strike fear into all who beheld her. She consulted the will of the gods by letting a hare escape from within her folded robes, which fled in a fortunate direction, and the crowd gave a tumultuous cheer. She then raised her hands heavenward and shouted 'I give thanks Andrasta, and call upon you as woman speaking to woman, to beg you for victory and liberty ... that you may be our eternal leader!

The British now embarked on an orgy of destruction, pillage and murder, offering up thousands of terrified prisoners as human sacrifices. But they had yet to face the Roman army. It is unclear at what point the first encounter with the legions occurred, but it was probably the clear defeat of a Roman army which forced Suetonius to sacrifice London. At Longthorpe, Cambridgeshire, the Ninth Legion had its base, and its commander, Petillius Cerialis, an impetuous and arrogant man, who thought he was facing a mere local uprising of peasants, marched his troops the 90 miles to Colchester in a desperate effort to relieve the city. By then the whole colony lay in blackened ashes, and the British, alerted to his advance, were waiting to ambush him. His legion was cut off and then overwhelmed by a furious British assault, and he had no choice but to ride with his cavalry to a nearby fort where he holed-up until the revolt was over, having lost 3,000 men. Another orgy of jubilant sacrificial slaughter followed, amid scenes of demented barbarism:

> Those who were taken by the rebels were subjected to every conceivable kind of outrage, but the worst and most bestial atrocity was this. They hung up the noblest and most highborn women naked, and then cut off their breasts and sewed them to their mouths, so that they appeared to be eating them: afterwards they impaled the women on very sharp stakes, which they thrust lengthwise through their bodies. Accompanied by sacrifices, feasts and sexual orgies, these things were done in their holy places, but especially in the sacred grove of Andrasta. This was their name for 'Victoria', the goddess they especially revered.

So the despised Britons under the command of a 'mere woman' were a force to be reckoned with. The vast British force, perhaps 200,000 strong, now converged on the doomed city of Londinium, and perhaps their outriders watched, as Suetonius and those fortunate enough to find protection with him rode out of the city to the north-west. Hours later the howling mobs of crazed British warriors engulfed the city.

They entered in the vicinity of Aldgate, nearby the heart of the modern financial hub of the City of London, or the 'square mile', approximately where the first Roman settlement was located.

Deep excavations in that area have revealed a layer of thick black soot – all that remains of the great Roman town. Smashed ceramic wares litter the area and glass turned molten in the intense heat. Tacitus remarks on the eagerness of the rebels, 'they couldn't wait to cut throats, hang and burn and crucify'. Catus Decianus's great stone headquarters building was ruthlessly demolished, but almost all buildings at this time were of timber construction, so the conflagration must have spread quickly as the looters ransacked wine and precious possessions. Thousands of civilians were slaughtered, and many were marched down to the river to be sacrificed. In the area near Liverpool Street station, a stream, the Walbrook, has been covered over by the bustling modern city for many years, but immense quantities of decapitated skulls have been found there, victims of ritual sacrifice. No prisoners were taken, and even if half of the population had made their escape, there must still have been thousands dead. Nothing remained of the first city of London and, with the jewel in the imperial crown gone, Boudicca's confidence must have been at an all-time high. Only one final detail remained – the complete annihilation of the Roman army.

Whatever we may think of the Roman regime, Suetonius's response was admirable. There was no panic, and his best hope was that he could combine three crack legions in the Midlands and at a suitable tactical location, confront the rebels and destroy them. Help may soon come from Gaul, where panicked refugees were already spreading the terrible news. But there was also potential help closer at hand. At Exeter, the Second Legion was based under the temporary command of a junior officer, Poenius Postumus. It was a desperate time. Tacitus says, 'Never before has Britain been in a more dangerous state, or since, we had to fight for life before we could think of victory,' and these must surely be words remembered from his conversations with Agricola, or drawn from his memoires. Suetonius ordered the Second Legion to march immediately and join the Fourteenth and Twentieth, who had now reached him somewhere in the Midlands. But Postumus refused to leave his fortress. The rebellion was now nationwide, and he feared the same fate as Cerialis and the Ninth Legion. The woods and hills along the

Fosse Way were infested with tribesmen and should Suetonius fail his only hope was evacuation by sea. This was a bitter blow to the old commander, and perhaps his only satisfaction was that a few weeks later Postumus fell on his own sword, having disgraced his command by his cowardice and disobedience. Suetonius's hand was forced. His troops would starve ultimately if no help was forthcoming, so even though he was outnumbered ten to one he resolved to conclude matters by a pitched battle, crucially on ground of his choosing. Meanwhile the avenging British host, perhaps swollen by even more recruits, was on the move, following him along the Watling Street. Fortunately for Suetonius, another doomed city, Verulamium, modern St Albans, stood in the way of the horde and the horrors enacted at Colchester and London were repeated there:

> A similar disaster overtook the municipality of Verulamium: for the barbarians, who rejoiced in plunder and shunned hard work, steered clear of fortresses and garrisons and headed for the places where the spoils were richest and the defences lightest.

Even if it only gave Suetonius 48 hours grace, this was a crucial delay. The immense British host, now loaded down with vast booty stashed in carts and wagons, became a huge chaotic traffic jam, proceeding only slowly up the Watling Street. For Boudicca this was a cause of grave concern, because at all costs Suetonius must be destroyed before Roman reinforcements crossed the Channel. The same devastation visited upon Colchester and London was meted out at Verulamium, but perhaps during the hiatus it became clear to Boudicca that the legion at Exeter would not be among her opponents. Now the warrior queen of the Iceni moved in for the kill.

This epic convulsion has no equal in subsequent British history, and the titanic battle that ended the affair was one of the most dramatic confrontations ever fought in the island – but where did it take place? Once again, Cornelius Tacitus, though he gives a blow-by-blow account of the fight, omits the exact location, but we may hazard a guess or two. It must have taken place somewhere north-west of St Albans, just off the Watling Street. Tacitus describes the position in some detail:

> At this time Suetonius had with him the Fourteenth Legion, together with detachments from the Twentieth and auxiliaries from the nearby forts, and he abandoned delay and chose battle. He selected a position in a narrow defile, protected to the rear by woods: he was sure there were no enemies except to his front, where the open plain was without cover, so that there was no fear of a surprise attack.

His force then was no more than 12,000 strong, against a British army of between 100,000 and 200,000. Even though many of the Britons would have been camp followers and other non-combatants, the odds against him seem staggering. A strong candidate for the battlefield is just outside Towcester, Northamptonshire, but some people think this too far south. Chester and Birmingham have been advanced as candidates, but the strongest candidate in recent years is the village of Mancetter, near Nuneaton – Manduessedum in Latin, meaning 'the place of chariots'. Roman coin hoards have been turned up of the precise period, consistent with soldiers hiding their wealth before battle commenced. Roman earthworks and fortifications have been discovered too, and High Cross a few miles away was the main road junction of Roman Britain, a place eminently suitable for the concentration of dispersed forces. Suetonius's original plan would have been for all three available legions to join him, so such a choice makes sense. Suetonius had taken every precaution to give his troops the maximum advantage, and to use the terrain to constrict and impede his ponderous enemy, whose immense wagon train now came in view:

> Thus he drew up his legionaries in close order, with the light-armed auxiliary infantry on either side of them and his cavalry massed in readiness on his flanks. The British forces, however, ran riot all over the field in their mobs on horseback or foot. They had never appeared in greater numbers, and they were so full

of confidence that they had even brought their wives to witness their victory, stationing them on wagons around the edge of the battlefield.

The great queen herself arrived to encourage her warriors:

Boudicca, with her daughters standing in front of her, was borne about in a war chariot from one tribe to the next. 'We Britons,' she declared, 'are accustomed to female war-leaders, but I do not stand before you as one of noble descent, fighting only for my kingdom and wealth: rather I present myself as an ordinary woman, striving to revenge my lost liberty, my lash-tortured body, and the violated honour of my daughters here. Roman lust and greed have reached the point where even our bodies – even those of old women and virgins – are not left unpolluted. But the gods are granting us our just revenge: we have already cut one legion to pieces, and the rest cower in their forts, or look to their escape. They won't even stand up to the raised battle-cries and shouting of so great a host as this, let alone endure our assault! Look at our numbers, and then at the reasons why we fight, and be sure that you will either conquer or die in this battle. That is what I, a woman, am resolved to do – you men may live as slaves of the Romans if you like!

It must have been a daunting spectacle, enough to demoralise even trained Roman legionaries, but Suetonius encouraged his men too, emphasising the difference between disciplined Roman troops and the motley collection of barbarians of both sexes who confronted them:

Don't worry about these yelling savages with their empty threats. Look, they have more women than warriors in their ranks! They are untrained and badly armed, and they'll break straight away when they see Roman courage and the weapons which have routed them before. Even when many legions are in the field, it is a handful of soldiers that decide the issue – so think what glory will be yours, a few men winning the fame of a whole army! Just remember, stick close together: throw your javelins – then push into them, knock them down with your shields and finish them off with your swords. Don't stop to consider plunder, when you've won the battle you'll have the lot.

It is a confident speech, and even if it was written down with the benefit of hindsight it tells us much about the killing machine that was the Roman army. The primary weapon of the legionaries was the *gladius*, a short stabbing sword, used from behind the protection of their huge rectangular shields, which were a weapon in themselves. As soon as the enemy came within range, massed volleys of *pila* were discharged, javelins with detachable heavily weighted spearheads, which would stick into the shields of their enemies rendering them useless. In wedge-shaped formations, like the teeth of some formidable beast, the Romans would then push forward into the melee, stabbing the exposed British in the upper body. Each legionary would be deployed at the front line for five frantic minutes until he was relieved by the man behind him, gaining valuable time to rest and prepare, as in rotation they rejoined the fight. The huge British numbers were in fact to their ultimate disadvantage in such a narrow position. As soon as the howling Britons were within 40 feet, 10,000 javelins arced into their ranks, and a few minutes later a second volley followed. Then the Romans moved steadily forwards and the massed British ranks faltered and fell back in disarray. Much worse was to follow. As they were compressed into the low-lying area, desperate to manoeuvre and use their swords, they found their exit blocked by the thousands of wagons that they had formed into a makeshift grandstand so that their families could watch the slaughter. This obstacle and the relentless advance of the legions, and now the charges of the Roman cavalry as well, trapped the Celtic warriors as the Romans systematically slaughtered everyone in front of them – men, women, children, and poor frightened horses gone wild with fear. This carnage continued for hours, until as many as 80,000 Britons lay dead. The Romans lost only 400 dead, with many more wounded. Boudicca escaped with her precious daughters, but clearly all was lost. There could be no recovery from a defeat on this scale. Shortly afterwards, Tacitus tells us, 'she ended her life with poison.' Her grave, if she was buried, was kept secret, but more likely she was cremated so that her remains could be kept from further Roman defilement. The fate of her daughters is a mystery. Cassius Dio says that some of the Iceni were prepared to fight on but Boudicca's death left them shell-shocked and leaderless. The survivors, traumatised and fearing that their goddess had deserted them, made their way home, but Roman revenge was merciless. The Iceni never recovered from the disaster. The Roman town built for them as a tribal capital, Venta Icenorum, failed to thrive. The tribe was so ruthlessly punished that its population could not sustain even a small provincial town. Tacitus's father-in-law Agricola, later governor of Britannia, was not the only young Roman soldier to be deeply moved by all he had seen of Roman misrule. The British had come within an ace of liberating themselves and humiliating the empire, and the Romans would never forget this irruption of hatred, or the courage of the woman who had so nearly defeated them. The Roman colony had survived, but it was to take many more years before they subdued most of southern Britain – the task of complete conquest of the island was to elude them.

5

A Desolate Peace

The Roman colony had been reduced to smouldering ruins. The relatives of those who had rebelled, where they survived, resorted to mendicancy and vagrancy. An entire generation of their menfolk had been wiped out. Agricola was not the only Roman to question the hard-line policies that had alienated and infuriated the Britons. The new financial procurator, Gaius Julius Classicianus, who had replaced the venal Catus Decianus, was faced with a monumental task, including the reconstruction of Londinium. He was so concerned at the situation he had inherited that he wrote to Nero himself, requesting a board of enquiry. His rationale was that it was the army that had caused all the trouble, and the man he blamed most was Suetonius, the very man whose superb generalship had retrieved the situation by defeating Boudicca. Nevertheless, it had been his determination to destroy the Druids that had left the colony open to insurrection, and his vicious punishment of the rebels afterwards threatened a virtual extermination of the most militant tribes, especially the Iceni. If there was no one left to labour for the Roman regime, or pay taxes, the entire colonial project was doomed. The 'bottom-line' was that Suetonius had to go. Nero sent Polyclitus, one of his close inner circle, to head up the commission. He was sympathetic to Classicianus's analysis, and the ageing Suetonius was accused of negligence and relieved of his command, to be replaced by Publius Petronius Turpilianus. Classicianus focused on rebuilding London, where he died in AD 65. His elaborate tombstone was later incorporated into the medieval city walls of London, preserving it for posterity.

This more liberal approach worked. The lowland tribes never rose again, and over the next century they adopted Roman ways until the point came where they no longer considered themselves to be 'Britons'. Latin began to be spoken, and written, because the benefits of literacy spread throughout the provinces of Britain. Successive more enlightened governors, of which Julius Agricola was the most famous, sought to 'root out the causes of war'. Tacitus says that his justice and fairness won the respect of the Britons and 'gave men reason to love and honour peace'. Taxes were reduced and educated Britons encouraged into the civil service. The South, the Midlands and eventually what is now the North of England were eventually absorbed into the Roman scheme, and precariously Wales, too, was incorporated. The Cornish peninsula and Caledonia, modern Scotland, were not as interpenetrated by the Roman culture, but they were nevertheless considerably influenced by the imperial provinces on their doorstep. Only in the desolate north, the barren highlands of Scotland, were the indigenous people left alone, and although Agricola contemplated an invasion of Ireland, this was never attempted and the Irish tribes remained free. The diocese of Britannia consisted of four, and possibly five provinces, self-contained political entities with their own local government. In the east was the province of Flavia Caesariensis, with its capital at Lincoln. In the west was Britannia Prima, with its capital at Cirencester. London was the capital of the province of Maxima Caeseriensis in the south-east, and in the north another province, Britannia Secunda, was eventually established with a capital at York. Another province may have been established later called Valentia, possibly in the north-west around Lancashire and Cumbria, or maybe in the intermediate zone between the Antonine Wall and Hadrian's Wall, but its precise location has not yet been established with any certainty.

Later, it seemed expedient to divide the Roman assets into two, with Britannia Superior in the south, retaining its civil administration, and Britannia Inferior operating a military administration in the north, again based at York. All these provinces were incorporated into a larger pan-national area called the

Prefecture of the Gauls, a vast bloc comprising all the provinces of Britain, Gaul and Spain. For over 300 years the 'Romano-Britons', as we should now call them, were an integral part of the empire and enjoyed all the splendid refinements of Roman life, under the protection of the army that had once brutalised them so grievously. The Romans took no chances with Britain again, and four of the elite legions of the Roman army were permanently garrisoned there, as insurance against further trouble. In fact there was still much to do in military terms. The two tribal areas that remained unsubdued were located in Wales and in the north, Brigantia. In AD 73, Sextus Julius Frontinus replaced Quintus Petillius Cerialis as governor and launched two major campaigns against the Silures and the Ordovices in Wales. A massive base for the Second Legion was constructed at Isca Silurum (modern Caerleon) with barracks for 6,000 troops. In AD 69, Venutius, the former consort of Queen Cartimandua, rebelled against her and drove her out but Cerialis intervened and Venutius was defeated at Stanwick hill fort, near Scotch Corner. It took many more decades to pacify the Brigantes, however. Agricola led a campaign against them and they rebelled regularly until the middle of the second century.

In essence Roman expansionism in Britain was geared towards harvesting the rich natural resources of the country, principally the rich grain lands of the fertile plains, but also the gold mines of Dolocauthi in Wales, and other areas rich in valuable ores and minerals. In around AD 80 Agricola attempted to bring Caledonia into the Roman imperial orbit. The intrepid governor, supported by a fleet sailing up the east coast, reached far into the northern highlands, confronting an army of 30,000 Caledonian clansmen under their leader Calgacus 'the swordsman'. The battlefield, known as *Mons Graupius* to the Romans, has never been identified with certainty, but may have been somewhere in Perthshire. Agricola triumphed, and another bloody slaughter left 10,000 tribesmen dead. In a famous speech to his men before the battle (probably an invented one) Calgacus says that the Romans 'practise robbery, slaughter and plunder and give it the lying name of empire. They make desolation and call it peace'. Agricola left a line of forts between the Clyde and the Forth and built a massive legionary base but gradually the lowlands of Scotland were abandoned in favour of a line between the Solway and the Tyne, upon which the extraordinary Hadrian's Wall was erected as a permanent fixed frontier. Should this formidable barrier be breached, one of the largest military bases in the whole Roman Empire was constructed at York, the headquarters of the Ninth Legion. Its *principia*, or administration building, was so enormous that it still stood in Viking times. The whole of this northern territory was under military, not civil jurisdiction, which tells us much about the divide that existed between the pacified South and the less predictable North. A further attempt at occupying the Caledonian lowlands was initiated during the reign of Emperor Antoninus Pius and another wall (or earthwork) constructed but, once again, this became untenable, and after thirteen years was abandoned in favour of Hadrian's line of defence. So, a military conquest was ultimately achieved of sorts, but the failure to completely eradicate Celtic and Pictish resistance left the civilised Romano-British provinces exposed to a resurgence of tribal militancy in the future. Moreover, as the prosperity and sophistication of the imperial areas went from strength to strength, the temptation to raid into the Roman dominions proved irresistible for the barbarian tribes, and it was this that was to finally undo all the work of over 300 years of Roman civilisation.

The potential for such incursions was an ever-present threat. As late as AD 154–55 an uprising of the Brigantes flared-up, which utilised the Pennine Hills as a base from which to attack Roman settlements as far south as the Peak District. Within a few decades the Caledonian tribes were active again, and many Roman troops mutinied rather than face the dangers of fighting these indomitable and ferocious tribesmen. In AD 208 Septimius Severus, an emperor who had been born in Libya, decided to restore order in Britain. He brought over a new army of 40,000 men and invaded the lowlands of Scotland again, repairing the Antonine Wall and refurbishing Hadrian's Wall (most of the remaining structure was in fact a result of his efforts). He may have taken as many as 60,000 troops into the far north, but the guerrilla tactics of the tribesmen, and the harsh conditions, wore out his men, and many resorted to suicide rather than be captured alive by the barbarians. Tens of thousands lost their lives, but

Severus, even though he was very ill and had to be carried on a litter for the duration of the campaign, was persistent. He tried again in AD 211 but became so ill that he was forced to return to York, where he died. It was his decision to divide Britain into two separate provinces instead of four or five, his rationale being to limit the personal power of the British-based legion commanders. By the end of the third century internal political, military and economic troubles were undermining Roman power, but ironically Britain was becoming wealthier and more sophisticated than ever. The increasing traffic by sea, although it was under the protection of a mighty navy, the Classis Britannica, was a tempting target for pirates such as Saxons, Franks, Frisians and Jutes. A commander was appointed whose knowledge of these peoples was second to none, Carausius, a native of what is now the Netherlands.

The Emperor Diocletian gave Carausius a commission to clear the seas of the pirate menace and, basing his fleet at Boulogne, he prosecuted the campaign with seeming success, but two years later he was embroiled in a scandal. In AD 286 the Western Empire had been divided between Diocletian and Maximian, with both men ruling as joint emperors. Maximian had investigated the activities of Carausius and alleged that he had been perpetrating what we would today call a 'scam'. He had been encouraging the pirates and allowed them to carry off booty, but had then intercepted them and taken their cargoes for his personal enrichment. The entire fleet was implicated and when Carausius was summoned to Rome to account for himself, he refused, and his fleet mutinied, declaring him to be their 'emperor'. This 'mini-empire' consisted of the coast of north-east France, Belgium, the Netherlands, and all the provinces of Roman Britain. Britain was essential to his secessionist project, because all the troops in the island were loyal to him, a very considerable force of three legions. To protect Britain against the threat from the legitimate Roman authorities, he commissioned nine massive stone-built forts, complete with artillery platforms all along the southern and eastern coast of Britain. These so-called 'Saxon Shore Forts' were originally thought to have been built as a bulwark against the Saxon and Frankish raiders under a new commander called the *Comes Litoris Saxonici* 'the Count of the Saxon Shore'. In truth, the fortifications, though they may have been legitimised by portraying them as a defence against piracy, were actually a defence against other Romans. This fragmentation of the unwieldy empire was the beginning of the end of the *Pax Romana* 'the Roman Peace' and when Carausius was assassinated by his second in command, Allectus, who seized control of the 'empire' of Carausius, a process began that was to bring about the ultimate disintegration of Roman Britain. The legitimate emperor, Constantius Chlorus, seized Boulogne and gathered a fleet, with which he reinvaded Britain. Allectus was confronted with his legions at Silchester, where he was defeated and killed, but all these complex and enervating internal struggles had not gone unnoticed elsewhere. When Allectus withdrew most of the garrison on Hadrian's Wall to provide a defence in the south, the Caledonian tribes broke through and ravaged the whole of the province of Britannia Inferior, even breaking into mighty legionary bases such as York and Chester. The Scotti, slave-raiders from Ireland, also took advantage of these power struggles and raided all along the coast of Britannia Prima, especially in Wales. In the east, the Germanic raiders – Saxons, Franks and Frisians – were also emboldened and they made hit-and-run raids as well. This was a sign of things to come, but eventually order was restored by Constantius. He invaded the lands of the Picts in AD 305 and compelled their surrender, but died at York the following year. For over a century Britain remained as part of the empire, but it was a different kind of empire, no longer expansionist and optimistic, but defensive-minded and preoccupied by insecurities, political intrigues and uncertainties, as well as dangerous external threats.

This potted history of Roman Britain is deliberately truncated. This book is mainly concerned with the Celtic resistance to various invaders, of which the Romans were the first. But in AD 306 an event took place that had a profound influence upon the way Britain saw itself in the world and, indeed, the way the world saw Britain. The son of Constantius Chlorus, Constantine, was hailed by his father's legionaries as the new emperor at Eboracum (York). This Constantine was to be the emperor whose conversion to Christianity changed the entire nature of the Roman imperial scheme. Henceforth, Britain was to become a nexus for powerful political intrigues, and control of the Roman island was to be crucial to the political power-brokerage process that installed Roman emperors in the western section of the empire. Far from being a remote colony with only limited strategic influence, Britannia was now right at the heart of decision making, and its large military complement became the makers or breakers of bids for the imperial purple. Also, even though Constantine's conversion came later, at the battle of the Milvian Bridge near Rome, the fact that the first Christian emperor had been elevated in Britain meant that its inhabitants began to associate it with the out-workings of a divinely ordained destiny, a magical place, as it had been in the olden times of the Druids. Its growing economic importance increased its negotiating power, and because it was the fulcrum of a huge bloc extending from the Netherlands to Gibraltar and from Hadrian's Wall to the Mediterranean, it was in a position to lend its weight to a procession of pretenders to the imperial authority. It was collusion in these internecine disputes which was to unravel Britain's relationship with the central Roman authority. All these developments left a legacy of insular support for dubious and obscure pretenders to the residual imperial jurisdiction, even after the Western Empire had fallen under the sway of the barbarians.

The most fearsome of the barbarians, from a Romano-British point of view, were the Picts of northern Scotland, the descendants of those hardy warriors who had survived the massacre at the Battle of Mons Graupius. They remain a mysterious folk to this day. In *Barbarians and Romans* (London, 1983 Edn), Justine Davis Randers-Pehrson states:

> The Picts were not a homogenous people. There was a Mesolithic stock in Scotland that may have represented a circumpolar culture like that of the Eskimos. Animals carved on standing stones by the Picts at a later time are especially charming and lively. Some are like Chinese brushwork in their fleetness; it is with amazement that we consider that the carvers slowly worked these skimming creations by incising a line in the rude, unyielding stone, first pecking it out and then patiently honing it to a shallow groove. This Bronze Age technique was

generally understood and used in Britain, but representation of natural forms in this way was peculiar to the Picts. No Celt had such a perception of the world about him. The configuration of animal joints and muscles in this simple, vigorous work is oddly reminiscent of Scythian metal-work from farthest Asia. This similarity, along with the philologists' judgement that the language of the Picts contained non-Indo-European traces surviving from the speech of the Bronze Age aborigines, justifies the thought that the Picts may have descended in part from some stock that once roamed across the polar regions all the way from China.

Whoever they were, and wherever they originated, in AD 360 they broke their treaty arrangements with Rome and combined with other Caledonian and Irish tribes to raid and plunder the north. Very possibly they had the assistance of the Roman auxiliary scouts in the debatable land between Antonine's (abandoned) Wall and Hadrian's Wall. Archaeological evidence seems to suggest a story whereby some of these auxiliaries had intermarried with local women and had children by them. They had a stake in the island and rather than be redeployed to far-off lands, many of them simply defected to the Caledonian and Pictish confederations. The empire had been sending these tribes tribute payments for many years and it could be that, for some reason, these stopped arriving. The military zone was interpenetrated by spies and informers who kept the Roman authority up to speed with developments. How, we do not know, but it seems that by AD 364 the Saxons, Frisians and Franks were privy to this intelligence. Then, in AD 367, a *conspiratio barbarum* – a full-blown alliance between the Irish, the Picts and the Germanic raiders – engulfed the entire Roman provincial scheme in Britain. This signified the beginning of the end of Roman authority in the island.

The Roman scouts and intelligence officers fomented mutiny among the garrison of Hadrian's Wall and the gates were opened to the barbarians, who poured through and ransacked the whole of the North and the Midlands. By spring they had even reached the South and were joined by large numbers of Roman soldiers who, not having received their salaries for some while, joined them. They were also joined by the liberated slaves of the large Roman villas that had been ransacked and burned, who wandered around pillaging, raping and slaughtering the well-to-do. Those loyal to the Roman emperor were forced to take refuge behind the walls of the larger towns, especially London. The Germanic elements penetrated far inland on their raids too, and two of the leading Roman commanders were killed by them. The catastrophe was the most serious disorder to befall Roman Britain since Boudicca, and desperate pleas for aid were sent to the emperor, Valentinian I, who was campaigning against German tribes and so was unable to personally assist. After reconnaissance and information-gathering had been completed, the emperor sent Count Theodosius, one of his most efficient commanders, with a force of four divisions of various auxiliaries, which embarked at Boulogne. They encountered the parties of brigands and pirates as soon as they landed, and soon chased them off. Theodosius reached London and relieved the siege, to the joy of the frightened inhabitants. An amnesty was offered to all Roman troops who had deserted (but not to the traitorous intelligence officers and scouts) and many rejoined the ranks until a large enough army could be deployed to retake the regions that had been overrun. The line of Hadrian's Wall was reached and it could be that it was at this stage that the province of Valentia was established in the lowlands of Scotland, though this is only speculative. New treaty arrangements were made, whereby some of the tribes just north of the wall kept the peace on Rome's behalf, and were handsomely paid for their trouble. The emergency lasted about six to nine months in its main phase, but the situation was not completely stabilised until AD 369. The sudden and coordinated attacks showed just how vulnerable Britain was; the provinces never truly recovered from the assault.

Constantine's mother, Helena, had been granted the title of *Augusta*, the equivalent of an empress, and had used her new-found gravitas to go on a pilgrimage to the Holy Land, where, in Jerusalem, she was supposed to have had a vision of the secret burial place of the True Cross. Excavations were carried out under her direct supervision, and the cross was (allegedly) found. A British origin was later claimed for this visionary lady, but as the imperial family were discovering the benefits of the new faith, back in Britain the opposite process was happening. The breakdown in the social order there caused many wandering unemployed or mendicant folk from the lowest social strata to re-embrace forms of paganism, which had long been practised in an underground, bowdlerised form. Old Celtic god-forms, guardian spirits, faeries and goddesses of wells and springs re-emerged, along with the almost forgotten war gods and battle heroes. Those who promulgated this Celtic cultural renaissance were the bards, despised and marginalised inheritors of the traditions of the Druids. As urban culture became more and more the preserve of the elite, aligned with an overseas authority, so in the countryside the pagan elements long dormant in the British psyche were reawakened. 'Pagan' means 'rustic' – the Roman Church was a predominantly urban affair. The name of the kingdom of Powys is possibly derived from *pagenses*, 'the rural disticts'. At Lydney in the Forest of Dean, a temple to Nodens, or Gwynn ap Nudd as he became known, was built at around this time; other ancient Celtic god-forms were worshipped once more too, such as Bran, Beli, Maponus, Cuda and Brigit. The lowest social strata had never abandoned the British language to learn Latin and, as the villas were looted or failed for want of reliable labour, the old language spread in the countryside, while Latin only thrived in towns, which were shrinking and losing their economic viability as the country estates that supplied produce for sale at markets became less productive and secure. Very many of the wealthy town dwellers were lawyers who had received tertiary education in the classics. The magistracy formed the natural nucleus of local government, and by this time was also the core of the Christian community in the towns. After nearly four centuries of being overlaid by a rational, scientific and materialist culture, Britain was reverting to magic.

The final meltdown in Britannia commenced in AD 381. In that year a senior Roman army officer, Magnus Maximus, a Spaniard by birth, took control of the army units in Britain, which was a very considerable force, following on from the troubles of 367–69. He declared himself as emperor, not only of Britain but of Gaul and Spain as well – the 'Prefecture of the Gauls'. To back his imperial claim Maximus gathered an army, including many British recruits, and marched on Rome itself. The Eternal City fell to him, but in 388 he was defeated and killed by the mighty Theodosius, the emperor of the Eastern Roman Empire, based at Constantinople. This failure would be a mere footnote in the miserable history of the declining years of imperial rule, were it not for the fact that his adventurism had denuded Britain of nearly all its garrison, including many of the 30,000-strong complement that manned Hadrian's Wall. Maximus seems to have had a British wife called Elen (St Helen) known in Welsh tradition as *Elen Luyddog* or 'Helen of the Hosts'. Their daughter, Severa, was supposed to have been married to a British nobleman by the name of Vortigern, who will shortly be of considerable importance in this story. Garbled folk-memories recalled the Maximus expedition and his exploit of having 'killed the king of Rome', which Arthur's similar campaign against Rome is probably based on. The later commentator and historian Gildas castigated him for having left Britain defenceless. This parlous situation led to a new upsurge in Irish raiding, and possibly the beginnings of Irish settlements in south-west Wales. On the last day of AD 406 the River Rhine froze over and a vast horde of Vandals, Alans, and Suevi crossed over and overran Gaul. A half-Vandal Roman army officer called Stilicho managed to restore some sort of order to Britain, but in 407 the last act of the Roman imperial story in the island took place when Constantine III was proclaimed as yet another usurper 'emperor'. He took what units of the Roman army remained in Britain on another doomed adventure overseas. Constantine and his second in command, Gerontius, never returned. Britain came under attack from Germanic pirates again. On 24 August AD 410, Rome itself fell to the Visigothic king Alaric. Britannia was advised to take measures for its own defence by Honorius, the Roman emperor. There was little else he could do.

The Western Empire was effectively finished – but perhaps the people at the time failed to see this stark fact. There had been many disturbances, intra-imperial wars, economic and military disasters, but people had always muddled through somehow. The Roman people of the empire shared a religion, way of life, language and common culture, and they did not suddenly all revert to their former tribal ways after 410. They were, however, on a road that took them, whether they knew it or not, backwards, because 'the eternal light of Rome' was a guttering candle and dark days were coming. Of all the provinces of the empire, it was to be Britannia that was to endure the most savage and remorseless assault. In the rest of the Western Empire Latin formed the basis of the languages and culture of what came later – but not in Britain. A Teutonic language came to predominate in what is now England because the people who migrated there from northern Germany and southern Scandinavia – Angles, Saxons and Jutes – were, unlike the Goths and Vandals, not even heretical Christians. They hated and despised Roman culture and had no use for its refinements and innovations. To them, cities were centres of psychic pestilence, cursed places infested with unclean spirits. Together with the traditional Irish and Pictish assailants, these Germanic pirates, who had formerly been content with hit-and-run raids, now looked at the abandoned island with a view to permanent settlement. It was precisely because of these unique threats that, eventually, the British rallied and did something that no other province of the former Roman Empire managed to do. They organised resistance using their own resources, and for a while, they halted the barbarian advance.

The Romano-Britons were hopelessly exposed and the Saxon 'plague' is evidenced by the widespread burial of silver plate and precious objects, such as the Mildenhall Horde in Suffolk. The end of Roman Britain was marked by burning villages and farmsteads, ransacked villas, and desperate attempts to hire barbarians as a defence against their compatriots. Settled bands of warriors, known as *Laeti*, some of them Germans of other tribes, protected regions with an aristocracy wealthy enough to pay and feed them. As early as 372, a German tribe, the Alemanni, had been transported to Britain under their king, Fraomar. In the Thames Valley another German mercenary group, the Gewissae, had been settled for generations, and had probably interbred with local womenfolk. Procopius of Caeserea tells us that in the absence of a central authority decision-making had devolved upon *tyrannoi* officials based in the *civitates*, analogous to county towns. Some kind of national federation of these local leaders seems to have recognised Magnus Maximus's son-in-law, Vortigern, as a *superbus tyrannus*; curiously, Vortigern's name is a title in Brythonic, 'Vor' is 'great' and 'tigern' is the head of the clan or folk – literally the 'great leader', his high-sounding title inverse to his real power. His credentials may have had something to do with his connections to Maximus, who may have been regarded as a 'national' hero – even though he had been born in Spain.

It is around this time, as the twilight turned to darkness proper, that history begins to shade into legend, but nevertheless history still records contacts between the Continent and Britain, including two visits by a bishop called Germanus (later St Germanus) of Auxerre in Burgundy. A Briton named Morgan, Latinised as 'Pelagius', was responsible for a heretical and revolutionary theological doctrine, which he promulgated in Rome and Sicily with the aid of an anonymous supporter known as 'the Sicilian Briton'. One of the tenets of the heresy was that man is basically good and capable of attaining grace by his own efforts – a doctrine not only extraordinarily optimistic but also unsupported by scripture. Another of its tenets was that the cause of extreme poverty is extreme wealth, and that Christians should aspire to a middle way, a sort of socialistic utopia. This latter message was most warmly received by the urban poor and the redundant slaves who relied on the doles for survival, but was viewed with suspicion by the Church, who feared the potential for politicisation of the divine message. In fact, much of what Pelagius said was in a direct line to the old morality of the Druids, and when Agricola, a student of Pelagius, returned to Britain and promoted his ideas in his own homeland he found a respectful and sympathetic audience. Determined to prevent the heresy from perverting the true Christian message, Germanus was sent by Pope Celestine I to tour the cities and chief churches of Britain and defeat the heretics in argument. This version of Christianity, ill-informed, or mixed with paganism or pseudo-Christian beliefs, was very strongly supported, especially because it was 'made in Britain' so to speak. It seems that Vortigern was an adherent of the heresy, so these religious missions in 429 and 444 provide us with a glimpse into life in Britain at just the time when the barbarian invasions were making their first impression.

They are the last known records of the civilisation that had existed in Britain for 400 years – so, what was happening, just before the darkness fell?

Firstly, it is clear that the war between Britons and Saxons had already begun. Germanus travelled to Verulamium, the city Boudicca had once destroyed, to meet a council of bishops and leading magnates, some of whom must have recruited local levies and militiamen. Germanus had extensive military experience, and despite his cloth he organised a campaign to sally out against the barbarians. They were said to have been interdicted and defeated without any blood being shed, with Germanus's host simply hiding in a wooded valley and shouting out 'Allelulia!' three times. This sonic attack proved sufficient, according to the chronicler, to put the enemy to flight, but reading between the lines we can perhaps see here the beginning of the British resistance movement. Secondly, town life was still going on at some level, and there was still a political infrastructure. The combined barbarian forces of mixed Irish, Pictish and Saxon raiders were operating in a similar way to the insurgents and invaders of 367. But by the time of Germanus's second visit, the situation had deteriorated markedly. The Saxons were arriving in large numbers and had settled in East Anglia and Kent. The control of the latter gave them a stranglehold on cross-Channel trade and, crucially, control over the traditional landing place for Roman forces sent to support Britain in times of crisis – Rutupiae (Richborough).

In 446 an appeal was sent out to Aetius, the famous general who later defeated Attila the Hun. The people who sent this desperate appeal are described as 'the miserable remnants of the Britons'. Clearly, something awful had taken place in Britain. The wretched British describe how 'the barbarians push us into the sea, the sea back to the barbarians, between these two kinds of death, we are either drowned or slaughtered'. But Aetius was too preoccupied with the Franks and Huns to help Britain, and the failure to respond consolidated the regime of Vortigern, whose Celtic Nationalism tinged with heretical religion, was peculiarly British. If Germanus's visits were designed to challenge him politically, the lack of a 'Roman' military response doomed the party in Britain, which still cleaved to the vestiges of empire.

In all probability, the enemies that had caused so much trouble were the Irish *Scotti* and the Picts. The later historian, Gildas, thought that Vortigern had hired a band of mercenaries – Jutes and Saxons – to fight against the Picts, a long-established imperial policy that had been resorted to for nearly a century. We cannot be quite sure that Gildas is accurate in this presumption, but what is claimed is that Vortigern's resources were so meagre that he could no longer keep up the regular provision of food supplies to the mercenaries. They immediately threatened rebellion, and soon acted on the threats by bursting out of their enclaves and sacking and burning southern Britain from coast to coast. This sounds like an organised campaign of terrorism and plundering, and it broke the will of many of those with enough resources to leave Britain by sea. Since the time of Maximus, a British colony had existed in Armorica – what became 'Brittany' in Gaul. Tens of thousands fled abroad, not only there but also to Spain, including some of the best educated and wealthiest of the Britons. Less fortunate folk had to content themselves with flight into the western lands, Wales and the West Midlands, and the peninsula of Devon and Cornwall. The intensification of the Saxon operations implies that by now they were operating along the same lines as the 'Great Army' of the Danes in the 860s. With nothing to stop them their ravaging proved sufficient to gain them control of the most Romanised part of the island, and the British population fled before them, leaving behind abandoned towns and ruined villas. Brutal massacres left the British bewildered and powerless, and Vortigern's regime must have faltered. It is recorded that at a conference, later known to the Britons as 'the treachery of the long-knives', that the Saxons drew concealed knives on their British hosts and massacred them.

A new leader, Ambrosius Aurelianus, emerged. He rallied the nobility of the south-west and the Cotswolds, Wiltshire and Dorset, and perhaps utilising previous military experience – or tactical innovations he had read about in military manuals – a British self-defence force was created. Ambrosius is described as a *gwledig* or commander in later Welsh legend, and he was said to have been descended from a family who had 'worn the purple'. This, and his prestigious Roman name – J. N. L Myers, in his *The English Settlements* (Oxford, 1986), points out that Aurelius Ambrosius was the name of the Bishop of Milan, whose cult status in the Church was very powerful at this time – suggests that Ambrosius was a member of a devout wing of the nobility. His authority may have extended beyond Britain to Brittany, and in the late 450s he managed to contain the Saxon advance and secure the sea-lanes between Britain and Armorica. The village of Amesbury in Wiltshire was originally called Ambresbyrig 'the fort of Ambrosius' and this puts the headquarters for his campaigns on Salisbury Plain, near to the ancient monument of Stonehenge. In Geoffrey of Monmouth's *Historia Regum Britanniae*, it is recorded that Vortigern was an enemy of Ambrosius, or Emrys as the Welsh remember him, and Ambrosius is described as a son of Constantine III. Ambrosius has two brothers in this account, including one called Uther 'Pendragon', and he is the putative father of another legendary resistance fighter – Arthur. He was to become the most famous Celtic warrior-king of all time, and a folk hero – but did he really exist?

6

The Enigma of Arthur

The historian J. N. L Myers in his *The English Settlements* (Oxford, 1986) thought that more time had been spent by academics delving into the issue of 'Arthur' than enough, and that serious analysis of the Anglo-Saxon intrusions in the fifth century had been obfuscated by these pointless researches. Another serious scholar, John Morris, published a groundbreaking study in 1973 called *The Age of Arthur: A History of the British Isles from 350–650 AD,* which took quite the opposite view. It was an attempt to reconstruct the jigsaw puzzle of source information that was indisputably legitimate around a 'missing-piece', which the reader was invited to infer must have been Arthur, the last of the sub-Roman pretenders to the imperial tradition to have emerged from Britain. In effect, he posited an 'Arthur shaped-hole', which he proceeded to fill with cleverly argued connections between historical fact and legend. Myers is quite correct to say that no really convincing archaeological or reliable documentary evidence exists for 'Arthur', but, as they say, 'absence of evidence is not evidence of absence'. John Morris, though he wrote with a convincing passion and adduced material from primary Celtic sources rarely considered in more Anglo-centric scholarship, came across as an advocate for an Arthur who was perhaps even more heroic than the man presented by Geoffrey of Monmouth. We will see later on how the folk legends about Arthur were recycled in the post-Anglo-Saxon period. However, the question we have to consider is whether he existed at all, and, if so, why is there such a dearth of evidence about him? If not, why was such a personage invented, what consolation or incitement was intended by the promotion of such a story? But most crucially, was he the mastermind behind a crushing defeat of the Saxons, at a place known as *Mons Badonicus*, or 'Mount Badon' – and if so, what were the implications of this Romano-Celtic victory?

The name Artorius, 'Arthur' is the Brythonic version, while it is not very common did have a precedent in Britain, and perhaps he was descended from one Artorius Justus, who served in the legions in the province in the third century. Curiously though, the name becomes more popular in the sixth century, which may have come about because of a desire to preserve the memory of the popular saviour – in the same way 'Winston' became briefly popular after the Second World War in Britain and its former colonies. Considering the cataclysm that had befallen the Britons, it is unsurprising that little material or documentary evidence was left behind for Arthur's existence, but folk legends and bardic poetry were already referring to him early on. A Welsh poem mentions him, which may have been translated from an original contemporary Brythonic source:

> At Llongborth I saw Arthur's heroes who cut with steel
> The Emperor ruler of our labour
> In Llongborth Gereint was slain, heroes of the land of Dyfneint
> Before they were slain they slew.

The use of the word *ameraudur* in Welsh, meaning 'emperor', may well be some garbled recollection of an authority superior to the petty tribal chieftains, rather like Cassivellaunus, Cunobelinus, and Caratacus in pre-Roman times – someone like a Celtic high king. There is also a connotation of it meaning a commander chosen according to respect or merit rather than hereditary entitlement. Llongborth may be Langport in Somerset, an area rich in folklore about Arthur. Dyfneint is Dumnonia, Devon and Cornwall. Again the peninsula is saturated in Arthurian folklore, as we will see. Gereint or Gerontius may be the same person as a noble of the Cornovii of the Midlands, elements of whose royal house seem to have been transplanted to the south-west at this time. Another early poem may mention Arthur too, called the '*Canu Heledd*'. It is a poem of mourning or keening, allegedly composed by the surviving sister of a band of brothers who rode into battle against Anglo-Saxon forces in the 650s and who were all killed in a counter-raid:

My heart is aflame like a firebrand ...
Brothers I had, better it was when they lived,
The whelps of Arthur, our mighty fortress
Before Caer Luitcoit they triumphed.

It has been objected that the line in the Canu Heledd may have been mistranslated, but there are other early references too, including one by Aneirin, a north-country Brythonic bard, who says that a warrior, although famously strong and brave, 'does not compare to Arthur'. I think those who try to suggest that the entire corpus of material adduced to support Arthur's early *literary* existence at least, is too weak or suspect, have not fairly considered these poetic references. Whether or not they referred to a real flesh-and-blood person or a fictional folk hero is quite another matter.

Our first real historical documentary encounter with Arthur comes in Welsh annals dating from the ninth century onwards, considerably after the events they purport to record. Nevertheless, they may well have been based on earlier sources recorded nearer the time, and so are by no means valueless. Arthur gets a mention in them twice, and battles are involved on both occasions:

490–516: Battle of Badon in which Arthur carried the cross of our Lord Jesus Christ on his shoulders (or possibly 'shield') for three days and nights and the Britons were victorious.

And later on:

511–537: The fight at Camlann in which Arthur and Medraut were killed.

In the case of these brief, enigmatic entries, whose sole purpose appears to be to intrude the name 'Arthur' into some sort of respectable history, the possibility of interpolation by a later scribe who has altered the document cannot be dismissed, and they must be viewed in that light. There was a frantic effort to collate evidence in Wales in particular during the ninth century, when Wales was in the process of becoming a united nation and presumably in need of a heroic foundation tradition. One of the participants in this effort was a clerk from Bangor called Nennius. He sought out any written documents relating to Arthur and 'made a heap of all I could find'. His *History of the Britons* contains the summation of all he had found out, and it is interesting:

> Then Arthur fought against them (the Saxons) in those days with the kings of the Britons, but he himself was the leader of battles (dux bellorum). The first battle was at the mouth of the river Glein. The second, third, fourth and fifth on another river called Dubglas in the district of Linnius. The sixth battle was on the river Bassas. The seventh battle was in the Forest of Celidon, that is Cat Coit Celidon. The eighth battle was in the fortress of Guinnion in which Arthur carried on his shoulders an image of St Mary the Virgin, and the pagans were put to flight and a great slaughter made among them through the virtue of Our Lord Jesus Christ and his holy maiden-mother, Mary. The ninth battle took place at the City of the Legion. The tenth battle was fought on the banks of a river called Tribruit. The eleventh battle took place on the mountain called Agned. The twelfth battle was on Badon Hill, in which on that one day, by one onset of Arthur, nine hundred and sixty men fell, and no-one slew them but Arthur. And in all the battles he was victorious.

What seems fairly certain is that this list comes from an original document, which may have been compiled from oral or poetic histories relating to Arthur, his victories, and his status. It openly admits that Arthur was no 'king', and indeed implies that he was not a man of high rank, but had succeeded because he was beloved by the people (like Caratacus?) or on pure military merit. If it were a forgery, designed to portray Arthur as an exemplar, why include this awkward fact? The places mentioned are obscure, widely dispersed, with no obvious connections between them. Rivers feature frequently and the four battles on the River Dubglas or Douglas indicate a long, hard-fought campaign in Lincolnshire or thereabouts. There are reasons to commend this as genuine too.

We have seen how the defence of river crossings was a crucial part of the Celtic military mindset, and the area around Lincoln was strategically vital to the defence of a contiguous zone inhabited by Celtic or Latin speaking folk. Nennius refers to Arthur's connections to the area of Herefordshire and Brycheiniog in south Wales in a footnote, and records that Arthur had a son called Anir, for whose death Arthur was responsible. These must be fragments of stories which recorded something of Arthur's background and family life, and again, if they were forgeries or cynical interpolations, why limit oneself to such an obscure area, and include what looks like scandal? My view is that the Nennius material contains genuine tales of some folk hero, based on a real person.

Arthur was not a 'lone wolf' but a captain of a Celtic war-band, the template for the later 'knights of the Round Table'. The *Black Book of Carmarthen* records some of their names, like Bedwyr and Kei, the prototypes for 'Sir Bedevere' and 'Sir Kay', and in a tale in the *Mabinogion* a medieval compendium of ancient Welsh oral folk tales, Arthur's men set out on a quest for a magical cauldron, an ancient motif in Celtic mythology, later to be Christianised and recycled as the Quest for the Holy Grail. In fact, as Peter Berresford-Ellis notes in his *The Celts* (London, 1998), Arthur and his men closely resemble the Irish Fianna, the elite warrior companions of Fionn Mac Cumhail, and the magical sword Excalibur is paralleled in Irish myth as 'Caladcholg', an equivalent weapon wielded by Fergus Mac Roth, another fabled Irish hero. Arthur's fame, indeed, spread to Ireland from west Britain, but the mythological themes in folklore about him must surely have been inspired by similar Irish tales in the first place. As we will see, for the Celts gods and heroes were interchangeable, and the pent-up outpouring of mythological archetypes which had been sublimated during the Roman occupation, the breakdown of religious conventions, and the deep folk need for a unifying 'national' story for the Britons – whether they were Latin-speaking or Celtic – gave a powerful impetus for folk tales that attached themselves to someone who was in all probability quite obscure. 'Arthur the Soldier', as he was known, was not uncontroversial. With the cities abandoned and many of the wealthier citizens having fled overseas, a big problem for Ambrosius and Arthur must have been how to raise taxes and foodstuffs or fodder for the cavalry from hard-pressed landowners, including the Church. The *Life of St Cadoc*, although it is a hagiography, contains all sorts of petty details about Arthur and his doings. Other saints' lives describe Arthur as a *tyrannus* that is, one not eligible to rule by virtue of birthright, and again they disparage him for his hard bargaining with the monasteries. According to a *Life of St Gildas* written by Caradoc of Llancarfan, Gildas (the same man who wrote the *Liber Querulous*, or 'book of complaint', which became the most reliable historical document for the period immediately after Arthur's putative reign) had good reason to hate the 'tyrant'. Arthur, it is claimed, had killed Hueill, the holy man's own brother. According to the same hagiography, Arthur's wife Guennuvar had been abducted by Melwas, a chieftain based at Glastonbury, and it was Gildas who negotiated her release. It seems all the more strange then, that Gildas – who was a real historical personage without any doubt – fails to mention Arthur at all in his history of the times, but there may be a solution to this anomaly.

The real problem which has bedevilled researchers into a 'factual' Arthur is that his rise to power coincided with the collapse of Roman Britain and the re-emergence or revival of Celtic culture – combined with a barbarian onslaught of unprecedented intensity from the Saxons. In times so troubled few contemporary records were kept up, but a little later, after the events but close enough to them to be reliably informed, Gildas wrote his *De Excidio et conquestu Britanniae*, his 'complaining book', about the 'ruination of Britain'. This was no conventional history but a diatribe against the petty warrior kings of the various British kingdoms of his day, whose immorality, apostasy and sin he believed had brought the Britons to their knees. John Morris thought that this emphasis on the failings of contemporary rulers was meant to be read in deliberate contradistinction to the 'glory days' of Arthur and Ambrosius, whose exploits had given the Britons an opportunity for national repentance for their collective sin. There was no need to refer to Arthur, in this view, because his achievements and legacy of good governance were well known to everyone. The reticence of Gildas to mention him by name could be ascribed to Arthur's slaughtering the cleric's brother. There is a theory that Gildas *did* mention Arthur, but that he disguised this using a sort of acrostic code, which when broken reveals him to be Cuneglas, a Welsh chieftain he describes as a 'red butcher', and a 'bear' – *Art*, or in Breton, *Arz*, is a root word meaning 'bear'. Gildas has a phobia about mentioning people by their real names, and perhaps his own personal vendetta against Arthur (although he was supposed to have forgiven him, even prescribing Arthur's penance for the killing) made it impolitic for him to become embroiled in an excoriation of a man who was, by his time, a national hero. It is important to take note that Gildas was not an 'historian' as we now think of that term, though his 'complaining book' is a *historia*. Knowledge of the past implied an ability to foresee events to come, prophetic visions, in other words. Gildas is berating his countrymen, who have neglected their moral duty, but he reserves his most bitter invective for their rulers. It may be that the king who morphed into 'Arthur' was a Welsh ruler called Cuneglas, who was too dangerous for Gildas to denounce openly. Instead he conceals his criticism in the form of a complex code and punning wordplay. But Gildas has no problem in mentioning Ambrosius, and he gives us the important information that he (Gildas) was actually born in the year of the victory at *Mons Badonicus* and confirms that it was a spectacular defeat for the 'gallows-crew' as he disparagingly calls the Saxons.

If we accept the date range of AD 490–500 as being about correct for Gildas's year of birth, this makes it impossible for Ambrosius to have been the British commander at Mount Badon. But if Ambrosius had trained a new generation of young lieutenants, maybe his own nephew among them, then they would have been the field commanders of the Romano-British army at Badon. Nennius says the victor was Arthur, and there are strong traditions for the battle being fought somewhere in the south-west of modern England. Bath has been postulated, and Solsbury Hill near Batheaston. Liddington Castle and Great Bedwyn are also strong contenders, and all these places are easily within reach of South Cadbury Castle hill fort in Somerset, which has an ancient tradition of being 'Camelot', and other folk connections with 'king' Arthur. Archaeological excavations revealed that a powerful Celtic chieftain refortified this hill fort as a base for a personal war-band, complete with watchtowers, a huge gatehouse, a chapel and stone-reinforced revetments around the ramparts, in around AD 470, just at the time a personage corresponding to Arthur would have been marshalling his forces for war against the Saxons. This fortress was still in use a century later and remains one of the most dominating hill fortresses in Britain. If it was not Arthur who accomplished this, then it was some other Celtic Brythonic warlord, and his anonymous achievements are just as impressive from an historical point of view. Some scholars have suggested a chieftain or petty king called Arthwys ap Mar who may have originated in Gwent as the model for Arthur, but as yet this is purely speculative, a fresh contender emerges almost annually. This odd melange of history, folklore, archaeology, and poetry does not lend itself easily to conventional historical scholarship, but it seems to me that far from Arthur obfuscating the 'facts', rather it is the other way around, that if we exclude the possibility of his being the organiser and victor at Mount Badon, we are no further forward, whereas if we triangulate archaeology, folk tradition, and the scanty historical references, a story of Romano-British revival is revealed, a heroic struggle that preserved the indigenous population in the island, and saved the Christian faith from utter extinction. It does not seem to the author too unreasonable that such feats should have passed into the legends and folk memory of the British people. His Saxon enemies, for whom defeat in battle was the ultimate humiliation, would have had no reason to preserve his memory. Sir Frank Merry Stenton in his *Anglo-Saxon England* (Oxford, 1970) comments that good evidence exists for a flight from southern Britain by Saxons to the Continent at this time. Badon was a crushing blow to the incomers, the culmination of a long and bitter war of attrition, so decisive that some sort of territorial partition was enforced on the Anglo-Saxons. This tells us something important, and perhaps crucial. The Britons were capable of offensive operations against the Saxons. The ancient stories about Arthur and similar Celtic warlords always refer to mounted troops, and the widely dispersed locations of the battlefields in Nennius's battle-list suggest a mobile cavalry force that roamed around the country from Scotland to Cornwall. Could this method of warfare provide clues as to Arthur's strategy?

The fact is that cavalry had long been the main arm of the Roman military just before they departed from Britain. There was a 'heavy' type, with both horse and rider clad in mail, the *cataphractarii* and a 'super-heavy' variety called the *clibanarii*. Count Belisarius reconquered Italy with a force of less than 1,000 cavalry at just this time. A force of Sarmatian cavalry over 5,000 strong actually served in Britain under a leader called Lucius Artorius Castus, and many features in the ancient legends seem to correspond to customs which the Sarmatians brought with them, in particular etiquette and ritual pertaining to their swords. Cavalry were more flexible than infantry, and whole tribes of peoples with a rich tradition of horsemanship could be recruited under the Roman banners. They were increasingly resorted to in times of straitened circumstances, which supervened as the empire declined because their mobility provided a strike force that could be deployed in surprise offensive operations, or for harrying settlers as they cleared woods and ploughed in clearings, or attempted to erect dwellings. As soon as Saxon war-bands departed on campaign (although the elite rode to battle, they fought as infantry by and large) their settlements were exposed to attack by British horsemen, a situation most enervating in terms of morale, but the Britons could also use the cavalry force as a mobile reserve, kept well behind the front line, to be used in an elastic defence utilising the still existing infrastructure of the Roman road system with its many posting-stations.

Such long-range campaigns were a feature of Penda of Mercia's strategy a century later. He operated from Exeter in the south-west all the way to Stirling in Scotland. The most we can say about the Badon campaign is that it was a siege, of a *mons* (hill fort), therefore it was the Saxons who were the aggressors, and they had struck deep into British-held territory. If the British field force or its core elements at least, were cavalry of some sort, they relied on a secure base for breeding quality mounts. Without this the entire project was in jeopardy. Arthur's curious status becomes explicable if we think of him as the leader of some mobile reserve that moved around the country in support of local tribal militias – the *dux bellorum*, the 'leader of battles'. In fact we know that a Roman military command *did* exist, whose commission was to act in just such a way, the *Comes Britanniarum*. If this position was revived, perhaps under a commander trained under Ambrosius, it absolutely depended upon a secure supply of mounts, and a large open area where the force (which may not have been very numerous) could train on manoeuvres. A Saxon attack on the West Country then, makes sense, and it was a plan worthy of Von Clausewitz in its Teutonic efficiency. A coalition of Saxons and Jutes, perhaps under the overall command of King Aelle of Sussex, must have advanced swiftly using the Ridgeway or Ermine Street. Their plan was to break through the thin screen of British scouts and concentrate against Arthur's (or some similar commander's) elite force, and destroy it. A 'siege' is described, and this can only mean that the outnumbered British force (and its mounts) were trapped in a hill fort by the Saxons, but this was a high-risk strategy because the Saxons were deep in enemy territory and their provisions could not hold out for very long. Arthur's men must have been very anxious. Arthur himself 'carried the cross of Our Lord Jesus Christ on his shoulders for three days and nights'. This odd piece of information tells us that Arthur, like Ambrosius before him, saw the war as a holy war against the heathens. The Old Welsh word *scuit* means 'a shield' but *scuid* means 'shoulder', so there could have been a scribal error. Did Arthur perhaps display the design of the cross on his shield or was there some dramatic ritual, a self-mortification before battle? To surround a large hill fort was risky, because the observers high above could pick out weak points in the line, or identify where gaps appeared when foraging parties were sent out by the Saxons. An early morning charge by a large body of horsemen could concentrate upon one such weak point and break through, and once the enemy was broken there could be no escape in this open country and no refuge for the hated Saxons among the local population. In such scenarios more men are lost in the follow-up then in the initial melee and this would have been what made Badon so decisive. A whole generation of Saxon warriors was annihilated, and they were so insecure afterwards that many decided to leave Britain and try their luck on the Continent. Of course we cannot know if the British cavalry force was modelled on the late-Roman types, but the Brythonic Celts (indeed all Celts) were always famous horsemen. Their relatives the *Gaels* had provided cavalry for the Egyptian Pharaohs, and chariots too – *Gael* means 'hero'. Such war-bands of British cavalry are exemplified in a poem written by Aneirin, the bard who mentioned Arthur very early on. In his *Gododdin* we get an impression of such an elite fighting force:

> Men went to Catraeth, shouting for battle
> A squadron of horse,
> Blue their armour, lances poised and sharp
> Mail and swords glinting
> Though they were slain they slew,
> None to their homeland returned.
> Short their lives, long the grief of their kinfolk
> Seven times their number the Saxons they slew,
> Many the widows they made, many the mothers who wept
> After the wine and the mead they left us armoured in mail,
> I know the sorrow of their death
> They were slain and never grew grey,
> From the army of Myndog, grief unbounded,
> Of three hundred, but one returned.

In my opinion, this is the most likely scenario for Badon, and Arthur, or someone like him, would have been very much like the warriors in Aneirin's poem, written not very long afterwards. We will never know for sure, but if Badon was in the West Country as I have postulated, this may also account for the curious atmosphere that has attached itself to Arthur's name – an atmosphere redolent of Celtic myth and the curious particularism of western Britain that we have encountered in an earlier chapter. This strong association of Arthur with the west has seeped into our collective unconscious – but is it correct?

It is important to bear in mind that there was no concept of a united Britain at this time. The Anglo-Saxon conquests of East Anglia, Kent, Sussex, and probably smaller enclaves in the north, were a *fait accompli*. If there was a strategic objective for 'Arthur' it would have focused on preserving the integrity of the province of Britannia Prima with its capital at Corinium Dobunnorum, modern-day Cirencester. Arthur's associations with Wales, Devon and Cornwall and the Welsh Marches and western Midlands all then fall into place. All of these areas were once part of this huge province. The British emigration to Brittany and Britonia in Spain made it all the more imperative to preserve the security of the sea lanes of the western approaches and we know Ambrosius built a fleet. Contact with a newly Christianised Ireland had also become increasingly important, and from the monasteries of that island came a new influx of missionaries and pilgrims.

The memories of Arthur were so strong in Devon and Cornwall that in AD 1113 a group of French monks were attacked at Bodmin for scoffing at a tale that 'King Arthur' had not only been a real historical person but that he was still alive, waiting to redeem his stricken country. Somerset, and especially Glastonbury, has always had strong mythical associations with Arthur, and in the twelfth century his grave (and that of his queen) were said to have been excavated in the grounds of the abbey there, after the 'secret' location was revealed by an alleged holy man. Herefordshire, south Wales, north Wales, Powys, Shropshire and Cheshire also have enduring traditions. At Mitchell's Fold stone circle, near Priestweston on the Welsh border, Arthur is said to have drawn the sword Excalibur from the stone, and the nearby River Camlad is said to be Camlann, the site of 'The last dim weird battle in the west' as Tennyson envisioned it. Unfortunately other traditions insist that Arthur was a 'man of the north'. Much of this speculation focuses upon the candidates for some of the battlefields in the list Nennius provides. Cat Coit Celidon is quite clearly on the Scottish borders, and one wonders if this has anything to do with the campaign in which Gildas's brother was killed (Gildas may have been a native of the area which became Strathclyde) and it has been thought that the River Glen in Northumberland is the same as the river 'Glein' mentioned in Nennius's list. It has to be said that there must have been many rivers named Glein and Dubglas or Douglas before the Brythonic language was lost in these areas, but a more convincing sounding connection is with Camboglanna, the site of the Roman fort on the abandoned and ruined Hadrian's Wall at Birdoswald. This means 'crooked glen' but again, there must have been hundreds of places with this name in ancient Britain. Afon Gamlan, a small tributary of the Dyfi, and Slaughter Bridge on the River Camel in Cornwall are both identified as the site of Arthur's legendary final battle with Medraut or 'Mordred' in which he was fatally wounded. 'Camel' just means 'crooked' in ancient British speech. The Anglo-Saxon poet Layamon was sure the Cornish connection with Camlann was correct in the twelfth century, when he wrote down his 'Brut'. Cornwall has some of the strongest folk connections to Arthur of all. Dozmary Pool on Bodmin Moor is supposedly where Bedwyr was ordered to throw Excalibur into the lake. Tintagel has a long tradition of being Arthur's birthplace. When Arthur is taken by faerie women on a magical boat to be healed of his grievous wounds it is to no ordinary geographical realm he is conveyed, but to 'the isle of apples' or 'Avalon'. He becomes *Rex quondam, Rex que futurus* 'King once, King that shall be'. For Arthur's destiny is to sail into the misty otherworld in the west beyond the great ocean, that fabled land where all the ancestor spirits retire, the same place we observed in the deep collective memory of the Celts from the earliest times. In Caer Wydr 'the Glass Castle' he lies in an enchanted sleep, until the days when his fellow countrymen have sore need of him. Then he will return in glory, the great liberator from the Land of Shades. We are no longer in the territory of conventional history, but of a resurgent religion, not quite Druidic, not entirely Christian, certainly tinged with elements of heresy and paganism – a phantasmagoria of the Celtic psyche, projected, as it were, into this increasingly dangerous and uncertain world. Sir John Rhys thought Arthur was a late-Brythonic variant of the Badb, the Celtic goddess or director of earthly battles. She dwelt in the otherworld, beyond the great ocean in the west, but in times of supreme cultural stress she would be called forth to take up her position as director or commander in this corporeal world. Arthur occupies a similar position, but as a male, solar divinity, who, like Orpheus, descends into the underworld, there to do battle with the forces of wickedness, darkness, oppression and death, only to re-emerge triumphant and invincible, the ultimate liberator of his people. But night will fall again – it has to – and the *combrogi*, the 'fellow countrymen', must wait patiently for the return of the cosmic hero who is, at the same time, their own tribal 'superman'. We may perhaps think of a process that began with a small tribal warlord being elevated to overall command of some British national army, organised along the lines of the former Roman army. That man won many small but significant victories throughout north and west Britain, and was celebrated in bardic poetry. Eventually a decisive victory was won at Mount Badon, and this victory was attributed to 'Arthur' as well. When he died, probably in some 'fight' at 'Camlann' the process of disintegration of the Romano-British way of life was already underway. The spirit of the mortal man was released and manifested in the Puffin or 'Cornish Chough', or sometimes was seen in company with his hound Cavall, riding Lamrei, his magical mare, as he led the 'Wild Hunt' across the land. Arthur's empire, like so much else about him, proved to be ultimately insubstantial, ethereal – and all his achievements crumbled as soon as he was dead. We cannot know, possibly can never hope to know, the precise circumstances of Arthur's reign, but for a few decades the Britons won a respite for themselves. As soon as the respite was over they were stricken by the 'yellow plague' and their Anglo-Saxon enemies resumed their hostile campaigns, driving the Britons even further west. Economically the Brythonic Celts were less prosperous and technologically competent than their pre-Roman ancestors, destined, it seemed, to become a people at the cultural as well as geographical margins. But the last flicker of resistance of these benighted folk produced a tangible result. They had survived, they had kept their language and religion alive, and one day what they had preserved would be taken up, to be reworked for the consciousness of the high Middle Ages. The promise of the legendary lore was, then, actually fulfilled – Arthur was indeed reborn.

Justine Davis Randers-Pehrson in *Barbarians and Romans: The Birth Struggle of Europe, AD 400–700* (London, 1983) says,

Many of the small kingdoms of the Britons were ephemeral … As far as tactics were concerned, they fielded armies with great elan but without any detectable plan. They armed themselves mentally with the thought that theirs was the Roman tradition, though whatever contact they had ever had with Rome must have been tenuous indeed. The kingdom of Dyfed, for example, appears to have been made up of descendants of an Irish war band (the Deisi) who may have been enlisted as federates by the usurper

Maximus on the eve of his departure for the Continent in 383. About fifty years later the Dyfed dynasty was headed by a man whose memorial stone presents the curious inscription 'Votepor Protector' (Stilicho was a protector at the court of Constantinople as a young man). By the wildest stretch of the imagination, the only protector among Votepor's ancestors from whom he could have inherited such a title might have been an attendant or even a hostage of the usurper Maximus.

But there is another fascinating possibility. If Arthur's title really was 'emperor' as early Welsh poetry implies, then the close companions of such a man (Ambrosius may have claimed the title as well) would have been *Protectors* as John Morris pointed out a long time ago. In such a context the last vestiges of Christian Rome in the West take on a meaning which is no longer 'ephemeral' or marginal, a last beacon of civilisation which, had it survived, may have become a kind of Western European Constantinople. It was not to be, however. The struggle to survive had sapped the will of the Britons. They reverted to what they knew best, the comfortable life of the tribe, the enchanting stories told around the cooking fires by their bards – and chief among those tales, the deeds of Arthur and his men, in the days of honour and glory.

7

The Lost Lands

An ancient legend recorded by Geoffrey of Monmouth (his real name was Geoffrey ap Arthur – his father was actually named Arthur) in the twelfth century must record some kind of garbled origin myth for the nations of Britain. Three great kings ruled the separate nations. Locrine was King of Lloegyr or Loegria – the area corresponding to England. Albanactus was King of Scotland, and Wales was ruled by a king called Camber. It came to pass that the island of Britain was invaded by the Huns, so the three kings combined to drive the Hunnic army into the River Humber, which is (supposedly) named after them. Only one Hun was taken alive, the most beautiful woman in the world, Estreldis, the daughter of the Hun king. Locrine was infatuated as soon as he saw her and took her for his intended bride. But Locrine had previously pledged to marry Gwendolyn, the daughter of the King of Cornwall, who immediately demanded that Locrine repudiate Estreldis and honour his previous betrothal. Locrine could not bear to lose the lovely Estreldis, so he hid her away in secret chambers within his palace, where she remained even after he and Gwendolyn were married. Gwendolyn gave birth to a son, Madan, but secretly Estreldis had also given birth, to a young girl named Sabrina, after whom the River Severn was named. One day Corineus, the King of Cornwall, died and at last Locrine was free to release Estreldis from her confinement and to repudiate Gwendolyn. When they heard of this insult to their princess the people of Cornwall raised a great army and invaded Lloegyr. Locrine was killed and Gwendolyn lost no time in revenging herself on her rival, Estreldis, who was executed. Her blameless daughter, Sabrina, was taken down to the riverside and offered as a sacrifice – the river is still named in her honour to this day. This strange and garbled tale is undoubtedly just that, but it is derived from some deeply ancient origin myth. The kingdom of Lloegyr was supposedly named after Locrine and was a defined political area – roughly all of modern England south-east of a line from the Humber to the Severn Estuaries, excluding Devon and Cornwall. Although it came to mean 'England' to the later Welsh, in fact the two countries were not synonymous. Lloegyr or Loegria or Logres was associated with Arthur in the corpus of Celtic myth and history known as 'the Matter of Britain'. Before we examine these matters in more detail it is important to consider another meaning of Lloegyr. For the Britons these were 'the Lost Lands', the areas at the interface of modern England and Wales, which gradually, and after centuries of bitter warfare, became anglicised. But within them there remained a substratum of Celts, later called 'the Welshry' by the Normans (to distinguish them from the conquered 'Englishry'). The expulsion of the Britons from these lands was never entirely completed.

The most satisfactory explanation of the origin of the word 'Lloegyr' I have found so far, is that it may be derived from a proto-Celtic word *laiko* meaning 'of the army' or 'warriors', but also with a connotation of 'layman' and even 'pagan'. Tribes hired by the Romans to protect regions within the empire, such as the Alemanni and the Gewissae, were called *Laeti* from a Latin word cognate with *Laiko*. The word does not seem to refer to a folk or a people as such. To the Welsh all inhabitants of Lloegyr were *Lloegrwys*, whether they were Britons or Saxons. The conventional thinking is that for the Welsh, the Dumnonians of Devon and Cornwall, and the Britons bordering on the Anglian settlements of the north-east, the name referred to an occupied area – a place where 'warriors' who were also pagans, had settled in large numbers, that is the Anglo-Saxons. We have already observed that the most heavily settled areas by the Germanic folks roughly corresponded to the same zone, which had been most heavily Romanised, and before that Belgicised. Therefore, for a period of over 500 years, the lowlands had been associated with a different culture to that which prevailed in the north and west, which we examined earlier. Originally these western and northern British-speaking regions formed one contiguous bloc with a common language, culture and religion. They were one people and their common enemies were the Anglo-Saxon nations. I think it very unlikely that Lloegyr meant 'the Lost Lands' originally, because in the early sixth century the war was still very much in progress and could have gone either way. Only later, when the Celtic north and the Celtic west were divided by the expansionist Anglian kingdom of Northumbria, would a distinctive border zone appear where British populations were absorbed into the growing Anglo-Saxon states. This process began as soon as Arthur (or whoever the alternative British leader was) died. As the Britons were stricken by a virulent epidemic, the 'yellow plague' during the 540s, the indigenous population may have been halved or even worse. The epidemic had spread from Egypt and had reached Irish and western British ports on trading ships. The Anglo-Saxons did not trade with the infected areas and so were preserved from calamity, alongside those Britons they kept as slaves. So stark was the cultural divide within the island, and so bitter was the hatred between Britons and Saxons, that the incomers were protected from any contagion from that quarter also. As the disaster for the Britons unfolded, while the Germanic population thrived, the point was reached where the Anglo-Saxons felt emboldened to reinitiate hostilities. Fortunately, the records of these epic conflicts are much better preserved for posterity than their 'Arthurian' counterparts, and they relate one of the most exciting and formative periods in all British history.

One reason why we are now on surer ground historically speaking is that we have a contemporary commentator, Gildas, whose whole purpose in writing is to excoriate the leading British kings of his day. There were five rulers who he selected as especially worthy of his castigation, Maelgwn or 'Maglocunus' of Gwynedd, Constantine of Dumnonia (Devon and Cornwall), Vortipor (possibly a descendant of the man commemorated as *Votepor Protector* mentioned in the previous chapter) – Aurelius Caninus (possibly a descendant of Ambrosius Aurelianus?), and a king named Cuneglas. Aurelius may have been a king of a region approximating to Powys, but we cannot be sure. Cuneglas, who has been postulated as a prototype for (or the actual personage of) Arthur ruled Rhos around modern Denbighshire. Of all these kingdoms one in particular stood out, Gwynedd. The folk movements which had resulted in the Anglo-Saxon immigration into Britain did not stand alone. As we have seen, there was a mass emigration of the Britons overseas to Brittany and Spain. Irish tribes, such as the Deisi in south-west Wales had begun a sporadic settlement of parts of Wales, and as a result of the constant disorders on the northern frontier, around Hadrian's Wall, there were tribes who had long been in the pay of Rome, whose task was to act as a buffer against the Picts. According to Welsh legend, a descendant of one of these border-chieftains called 'Paternus of the Red Cloak' or Padarn, Cunedda by name, had been invited into the northernmost part of Wales, Anglesey and the Lleyn peninsula and Snowdonia, as a buffer to Irish settlers after the Roman collapse. This was a similar arrangement to that which had brought the Anglo-Saxons into Britain, and perhaps Vortigern was responsible for this settlement too. More likely though, some more eminent and powerful Roman official was involved, perhaps Magnus Maximus or Theodosius. The story of this plantation is only legendary, but records elements of older traditions dating from a time when the Britons still acknowledged some kind of high king. The tribe Cunedda led into north Wales were known as the *Votadini* in Latin, or the Gododdin among themselves. Such wholesale movements of populations were well-known in the late Roman imperial period. But there is another possibility, because this exodus from the north may have been arranged by someone whose authority and power reminds us that Arthur may not be so fictional a character as some have supposed. Like Arthur he is a legendary figure, a mighty northern overlord known as Coel Hen Guotepauc 'Old Coel the Magnificent' – 'Old King Cole' of the well-known nursery rhyme. If we can crack the riddle of this mysterious personage, we will understand the intricacies of sixth-century Brythonic politics all the better.

The Anglo-Scottish border country was a war zone until the early modern era, the 'debatable land' fought over by private armies of local clan chiefs, the 'Reivers'. But this culture of raiding and counter-raiding, family feuding, selective assassinations and cattle-rustling goes back to pre-Roman times. Hadrian's Wall is a monument to the rapacity and belligerence of these clans and tribes, but also to the ruthless efficiency of the Romans when it came to solving the problem. The late historian John Morris proposed that when Rome withdrew its forces, some powerful Roman military commander, probably the *Dux Britanniarum* or governor of the militarised area of Britannia Inferior, used the legitimacy of his imperial credentials to seize control of the area as his personal fief. Coel, in this scenario, was 'Coelestius', just as Arthur was 'Artorius'. In fact there is more evidence to support Coel as a warlord of this type than there is for Arthur. The north was one of the most militarised areas in the whole Roman Empire. Someone prevented the disintegration of these regions after the Roman withdrawal, and Aneirin's poem 'Gododdin' describes the kings of the British kingdom of Rheged as 'whelps of Coel's breed'. Eight lines of princes described in Welsh annals can be traced directly to Coel, among them, significantly, the royal house of Gwynedd. Coel 'Hen' ('the old') may connote the 'common ancestor' of many northern British and later Welsh royal families. Of course the Roman connection is speculative, and Coel was more than likely just a rough north-country Celtic warlord, ruling a kingdom which included territories on both sides of Hadrian's Wall, from Edinburgh to Cheshire and Yorkshire. It may well have been Coel, the nearest thing to a high king the Britons had left, who arranged the transplantation of the Gododdin, or at least important elements of the tribe, including noblemen, to north Wales. Cunedda was supposed to have married a daughter of Coel, and it could be that this sealed a contractual agreement between the two men. Maelgwn was Cunedda's grandson. They were a violent breed. Cunedda seems to have cleared the Gwynedd area of Irish settlement with ruthless efficiency so that they never returned.

Although Gildas describes Maelgwn as the 'Dragon of the Island' (we are unclear if the island referred to is Anglesey/Ynys Mon or Great Britain as a whole) and informs us that he is an exemplar among kings in beauty, strength and height, he also makes it clear that he is a bloody murderer, having slaughtered many kings, including his own uncle. To expiate these murders Maelgwn had repented and entered a monastery (in fact he was a fellow novice with Gildas for a while) but he ultimately leaves the holy life to seize control of Gwynedd, where at his splendid court at Aberffraw he luxuriates in the sins of the flesh. Maelgwn is '*hael*' meaning 'generous', and at first the bard Taliesin praises him:

> May Maelgwn of Mon receive the mead and offer it
> To us
> In foaming cups, the sweet blessed spirit
> Of the honey-bee which elicits our delight.

It was not just intemperance in alcohol that ensnared the king in sin. He imprisoned his own nephew Elffin, according to legend, and arranged for his wife to be seduced by Rhun, Maelgwn's son. Elffin's skilful and gifted bard, Taliesin, then called down a curse on Maelgwn which was to take effect with devastating consequences:

> May there be no peace or health
> For Maelgwn Gwynedd!
> Because of his wickedness and abuse of power
> May he suffer the utmost ills!
> May all his lands be wasted
> And may long exile be the fate
> Of Maelgwn Gwynedd.

Between Taliesin's cursing, and the invective directed at him by Gildas – one of the most influential men in the British Church – we have an impression of a greedy, ungovernable, immoral bully. Taliesin was a magician not to be trifled with. He invoked a 'strange creature' to punish Maelgwn, a beast that, like Grendel in *Beowulf* lurks in the bogs:

> From the swamps of Rhiannedd a strange creature
> Comes to punish Maelgwn for his iniquity,
> Its hair, its teeth and its eyes will be gold,
> It will bring destruction to Maelgwn Gwynedd.

In 547, the 'yellow' plague reached north Wales. Maelgwn, fearing the prophesied creature hid himself away, but as he looked through the keyhole of his door he is supposed to have seen the plague 'loping towards him'. Maelgwn 'the Tall' expired in the epidemic. Although we may discount Geoffrey of Monmouth's account when he claims that Maelgwn ruled an empire including Iceland, Ireland, the Orkneys and parts of Scandinavia, there is no reason to doubt that within those kingdoms of Britain not under the control of the Anglo-Saxons, he was acknowledged as a high king. His son, Rhun, was so powerful that he raised an army in Wales and marched it through the independent kingdom of Rheged all the way into Strathclyde where he overcame the kingdoms of Ystrad Cluth and Manau Gododdin. His army were away from home so long, it is recorded, that the women of Venedotia or Gwynedd were forced to sleep with their grooms. The projection of such power implied authority to compel lesser kings to provide levies for his armies. But these epic Celtic inter-tribal wars, though they were a gift for the bards, were a disaster for the Brythonic people as a whole. They dissipated the resources of the Celts just as the Anglo-Saxons were consolidating strong new kingdoms. The victory at Mount Badon had been won because the southern Britons had cooperated, but the northern kings were engaged in constant hostilities with each other.

It was this disastrous internecine strife which gave us one of the most famous characters in British folklore, 'Myrddin Wyllt', the original 'Merlin'. It is highly likely that his character was invented at a later date, and then retrospectively intruded into the annals that referred to a battle in north Britain in the 570s. At the Battle of Arfderydd, or Arthuret, in AD 573 a coalition of Christian Britons confronted Gwendoleu, Myrddin's supposed patron, who was either pagan or a heretic of some kind. Gwendoleu was killed in the battle, which is described in the Welsh triads as one of the 'three frivolous battles', the *casus belli* being a dispute over 'a lark's nest'. Although we cannot know the context of this legend, it implies a society where constant warfare and plundering meant British armies could be deployed across hundreds of miles to slaughter each other. For this to have been the case the Anglo-Saxon threat had not yet become serious enough to concentrate the minds of the British kings. No wonder that Gildas denounced these frivolous and small-minded rulers or that bards like Taliesin or Myrddin were angered or driven to despair. Myrddin was so stricken with grief at the death of his master and overwhelmed by the unfolding tragedy about to engulf the Britons that he wandered in the Caledonian forests as a madman, until poetic and visionary inspiration was granted to him. We will encounter him again later in our story.

If, as seems likely, a constellation of British statelets ruled by the sons of Coel or his sons-in-law (such as Cunedda) had emerged in the late sixth century, there was an inherent problem in this arrangement. By Celtic custom all sons of a king were entitled to a share of their father's land, which they ruled in their own right even while he was living in many cases, a principle known as 'partible inheritance'. Unlike primogeniture, where the eldest son succeeds to the entire realm, in the Celtic system all sons were legitimate heirs – even those born out of wedlock. This encouraged the assassination or elimination by murder or poisoning of collateral kinsmen and doomed the Britons to constant feuding and civil wars. It was a fatal weakness which dissipated the slender resources of what were already small kingdoms in bleak regions where poor peasants struggled to feed themselves, let alone pay taxes or provide billets for troops. Occasionally the process had the opposite effect, because the bitter family feuds threw up mighty kings whose charisma proved equal to the Anglo-Saxon threat. The plague seems to have been at its most virulent in Britain around AD 547, the year of Maelgwn's death, and this is also the year Bede recorded the arrival in Britain of Ida 'from whom the lineage of the Northumbrians takes its origin, and he remained in the kingship for twelve years'. The timing of this landing may have been in response to tales told by merchants of the catastrophe, which had overtaken the British in the aftermath of the plague, and Irish annals specifically state that the disease had decimated that island in the same year. Ida and his followers arrived on the north-east coast between Lothian and the Tyne, an old British kingdom called Bryneich around Bamburgh. This area may have been left depopulated even before the plague struck, because it was a neighbour of Gododdin from whence Cunedda and his followers may have emigrated. Ida soon annexed this territory, which became a small Anglian kingdom called Bernicia. To the south, in what is now Yorkshire, another Anglian group, the Deirans, had settled and beyond that in Humberside and north Lincolnshire another Anglian immigration had taken control of a region called Lindsey. By around AD 570 or thereabouts, York itself had fallen to the Deirans, who made it their capital. If all these Anglian territories linked up under one powerful ruler it was obvious that the *Gwr y Gogledd*, or 'Men of the North' as the Brythonic Celts called themselves, would be in serious danger and, eventually, this is precisely what happened.

Across the Pennines the unprecedented adversities had thrown up a strong man, Urien, a great-great-grandson of Coel as King of Rheged, a large nation that extended from the Dee around modern Flintshire into Cheshire and Lancashire and all of Cumbria and Galloway. The placename 'Rochdale' commemorates the name of this vanished realm, originally Recedham, and also Dunragit in Galloway. It extended east of the Pennines to include Catraeth (modern Catterick) but it was centred on the Solway around Carlisle, a region that passed into the Arthurian legends as 'Gore'. By the late 570s it was clear that several powerful Anglo-Saxon kings were poised ready to move westwards. In the north, King Aethelric of Deira commenced hostilities with Rheged. A bold Anglian attack thrust right over the Pennines and at Argoed Llyfein, the forest of Leven in Cumbria, Aethelric, nicknamed the 'Flame-bearer' by the Celtic bards (perhaps his army had marched through the mountain passes in a night attack), was confronted on a bleak Saturday morning by the mighty Urien. The Angles were soundly beaten, and Urien became a legendary Brythonic hero. This did not end the war, but intensified it until it became an epic conflict – truly worthy of poetry and legend, a contest between 'Dark Age' super-powers. In 592, a Bernician king took control of Deira, Aethelfrith – Aethelric's son, and he was determined to avenge his father who had been killed in battle by the Britons. Bede says he 'was a most powerful king and most desirous of glory, who, more than all the leaders of the English harried the peoples of the Britons. No one among the nobles, no one among the kings, made more of their lands either tributary to the people of the English or inhabitable by them, having exterminated or subjugated their inhabitants.' Aethelric's strategy

was clear – to obliterate Rheged – but in 590 Urien moved first.
With a combined force from several northern Celtic kingdoms
he invaded Northumbria and drove the Angles before him until
in desperation they were forced onto the tiny island of Metcawt,
now Lindisfarne. It seemed nothing could stop Urien from driving
the invaders into the sea, but one of his allies, Morcant, became
so insanely jealous of Urien that he hired an assassin, Llovan
Llawdivro, 'the Landless One', to murder him. It was a blow
that shattered hopes of a British recovery. The bards were beside
themselves:

> I bear within my cloak the head of Urien most generous of
> princes
> On his white breast a raven feeds, great were his deeds
> And far from the fame of Urien from Rhiw I have borne a head
> Whose lips are red with blood, woe to Rheged this day
> His slender white body will be buried this day
> Beneath earth and blue stones, sorrow to me and sad disgrace.

But all was not lost. Urien's son, Owain, was a 'chip off the old
block', a Celtic hero, so much so that he was eventually elevated
to the magical company of Arthur's Round Table as 'Sir Yvain'.
A last desperate attempt was made to throw the Northumbrians
into the sea but it was a suicide mission, a cavalry charge as
insane as the Charge of the Light Brigade many centuries later.
At Catraeth (modern Catterick) a small war-band of 300 heroes
was overwhelmed by a vastly numerically superior Northumbrian
army under Aethelfrith. Aneirin's elegiac poem 'Y Gododdin',
which commemorated the raid, is among the earliest examples of
Brythonic literature, according to the scholar Ifor Williams. For all
its glorious valour the attack stood no chance of achieving anything
of strategic value but, like the commando raids of the Second
World War by Britain against Nazi Germany, they salvaged some
honour at least. The desperate war had left one man in control of
the entire north and Rheged fell. Now Wales was separated from
Cumbria and Strathclyde by a powerful Anglian frontier on land,
and a Northumbrian fleet had the potential to disrupt and destroy
British and Irish sea traffic. No wonder Myrddin had gone insane.

As a *Homo Sylvester* he ran ragged through the woods conversing with trees and wild pigs:

> Sweet apple-tree who grows in the clearing
> The lords of Rhydderch's court do not see you
> Although they trample the ground at your feet
> I am hateful to the followers of Rhydderch,
> After Gwendoleu, no prince honours me,
> I have neither joy nor visits from my beloved.
> At Arthuret I lost all feeling
> And now I am despised by the swan-white woman...

The psychic disintegration was much the same process that the Druids had undergone, a massive ego-loss experience, but then a transfiguration, a sense of the connectedness of all things, the knowledge of the *awen* – the 'fire in the head'. It was impossible to attain without suffering. To break through the constraints of time and space, to be granted the visions of prophesy, the ultimate humiliations, degradations and privations must be endured – the price of truth:

> Listen little pig. I have trouble sleeping
> So shaken am I by sorrows
> For fifty years I have suffered so much
> That now I am pained by joy
> Listen little pig, it is not my purpose
> To hear the water-birds making their commotion
> My hair is sparse, my clothes are ragged
> I am cold and the vale is my barn for I have no corn,
> My summer harvest is poor indeed
> Since the battle of Arthuret I have lost all feeling
> Even were the sky to fall on me and the sea overflow.

The northern English offensive under Aethelfrith was a Northumbrian *Blitzkrieg* and turned that nation into the most dangerous force in the island, but elsewhere other Anglo-Saxon kingdoms were on the move, and two were a particular threat to the Britons: Mercia and Wessex. By the beginning of the seventh century the process had begun whereby the Anglo-Saxon kingdoms expanded at a rapid rate, with great violence, and British kingdoms were subdued or suffered to remain only on payment of tributes. At the boundary between the two peoples an intermediate zone was created, a shadowy territory that became 'the Lost Lands'.

Because the Venerable Bede, the 'father of English history' was a Northumbrian monk who spent most of his life at his monastery in Jarrow, our knowledge of Northumbrian affairs is well attested and he gives us an intimate account of the most important power struggle of the times – the conflict between Northumbria and the Britons – and then the wars between an alliance of the Britons and Mercia and Northumbria. This is extremely fortunate because it was these bitter and prolonged wars which decided the future of state formation in the island. Nowadays, of course, we are much more focused on the south of England as the centre of political and economic power, but this was not the case in the seventh century. Before we return to the main political action, however, we need to be aware of the progress of Anglo-Saxon expansion as it affected the south, where kingdoms were founded, one of which, Wessex, was destined to prevail as the strongest of the seven Anglo-Saxon realms, the so-called 'heptarchy'. Despite the fact that our reigning monarch is supposedly a descendant of the first King of Wessex, Cerdic, he is almost as much of a mystery as Arthur, with whom he was supposed to have been contemporary. His name is not Anglo-Saxon, but British, a variation on Ceredic, Ceredig, Caradog – and Caratacus. What was a Saxon king of Wessex doing with a British name? The *Anglo-Saxon Chronicle* says that he arrived with his son Cynric in AD 495 and settled around the Solent. A bitter local war was fought for thirteen years with a local British chieftain called Natanleod, but eventually Cerdic prevailed. Initially he is described only as an *ealdorman* but by 519 he had become king. J. N. L Myers postulated that Cerdic may not have been Saxon at all, but a nobleman of a Romano-Celtic family who had been left as the *de facto* authority over a subdivision of the 'Saxon Shore'. They may have hired Saxon mercenaries or augmented *Laeti* militias of Germanic origin, which were already *in situ* and, like Vortigern, perhaps Cerdic intermarried with the Saxons. Alternatively, his father may have been Saxon and his mother a Celt. Another possibility is that the Germanic Gewissae tribe of the Thames Valley may have prevailed in local infighting and that Cerdic originated from them, rather than Saxons, who were relative newcomers. The *Anglo-Saxon Chronicle* traces his ancestors back to the god Woden, ultimately, but this in itself seems suspect, drawn from an earlier regnal list that probably originated in Bernicia in Northumbria. The Gewissae had been settled for a long time, and the German troops must have intermarried with local women, which would account for the Celtic name. Many subsequent West Saxon kings have names that may be of Brythonic origin and, although we should not infer too much from this, the initial Saxon settlement cannot have been numerically very great. There must have been a considerable degree of intermarriage and children of mixed heritage, even if British men eligible to bear arms were, as Bede tells us was the case in Northumbria, 'exterminated'. We know this was not the case in Wessex because West Saxon law codes make special provision for compensation payments or *wergild* in respect of 'Welshmen' who were injured or killed many centuries later, and King Athelstan was said to have expelled Welsh speakers from Exeter as late as the tenth century.

All we know is that Cynric succeeded his father, another 'Saxon' king with a British or Irish name, who fought the Britons at Old Sarum in Wiltshire in AD 552, presumably Cynric was the victor. Another battle was fought, at Beranbyrg in AD 556, where Cynric was fighting with his son Ceawlin alongside him. J. N. L Myers doubted that Cynric even existed and said that he may have been invented to plug a gap in a falsified regnal list. Myers suggested that Ceawlin, although he is the first of the West Saxon kings who seems historically genuine rather than quasi-mythical, was in fact almost certainly *not* Saxon but was a leader of the Gewissae, who finally prevailed in the struggle for south-western Anglo-Saxon supremacy. Fortunately, a long and detailed saga recorded Ceawlin's wars and, like Aethelfrith in the north, he appears to have decided to make himself overlord of all the southern peoples – Saxon or Brythonic. The main objective of his campaigns was to overwhelm a fellow Anglo-Saxon kingdom, Kent, and in 568 at 'Wibbandun' a bloody battle was fought with King Aethelberht of Kent. A campaign in 571 took Ceawlin's army into Oxfordshire, where he attempted to wrest control of the area from the Britons. He seems also to have pushed west, and, in AD 577 at Dyrham in Gloucestershire, a combined army of Britons under a leader called Condidan was heavily defeated. This was a strategic catastrophe for the British cause, because Cirencester, the ancient provincial capital fell, as well as Bath and Gloucester. The south-west, Dumnonia (Devon and Cornwall) and parts of Somerset and Dorset – were now cut off from Wales, just as Aethelfrith had cut Wales off from Cumbria and Strathclyde. In the western midlands two Brythonic kingdoms held out within what is now modern England for a while longer, small and vulnerable state-lets called Luitcoit and Pengwern bulged east in a salient into Anglo-Saxon territory, and in West Yorkshire a Celtic nation called Elmet ('the Elm forest') still existed as the seventh century commenced. Recent DNA research by the University of Oxford has revealed a surprisingly high number of the modern population still show genetic traces of Celtic ancestry thereabouts. Such studies are always contentious of course, but they do seem to confirm distinct fault lines in the presence of 'Y' chromosones in men along geographical borders corresponding to traditional accounts of the ethnogenesis of the Anglo-Saxon and Celtic peoples. Economically the British Celts within the areas of Anglo-Saxon settlement were inferior beings, whose capacity to reproduce was restricted, and whose 'human rights' were negligible. Where the Celtic Britons were able to preserve their liberty this was similarly within a context of economic constraint and the emotional connection with the land was intensified. *Gwlad* meaning 'land' or 'country' was in Old Welsh *gulat* meaning 'sovereignty'. But at this time there was no notion of a 'Welsh' nation, and each Welsh or British kingdom was a small cultural islet, ruled by its own petty king. This fragmentation was almost fatal for British resistance, but fortunately the Anglo-Saxon kingdoms fell to fighting among themselves for a while. In 584 Ceawlin tried once again to subdue Oxfordshire, but at Fethanleag, modern Stoke Lyne, he was defeated decisively and his ally, Cuthwine was killed. The old commander was so humiliated that his young nephew, Ceol, rebelled against him and Ceawlin died as he had lived – by the sword. Garbled and unclear as all this is, we can at least surmise that the British fortunes in the south fared little better than they had done in the north. But there was one more frontier zone where Anglo-Saxon pioneers were pushing west – Mercia.

A king called Creoda or Crida has been postulated as the founder of the Mercian dynasty, who was reputedly the great-grandson of Icel, the Anglian king who had first landed in Britain. Since Icel was supposedly a great-grandson of Offa of Angeln on the borders of Germany and Denmark, the Mercian kings claimed a direct descent from Offa, who could trace his ancestors back to the legendary god-hero, Woden. We know very little about Creoda and even his existence is disputed, but he was supposed to have been the father of another Mercian king, Pybba, in turn the father of a king who was to play a crucial role in the dramatic events about to unfold, Penda. The issue of genealogical descent was absolutely crucial to the establishment of the Anglo-Saxon kingdoms, and we have already seen how murky these waters could get with the case of Cerdic of Wessex and his issue. In the Germanic traditions the tribal leader was believed to be a direct descendant of Woden, and therefore a semi-divine being who inherited in his person the exemplary military virtues of the god. We have only to consider the lavish trappings and adornments such men took with them when they departed this life, such as the Sutton Hoo treasures excavated in 1939, or the Staffordshire Hoard discovered in 2009, to appreciate the immense status and power the Anglo-Saxon kings embodied. For the Mercians, one of the last Anglo-Saxon nations to be converted to Christianity, the cult of militarism was especially important. They were a pioneering people who gradually moved east along the rivers, such as the Trent. A chieftain called Snota founded the city of Nottingham and the East Midlands gradually fell under Mercian control. Originally the Celtic kingdom of Powys had extended east as far as what is now Northamptonshire, but the Mercians seized control of Cynwidion another Celtic statelet in that area and shared out the land. John Morris thought that the Cornovii tribe of Staffordshire and Shropshire had such a strong military pedigree that further Mercian expansion to the west was contested, and this may be why Tamworth, which became the Mercian capital, was located on the western frontiers initially – as a forward base, rather than being 'at the heart' of Mercia. The very name which the Mercians took gives a clue as to how they saw themselves – wild frontiersmen; *mierce* means 'borderers', as in the Welsh Marches or Tolkien's 'Riders of the Mark'. One of their kings, Ceorl, seems to have used a nickname or joke name as a 'badge of honour'; *ceorl* means 'churl' – a country yokel – and that is exactly what these people were. They were not one people, but a coalition of many different subtribes with exotic sounding names, the Unecungga and Noxgaga among them. They operated independently, and it has been suggested that the Mercian expansion was in many ways analogous to the expansion into the western United States during the nineteenth century. These people may have been in a state of rebellion against the notion of overlords and kings, and their dreams were of finding a place where they could find 'good drainage and clear springs (giving) ... hope of a settled life. Here they staked out their claim as a family or group, chopped down trees and built their elementary stockade to keep out the rest of the world...' as Edward Chitham put it.

These free spirits soon ran up against harsh realities. The regions into which they had penetrated were inhabited by Celts with an ancient military tradition and it was impossible to ignore the threat they posed to isolated outposts far from their fellow countrymen's main armed forces. Small groups of settlers needed to cooperate to defend themselves and so they formed a federation, which acknowledged two over-kings: one for the north of the Mercian area, another for the south. This is the kind of simple but effective system still used by chapters and gangsters to this day, and the kings were 'hard men' whose sole recommendation for rule was their ferocity and skill in war. But the threat to the Mercians from the Britons was less serious, perhaps, than that which came from Northumbria on the northern frontier or Wessex to the south. Indeed, as they entered the seventh century there were good reasons why the Britons and the Mercians should make common cause, particularly against Northumbria, the main threat to them both. The terrain prevented easy Mercian expansion into the western Midlands too. Sir Frank Stenton in his *Anglo-Saxon England* (Oxford, 2001 Edn) thought that the limit of their advance was the watershed between the Trent and the Severn, marked by significant place names such as Wednesbury and Wednesfield ('Woden's fortress' and 'Woden's plain'). The 'belt of high land connecting the hills of Cannock Chase with the Forest of Arden' he contended, was the 'border' from which the Mercians took their name – not, as is so often supposed, the present-day border with Wales. The area approximating to the modern-day conurbation of the county of the West Midlands was under Anglo-Saxon control, as was Gloucestershire and Worcestershire, which had fallen to a mysterious folk called the Hwicce (pronounced 'witch-a') who may have morphed out of the Gewissae. They had emerged from the Forest of Wychwood in Oxfordshire and occupied the lands of the Dobunni. At first they had their own kings, but in time they too became part of the greater Mercian project. To the west, amid the forests and marshes of Kinver and Morfe (which retain their Celtic names to this day), British people still survived in tiny independent cantons well into the eighth century, but these fragile and poor kingdoms, such as Pengwern in Shropshire and Luitcoit in Staffordshire must have come to some sort of tributary arrangements, particularly with Penda, and these soon became formal alliances.

So, by the end of the sixth century great swathes of British territory had been lost, and this loss grieved the Celtic mind so deeply that 'the Lost Lands' became a metaphor for their national decline, which Gildas had warned of. The odds were stacked against the proud descendants of Caratacus, Boudicca, and Arthur, but deep in the British consciousness an idea of national resurgence was stirring, and a mighty warrior was being inculcated with prophetic adjurations to reconquer the 'Lost Lands' – Cadwallon ap Cadfan of Gwynedd. What is incredible is that he very nearly succeeded.

8

The Resurgence of the Britons

We have followed the fortunes of Myrddin in the previous chapter, but such bards, inflamed by the knowledge of the *awen*, were much more to the Britons than mere soothsayers or 'cunning men', they were akin to primordial tribal Shamans and their sayings were revered as direct revelations from God. Another bard has already been mentioned, Taliesin, and he was said to have cursed Maelgwn of Gwynedd, before AD 547. The so-called *Book of Taliesin* in the National Library of Wales is a collection compiled in the fourteenth century from much older manuscripts. It contains a prophetic poem called '*Armes Prydein Vawr*' or 'The Great Prophesy of Britain'. Like their Druidic forebears these bards were agitators, whose panegyric poetry in praise of their royal or noble patrons exalted the Celtic kings and recited the lineage of their ancestors, which they had preserved using the same mnemonic techniques as the Druids. A really powerful bard could do more: he could see into the future and know the fates of future kings and their nations. Another interesting insight into the way in which prophetic propaganda could seep into the consciousness of kings, affecting their political strategies, can be seen in a poem called '*Cyfoesi Myrddin a Gwenddydd ei Chwaer*' or 'A conversation between Myrddin and his sister Gwenddydd'. His sister questions Myrddin about future rulers of the Britons and in response he gives a long regnal list, starting with previous kings but extending (supposedly) into kings in the days to come. Asked about the fate of the Britons he replies, 'There will be resurgence.' A problem with these bardic traditions is of course, that they probably postdate the events, which they purport to have foreseen but nevertheless preserve, I believe, a sacred tradition that may have its ultimate origins in early Celtic times. I am not alone in believing this to be the case. Robert Graves in his *The White Goddess* (London, 1961 Edn) made a convincing case for a tradition of magical poetry, which endured from the Old Stone Age until the modern era. We will encounter this again, but suffice to say that by the early seventh century folk legends about 'Arthur' and bardic visionaries inculcating the need for a British counter-stroke were rife throughout the British-held territories. Whatever their true powers, the bards had divined that a tipping point had been reached and Northumbria was becoming a threat too powerful to ignore. In AD 613, Aethelfrith 'the Twister', as the Britons called him, wiped out a combined British army at the Battle of Chester. Kings Selyf of Powys, Iago of Gwynedd, and Cadwal of Rhos were all killed, but the most notorious result of the battle was that a very large number of British monks who had gone to the battlefield to pray for a British victory were massacred by Aethelfrith, who thought their prayers may be magical spells. He showed no remorse, saying that since their prayers were against him this made them effectively combatants. It is claimed that as many as 1200 British monks were killed, and though this may well be an inflated figure, that some hundreds of such men took such risks shows how important the fate of the battle was to the Celts. It was an atrocity which shocked the Britons, but the severe defeat was an omen of even more dangerous times ahead.

King Aethelfrith of Bernicia had driven Aethelric of Deira's brother, Edwin, into exile when he had seized York and become king of a unified Northumbria. Geoffrey of Monmouth recorded that Edwin had sought sanctuary with the kings of Powys and Gwynedd, but this may have been designed to add a frisson to his tale of rivalry between Cadwallon and Edwin. We know that for a while Edwin was a wandering exile. He was a marked man, so much so that his presence attracted the prospect of retaliation by Aethelfrith against those prepared to play host to Edwin. King Ceorl of Mercia did take him in for a while, and even married his daughter to Edwin, but feared provoking Aethelfrith. The hunted fugitive arrived next in East Anglia, to seek the protection of King Raedwald, the king whose treasures were probably those discovered at Sutton Hoo in 1939. Raedwald was called a *bretwalda*, a word meaning something like 'wide ruler', which denoted a special status among the Anglo-Saxon kings. It was Edwin's last hope. If Aethelfrith decided to intimidate Raedwald, he would be making a diplomatic faux pas and any undue pressure could be construed as disrespect to the *Bretwalda*. Fortunately for Edwin, Aethelfrith did just that. He sent a messenger to Raedwald requesting that Edwin be executed. But Raedwald's queen pleaded to her husband to stay his hand. Edwin had cleverly befriended Raegenhere, Raedwald's heir, and Aethelfrith's ultimatum backfired. *Bretwalda* Raedwald marched on Northumbria and on the River Idle in Lindsey the East Angles and Northumbrians met in a desperately fought battle, which turned the river red with blood. There is a legend that Edwin and Raegenhere had swapped armour to bring them luck in battle. Aethelfrith was so incensed with all the troubles Edwin had caused him that he immediately charged what he thought was Edwin, whose armour was distinctive, and slew him – but in fact he had killed Raegenhere. Raedwald, discovering that his son had been killed, immediately sought out Aethelfrith and killed him, and the victory went to Raedwald. The East Anglian king was so broken-hearted that he immediately turned for home as soon as he had installed Edwin as the new King of Northumbria in 616. This was a major turning point in Anglo-Saxon and British history because Edwin realised the enormous potential of his new realm, especially its military power. The small Celtic kingdom of Elmet in modern West Yorkshire, ruled by Ceretic ap Gwallog (yet another reputed descendant of Coel) was now extremely vulnerable.

In AD 619 Edwin made a trumped-up accusation against Ceretic to the effect that he had poisoned a Deiran nobleman called Hereric, Edwin's nephew. The outnumbered Celts made a last hopeless stand on the River Idle near Bawtry but were soon overwhelmed. Ceretic managed to escape but died shortly afterwards. Mercia and Gwynedd were both very disturbed by this development, Mercia because they now had a volatile frontier to patrol in the north instead of a fairly harmless Celtic enclave, and Gwynedd because it showed that Edwin now considered himself ready to take offensive action against his neighbours, particularly by sea. It was just a matter of time until hostilities commenced, and when Raedwald died in AD 620 Edwin assumed the title of *Bretwalda*.

This may have gone to his head, for he began to lead processions around York with a standard-bearer in front of him carrying a *tufa*, a winged globe on a tall staff as the Romans had done. York was still visibly Roman, with standing ruins and powerful city walls. Edwin's second wife Aethelburh of Kent, who he married in AD 625, was a strict Catholic, and the marriage was conditional on Edwin's conversion. Paulinus, her chaplain, was sent north with her to facilitate mass baptisms at Yeavering Bell, one of the king's most lavish residences. Thousands upon thousands were baptised in the nearby River Glen, after hearing sermons declaimed before a huge timber auditorium. Although Edwin prevaricated, he finally became a genuine Christian convert after he recovered from an assassination attempt. King Cwichelm of Wessex, Edwin's main political rival, had sent an agent with a poisoned dagger to Edwin's court. He lunged and made contact and Edwin drifted in and out of consciousness for some time, promising that if he survived, he would become a sincere Christian. He did survive, and was true to his words, but his decision to opt for the Roman Catholic variety of the faith was a calamity for the other kingdoms. Edwin saw himself as a holy warrior for Christ, destined to bring the true faith to the 'heretics' of the British Celtic Church, and to convert the pagan Mercians at the point of the sword. In AD 629 Edwin's powerful new fleet showed just how serious he was about imposing his hegemony. The Isle of Man and Anglesey were suddenly attacked, and Cadwallon was taken by surprise at Penmon. He only just escaped, and was taken by boat to the tiny island of Glannauc or Priestholm off the coast of Anglesey. According to the '*Moliant Cadwallon*' a Welsh poem inspired by these events, Cadwallon was rescued and taken to exile in Ireland. Gwynedd was occupied by a Northumbrian garrison. These events soon had dramatic repercussions that were to engulf nearly the whole of the island south of Hadrian's Wall. We cannot be sure what Cadwallon did next, but there are hints that he sought the backing of Brittany, for it is recorded that he eventually gathered a fleet at Guernsey in the Channel Islands. For the time being, however, Edwin reigned supreme, the most powerful king to have emerged since the Anglo-Saxons invaded – but his success was to be short lived.

Meanwhile Edwin was attempting to overawe Wessex, whose king, Cwichelm, had been responsible for the assassination attempt against him. This campaign necessitated an arrangement with the two brothers who ruled Mercia – Eowa in the north and Penda in the south. The Church blessed the campaign against the West Saxons and Edwin's marriage to Aethelburh of Kent secured a powerful ally against Cwichelm in the south. In AD 628 it is recorded that Penda fought the West Saxons at Cirencester, probably a proxy campaign ordered by Edwin, and the West Saxons 'came to terms' indicating that they were defeated. Penda was young and powerful, a noted warrior and 'fighting man of the royal stock of the Mercians' as the *Anglo-Saxon Chronicle* states. Edwin may have been forced to delegate in this way because he had other troubles on his hands. A war with an Irish king, Fiachne of Ulaid, modern-day Ulster, must have preoccupied Edwin and kept him in the north because it is recorded in Irish annals that Fiachne struck across country as far as Bamburgh, which he put under siege. The struggle for control of the Irish Sea affected all the pan-Celtic realms, Brittany, Cornwall, Dyfed, Gwynedd, Man, and Ulaid. The backing of the Roman Church had, moreover, turned the conflict into a war of religion, for Edwin's bishop, Paulinus, had expelled the British clergy from Elmet, and it was clear that schism would not be tolerated under Edwin's 'imperium' as Bede called his regime, deliberately invoking the idea of Roman imperial power. So Cadwallon must have found powerful backers everywhere, determined to resist Edwin's domination. For the later Northumbrian monk Bede, Edwin was a national hero and an exemplary Christian who had brought strong rule to his country, such that a 'woman with a babe might travel from sea to sea without fear of molestation'. Yet for the kings of neighbouring kingdoms at the time his rapacious expansionism was an existential threat, and the desperate attempt to assassinate him points out just how fearful they were of him. Resentment against his power was widespread but no one kingdom was powerful enough to challenge him, as Raedwald had challenged Aethelfrith. Edwin's able and ruthless lieutenant, Penda, is recorded to have laid siege to Exeter, probably in an attempt to secure tribute from the King of

Dumnonia that had previously been due to Cwichelm. Our source for this is the twelfth-century *History of the Kings of Britain* by Geoffrey of Monmouth, much of which is legendary, but a sequence of events can be dimly discerned which resulted in a complete reversal of fortunes for Edwin. Cadwallon, so Geoffrey tells us, set sail with a fleet of Breton and Irish mercenaries from Guernsey and landed in Devon just at the time when Penda was laying siege to Exeter. This may well have been in response to an appeal sent out from Dumnonia to Brittany for military assistance. Reinforced, the Devon men sallied out and defeated the Mercians. Penda was forced to come to terms and, in a remarkable turnaround, he now pledged fealty to Cadwallon. This was a spectacular military and diplomatic coup for Cadwallon. Now Penda, the most feared warrior in Britain, was his deputy, and the road to Gwynedd, through Mercia, lay open to him. These events are extremely hazy, and we have only the merest clues to guide us, but I have postulated elsewhere (in *The Anglo-Saxon Age: The Birth of England,* Stroud, 2015) that a legend of a 'battle' between Penda and Cadwallon, which supposedly took place at Onnenau Meigion (now called Six-Ashes), a tiny hamlet right on the border of Staffordshire and Shropshire near Bridgnorth, may be a mistaken reference to a combined hosting of the Britons and the Mercians at that place in AD 630. The sacred grove may be in the neighbourhood of Holy Innocents Church, Tuck Hill, with a magnificent view across the Severn Valley to the Clee Hills. Cadwallon had suborned Penda's support with promises of rich plunder from the new Northumbrian churches and monasteries (monasteries functioned as an early form of banking system for valuables).

In Myrddin's prophesies it was said that a 'great eagle' would host with a British army at Onnenau Meigion and that this British army would then recapture 'the Lost Lands', recovering the sources of the rivers Trent and Mersey, and secure a frontier for British lands with the 'Saxons' somewhat to the east of the River Severn as far as its mouth. This prophesy was to have potency for many centuries as we will see, and what I believe is that for propaganda and pseudo-magical purposes, Six Ashes was the agreed venue for the junction of the allied British/Mercian forces before they set out to liberate Gwynedd. If I am correct, the combined army crossed the Severn at Quatford near Bridgnorth, 4 miles away, and then proceeded into Wales. At Cefn Digoll, Long Mountain, just outside Welshpool, the Northumbrian army lay in wait. They would have known that the allies would have to cross the Severn near Forden Gaer in Montgomeryshire (the so-called 'key to Wales'). In fact we are not even sure if Edwin was present, and the Northumbrians may have been commanded by a mere ealdorman. The result was a triumph for Cadwallon, and a severe reverse for Northumbria. Edwin was forced to abandon Gwynedd and Cadwallon's status as a 'high king' was massively enhanced. He was now free to recruit levies from all the free British realms for an invasion of Northumbria. Penda had enhanced his reputation and status too, and it was perhaps not clear at first just how crucial his support had been in gaining victory. After two years of planning, the two men joined forces again, and this time their objective was nothing less than to kill Edwin and to wipe Northumbria off the map.

Once again Penda was the key to success in the campaign, which took place in October AD 632. The allies may have utilised the cover of Sherwood Forest in Nottinghamshire for the campaign, or perhaps Edwin had waited for them there, near the village that still bears his name – Edwinstowe. In 1951, skeletons of over 200 males were discovered in the churchyard of St Mary's Parish Church Cuckney nearby, and there is a theory that these may be fallen warriors from the battle. The battle, which took place on 12 October, was called *Haethfelth* by Bede; many centuries later, the historian William Camden thought the place was Hatfield Chase near to Doncaster in South Yorkshire. He was told that a mound called Sley-Burr Hill contained the remains of fallen warriors from the battle. We will perhaps never have a definitive answer as to the location for the Battle of Hatfield, or Heathfield, as it has been known for centuries, but the result was a catastrophe for Northumbria. Edwin was killed, alongside his son, Osfrith. Another son, Eadfrith, managed to escape but was hunted down and captured by Penda, and later killed. Penda's part in the victory cannot be overstated, and Bede says that after the battle he was made king of the entire Mercian people. The *Historia Brittonum* tells us that 'he was the first to separate the kingdom of the Mercians from the Northumbrians', meaning that tributary arrangements that had previously subordinated the Mercians to Edwin were ended. The loot from the battlefield must have been immense, and I believe the Staffordshire Hoard may comprise elements of the booty Penda took from the fallen warriors. Elite jewellery, including Christian crosses (which may have come from Northumbria), and state-of-the-art weaponry, including a helmet decorated with stamped gilded foils, and exquisite hilt-decorations and pommels from up to 150 swords, were not the accoutrements of any common soldier – and look in every way fit for a king with holy imperial ambitions such as Edwin. These ambitions were now thwarted, for the great battle had been so decisive that Northumbria completely disintegrated. The 'Great Prophesy of Britain' and the visions of Myrddin seemed about to be fulfilled. Penda looted, ransacked and burned throughout the autumn before returning home with his spoils (perhaps by way of the Watling Street, near to which the Staffordshire Hoard was discovered in 2009). Cadwallon marched his army into York, and the British army reoccupied the ancient capital of Britannia Inferior. It had been an incredible comeback – even the achievements of Arthur paled by comparison.

The occupation of Deira during mid-winter necessitated widespread foraging and raiding by the British army, and perhaps this is what lies behind Bede's calumniation of Cadwallon, who says that he proved himself 'a barbarian worse than any pagan' and that no English were spared, not even women and children. Bede's assertion that Cadwallon's aim was to 'exterminate the whole English race within the island of Britain' does not seem credible, because his alliance with the Mercians showed him to be eminently practical in these matters, not swayed by xenophobia against the Anglo-Saxons. But it may well be true that there was a bitter hatred for the Northumbrians, who had driven him into exile and occupied his country. British soldiers billeted uncomfortably in a foreign land were probably little better behaved than Anglo-Saxon pillaging armies, and there are hints that Cadwallon was cunning and cruel. Edwin's queen and her young children had fled to Kent for sanctuary, and the demise of Edwin meant that a claimant to Bernicia, Eanfrith, whom he had driven into exile, now returned to claim his former kingdom. A cousin of Edwin, Osric, claimed the throne of Deira and both men were prepared to pledge fealty to Cadwallon and offer up large tribute in order to secure their thrones. But Cadwallon was determined to eliminate any prospects of a future Northumbrian resurgence. Eanfrith was invited to negotiations with Cadwallon, only to be ruthlessly murdered by him. The Church had disintegrated in Northumbria. Paulinus had fled, leaving behind his faithful deacon, James, to minister to the stricken population. Eanfrith and Osric both reverted to paganism, and perhaps this reaction against the Church was due to a perception that Aethelburh and Paulinus had compassed the destruction of Northumbria by their meddling. Clearly the Christian God did not guarantee victory in battle as had been promised. Osric raised an army and besieged Cadwallon's forces in 'a strong town', perhaps York itself, but Bede is not specific. Cadwallon sallied out and attacked the Deiran army and destroyed it, killing Osric. The King of Gwynedd now ruled supreme in York, a latter-day *Dux Britanniarum* and the resurgence of the Britons seemed complete. Nothing, or so it seemed, could save Northumbria – but the humiliated, impoverished and traumatised people of that country were now to be granted a miracle.

In AD 617 Aethelfrith's two sons, Oswald and Oswy, had been exiled by Edwin, and had sought the protection of the King of Dalriada, an Irish kingdom which extended from eastern Ulster to western Scotland. The boys were sent to the tiny island of Iona, where they were placed under the protection of Irish monks who converted them to Irish/Celtic Christianity. Both boys became exceptionally devout and may even have been educated to some degree during their long exile. Now Oswald saw his chance and gathered an army from Dalriada consisting of Gaelic-speaking clansmen. Although his army was not large, it was of good quality, and Oswald claimed that he had seen a vision of St Columba assuring him of victory. As soon as he heard that Oswald had marched south, Cadwallon left York and marched out to meet him, completely confident of yet another victory, for his army was much the larger. The two armies met at a small stream, the Denis Brook (now called Rowley Burn) outside Hexham, within sight of Hadrian's Wall. The Welsh remember the battle as 'the strife at Catscaul' – that is 'the battle on the Wall' – but to the Northumbrians it became known as 'Heavenfield'. Oswald erected an enormous wooden cross beneath which his Irish soldiers prayed, and when battle was joined the Britons were driven back and a bloody slaughter ensued. In such wild country there was little hope of escape for an army which had been routed and nearly all of Cadwallon's soldiers were wiped out, very few ever returning to their homeland. Cadwallon was discovered and killed, and Oswald's victory was a triumph that must have seemed literally heaven-sent. The resurgence of the Britons had lasted for a few short years, but this total annihilation of British arms ended all hopes for the recovery of 'the Lost Lands'. We should not underestimate how much of a catastrophe this was, for it seemed to confirm what Gildas had said, that the Britons were being punished by a God who had abandoned them, giving succour instead to their enemies. Indeed, the very soldiers who had destroyed the Britons at Heavenfield had been Celtic, Irish tribesmen from Scotland who had delivered victory to a 'Saxon' enemy. In the face of these stark facts the tales of the bards and the prophesies of visionaries seemed empty, even treacherous, except perhaps for a few lines by Taliesin:

> Their Lord they shall praise,
> Their speech they shall keep,
> Their land they shall lose,
> Except wild Wales.

The focus now was on resisting a Northumbrian counter-attack. The British kingdoms and the Mercians both had much to fear from a revitalised Northumbria, but that country had been so devastated that it would be some years before Oswald was ready to resume hostilities.

The history of these islands, as it has been taught for countless generations, owes much to Bede – the 'father of English history'. Bede was very influenced by Gildas, whose history and adjurations to moral rectitude he had read assiduously before he wrote down his own *Ecclesiastical History of the English People* in the late 720s. Gildas's message seemed clear, that the Britons were an accursed nation, duly humbled by God in the shape of the Anglo-Saxon invasions. The irony was that God had chosen pagans to chastise his own faithful flock. Cadwallon was portrayed as a cruel, ravaging barbarian, and a murderer. This denigration of the Britons legitimised subsequent English dominion over them, for punishment of the 'Welsh' was seen as God's work. This prejudice affected all subsequent English historical accounts, and was one of the factors that gave rise to institutionalised racism towards people of British descent. In fact Cadwallon had been a Celtic hero to equal Arthur, and had very nearly defeated the most powerful of the Anglo-Saxon nations at that time. It was no coincidence that a later West Saxon king, Caedwalla, was named in honour of Cadwallon, so Bede's story that he was the implacable enemy of the entire English race 'within the boundaries of Britain', cannot be credible. Cadwallon left an infant son, Cadwaladr, whose Red Dragon emblem remains the national flag of Wales to this day. He may have fought in the so-called Second Battle of Mount Badon in AD 655. Unfortunately, the two battles do not refer to the same location, and the site of the second battle has been identified as Myndd Baedon in mid-Glamorgan. Morcantius, or Morgan, who was killed in this battle, may have been a great-grandson of Arthur.

In the immediate aftermath of the British defeat, Cadwaladr was too young to take the throne of Gwynedd and a regency, under an obscure king called Cadfael, nicknamed Cynfedw, or 'the battle-shirker', took control until Cadwaladr came of age. All sides in this terrible war were now exhausted, but a resumption of hostilities was inevitable. Northumbria's strategic aim, according to the excellent analysis by Thomas Charles-Edwards in his *Wales and the Britons 350–1064* (Oxford, 2012) was to control the former territory of the Cornovii tribe, which extended from Cheshire into Staffordshire and Shropshire. Aethelfrith and Edwin had done their utmost to annexe this area, and now Oswald resolved to do the same. In AD 642, the Northumbrian king, possibly in alliance with Penda's brother, Eowa, invaded Mercia and confronted a combined army of Mercians and Britons. This was almost the last occasion, perhaps, where we can refer to a 'British' army rather than a 'Welsh' one, and the fascinating political machinations that preceded the war have been obscure for a long time. One of the great benefits of the discovery of the Staffordshire Hoard is that it forces us to focus on this time and these protracted and bloody conflicts, which changed the course of British and Anglo-Saxon history. It is worthwhile, therefore, for us to refamiliarise ourselves with that area, which had once been the homelands of the tribes described in chapter two – the western Midlands and the Welsh borderlands, as they were in AD 642 when Oswald's army invaded the area.

It cannot be stressed too much that the western Midlands was still largely Celtic at this time. A crucial kingdom was Powys, which was not as now a Welsh county, but a kingdom extending far into what is now England. It is a mystery as to when it emerged. One of its constituent parts, Gwertheyrnion, was almost certainly the homeland of Vortigern. He is mentioned as being a founder of the dynasty of Powys, and it has been speculated that his original power base may have been the city of Viroconium (Wroxeter), which still functioned as a viable urban centre well into the sixth century. Dynasts such as Cynan Garwyn and Selyf ap Cynan, who was killed at the Battle of Chester, are mentioned in early praise poetry, which was not written down until the ninth century. The pressure on the kingdom of Powys did not come just from the English. Gwynedd was hostile to Powys and may have supported a subkingdom called Dogfeiling or Pengwern. Dogfael was the putative eighth son of Cunedda in the legendary foundation myth, but there is a possible link to the 'Dagda' or 'good god' – an Irish deity that may have been introduced into north Wales by Irish immigrants. The Dogfeilion were the 'Servants of the Dagda' originally, a cadet branch of the kings of Gwynedd, and it was that nation which encouraged its encroachment on the territory of Powys. Dogfeiling seems to have been centred on Shropshire, and Llys Pengwern, its royal seat, was somewhere in the Tern Valley near to modern Shrewsbury, possibly near Baschurch. It was ruled by a man named Cynddylan ap Cyndrwyn, about whom a corpus of poetry was written, supposedly by his sister, Heledd, or a poet writing from her perspective – the *Canu Heledd*.

We have already seen how the principle of partible inheritance led to a fracturing of small Celtic realms, or *cantrefs*, as they were apportioned to various sons. Three old Roman towns formed a triad of interconnected statelets ruled by kin of the Dogfeilion royal line at Caer Guricon (Wroxeter), Caer Magnis (Kenchester) and Caer Luitcoit (Wall-by-Lichfield). The Mercian presence on their

frontiers, particularly after the powerful Penda became the overall
Mercian king, must have been sufficient for him to impose some
sort of tributary arrangements on these tiny kingdoms, but they
were tolerated by him and as John Morris and others have pointed
out, pagan Mercian graves of this period end quite abruptly at
Tamworth, fully 7 miles east of Lichfield, and at Yoxall the same
distance to the north. Luitcoit ('the open pasture by the blue-grey
wood-shore' it may mean) had been Letocetum, an absolutely
crucial posting station on the Roman route of Watling Street – the
impressive ruins are still visible today. It was uncomfortably close
to the Mercian frontier but relations were not hostile, so long as
tribute payments were kept up, and indeed the Brythonic Celts
and Mercians of the region were close allies. Virtually no artefacts
of Celtic origin have been found in the Staffordshire Hoard, for
instance. As Penda's allies they were exempt from his plundering.
Indeed on one famous occasion 'the Restitution of Iddew' (or
Iudeu) Penda forced Oswy, Oswald's brother and successor as King
of Northumbria, to give up 'all the treasures which he had with
him in that place, and then distributed them to his British allies',
according to Bede. Iudeu, or Iddew, is probably modern Stirling in
Scotland. Penda is a name that contains the Brythonic word *pen*,
meaning 'head' or 'hill', and it is just possible that his name was a
punning nickname, like 'Attila' – the 'Little Father' – so 'Pen-da'
would have been 'the Head Father'. It is true to say that Mercia,
like Northumbria and Wessex, was to some extent an Anglo-British
kingdom, perhaps pre-eminently so. There may have been a degree
of bilingualism and we know that a class of men existed called
Walhstods who could act as interpreters. But although Penda had
become the leader of the allies after Cadwallon's demise, these
small Celtic kingdoms were still fiercely independent.

The traditional site for the confrontation between Penda and
Oswald is the town of Oswestry (originally 'Oswald's Tree') on the
Welsh border. The Welsh called the place Croesoswallt. The battle
itself was known as Maes Cogwy in Welsh, and Maserfelth in English.
The battle became notorious for an atrocity committed by Penda,
but apart from these bare facts we know very little except the date,
August 5 AD 642. Oswald may have had Penda's brother Eowa as
an ally, so there may have been many Mercians in his ranks whose

loyalties were divided. Penda's allies, by contrast, were fighting to protect their own territories from Northumbrian pillaging, and were traditional enemies of the Northumbrians. Cynddylan of Pengwern fought alongside Penda, and probably accompanied him on his invasion of Northumbria two years later. Penda was at the peak of his fighting powers and Oswald's army were driven back and annihilated. Oswald, seeing that there was no hope, fell to his knees and prayed for his soldiers, before Penda's vanguard broke through to hack him into pieces. Oswald's head, arms and legs were set on long poles, and attached to a tree (probably an oak) where they hung as an offering to Woden, pagan god of battle, as thanks for this stunning victory. The Northumbrians thought this had been done in a spirit of mockery of the pious king – giving them every excuse to hate Penda all the more. Even Penda's Welsh allies were shocked. They were Christians and they attributed Penda's victory to diabolical aid – a 'pact with the devil' cemented by this grim offering. But however the victory had been won, Penda, the 'Panta ap Pyd', or 'Son of Danger' as the British knew him, had broken Northumbrian power again and within two years he led a plundering expedition against the new King of Northumbria, Oswy. This may have been in retaliation for a raid by Oswy in 643 to recover his brother's sacred remains (he was now considered a saint in Northumbria). The war resumed in 644 when Penda took his army deep into the north, besieging Bamburgh. Only prayers by St Aedan himself prevented the immolation of that fortress and vast treasures were taken again.

Penda did not confine himself to wars of plunder against Northumbria either. Wessex and East Anglia felt the force of Mercian power and at the Battle of Bulcamp Penda slaughtered the East Anglian king. It seemed that nothing could stop the hoary old warlord, but in 655 Penda became too overconfident, like Aethelfrith, Edwin, Cadwallon and Oswald before him.

Penda, who was by now in his late-fifties or even older, assembled a huge army comprised of contingents from thirty different Anglo-Saxon and British nations. Such a vast host was unstoppable and Penda could only be appeased when yet more treasures were sent to him to desist. Not content with this, Penda took Oswy's young son, Ecgfrith as a hostage. The various contingents of

Penda's army were ranging throughout Northumbria, but in early November Penda called a halt. The army turned for home, via the old Roman road that led from York to Manchester and Chester. But Oswy, realising his chance, immediately called out his army and followed the invaders. On November 15 655 Oswy caught up with the retreating Penda just outside Leeds, where a river, swollen by autumn rains, had blocked his retreat, called *Winwaed*. We are unsure which river this actually was. It could be the River Went, which sounds remarkably similar, or the River Cock near to an area still known as Pendas Fields outside Leeds. Penda was forced to face about and prepare for battle, but in the night his ally from Gwynedd, Cadfael ap 'Cynfedw' – 'the battle-shirker' as he became known to history – sneaked away with his army and escaped via the Roman road to Manchester and the west. They were not the only deserters. Aethelwald of Deira was the son of Oswald, the man Penda had gibbeted on a tree, and he stood aside with his forces as battle was joined. Only the puppet king of the nation Penda had ruthlessly subordinated, Aethelhcre of East Anglia, remained loyal, and with his considerably diminished forces Penda awaited Oswy's assault. Oswy promised to give up his favourite daughter to a nunnery and to endow a dozen monasteries if he was victorious. His prayers were answered. The old Mercian king fought heroically to the last, but was finally overwhelmed and decapitated. At last, there was one nation and one king who was the victor of the long, complex and draining cycle of wars – Northumbria and Oswy. Mercia had been defeated and would soon be ruled by Northumbrian governors, but for Penda's former British allies the loss of his protection boded very ill. The writing was on the wall. A hostile Anglo-Saxon power now had a border with the British kingdoms east of the Severn, under a king whose state policy was no different to Aethelfrith's and Edwin's and more recently Oswald's – the elimination of the British kingdoms of the Welsh borderlands, but like their comrades, 'the Men of the North', they would not go quietly.

9

The Great Divide

The atmosphere of mutual tolerance between Mercia and its British neighbours was now exchanged for one of hostility and intimidation. Northumbrian governors were imposed on Mercia north of the Trent, but Penda's son Peada (ironically) had married Oswy's daughter, Aelfleada, as part of a diplomatic initiative a few years before where the young pagan had converted to Christianity. According to Bede he was a sincere and well-meaning Christian, but now, as King of Middle-Anglia – the rump of Mercian territory his father-in-law permitted him to rule – Peada was completely a tool of Northumbrian foreign policy. Increasingly, territorial and political disputes were now underpinned by religious considerations because with the exception of Sussex, pagan for slightly longer, Mercia was the main Anglo-Saxon kingdom not to have relinquished pagan worship and embraced the Christian faith. Bede sounds rather triumphant when he writes that Oswy, 'having cut off the wicked king's head, converted the Mercians and the adjacent provinces to the grace of the Christian faith'. We should not doubt that this missionary zeal was genuine and to some extent motivated by Oswy's evangelical duty, but there were also political and military considerations that informed his overall strategy. This process had been underway well before the dramatic events of AD 655. Two years before, following his marriage to Aelflaeda, Peada had accepted four missionaries from Lindisfarne into Middle-Anglia where they were free to preach and make converts and to baptise them. Those who still demonise Penda as an almost diabolical figure neglect the fact that he could very easily have forbidden this mission in his son's subkingdom. That he did not probably shows that for at least a short time he was sincere in trying to avoid conflict. The three English monks, Adda, Betti and Cedd (the last-named was the brother of Chad, later the Mercian bishop) were accompanied by Diuma, an Irishman. Diuma was consecrated as a bishop by Finan of Iona, and a see was briefly established at Repton in Derbyshire. This may have been the act that precipitated the war of AD 655 because Penda would not have countenanced what he regarded as meddling in Mercian affairs by what were effectively agents of King Oswy of Northumbria. But the catastrophe at Winwaed changed everything.

What Bede meant by 'Mercia and its adjacent provinces' referred to the satellite kingdoms of the Hwicce, Magonsaetan, and the Westerne. The first we have examined already, Worcestershire and Gloucestershire. The Magonsaetan inhabited Herefordshire and southern Shropshire. The Westerne may be the same people as the Magonsaetan, or perhaps were the people living in the area that Penda originally came from, east Worcestershire nearby the Cotswolds. Others think they may have lived in Cheshire and the north Shropshire plain. But it was not just these Anglo-Saxon folk who were affected by Oswy's evangelical ambitions. The Diocese of Lichfield was established in AD 669 by St Chad, but I believe that an earlier attempt was made to annexe that area, the small British enclave of Caer Luitcoit, ruled by a kinsman of Cynddylan named Morfael ap Glast. My theory is based on the fact that within a few months of being confirmed as king by Oswy Peada was poisoned by his wife, probably acting on instructions received from her father. The poem called '*Canu Heledd*' mentioned in the previous chapter makes reference to a raid by the war-bands of Dogfeiling on Caer Luitcoit (Wall-by-Lichfield). I suggest that Oswy may well have encouraged Peada to seize this desirable location with the idea of using it as a base for a new Mercian diocese. The Britons were, understandably, sedulously protective about their own ancient faith traditions and their indigenous ecclesiastical organisation, but on a more ancient level, the area was a sacred shrine of Brigit – one of the most august Celtic goddesses, a deity so revered that she became transformed into the Christian saint of that name. Morfael immediately called on mutual support from Pengwern. The object of such a surprise cavalry attack was plunder and seizure of livestock – a lucrative spoiling raid, but also a reminder that the Dogfeilion were nobody's vassals. Heledd describes the departure of her brothers, in words which recall Aneirin's '*Gododdin*':

> My heart is aflame like a firebrand…
> Brothers I had, better it was when they lived,
> The whelps of Arthur our mighty fortress,
> Before Caer Luitcoit they triumphed;
> There was blood strewn for the ravens, fierce attack;
> They shattered lime-shields the sons of Cyndrwyn…
> Glory in battle, great plunder
> Outside Caer Luitcoit, Morfael took it.
> Fifteen hundred cattle and five stewards,
> Four-score horses and splendid armour
> Each bishop rushing to the four corners,
> Hugging their books could not save the monks.

It has to be considered, I think, that the site where the Staffordshire Hoard was found is just 2 miles from Wall-by-Lichfield – 'outside Caer Luitcoit'. I have examined these connections elsewhere but if there was some botched plan to eject the Britons from Luitcoit, which then resulted in a disastrous battle with a small British army, it may explain why Peada was murdered by his wife. Cynddylan became a Brythonic folk hero, celebrated in poetry as 'the bright buttress of the borderlands'. But his success signed his death warrant. In AD 659, piqued by a Mercian rebellion led by Wulfhere, Peada's brother, and preoccupied by a war against Talorgan, King of the Picts, on his far northern borders, Oswy ordered the elimination of the Dogfeilion royal household. A party of raiders surprised Cynddylan and every member of the royal house with the exception of the eponymous Heledd, at Llys Pengwern near Baschurch. The entire company were massacred and the royal hall burned to ashes, the churches set on fire – an entire culture extinguished. Small wonder that Heledd's words (whether actually composed by her or not) convey such haunting sentiments of grief and loss, the epitome of the laments for the 'Lost Lands'. As she wanders through the inferno to the smoking ruins of her brother's royal hall, she witnesses the end of the Brythonic culture in the lowlands, scenes from a psychical apocalypse:

> The hall of Cynddylan is dark tonight
> Without fire, without light,
> And what a silence surrounds it!
> The hall of Cynddylan is dark-panelled,
> It shelters no more the laughing company
> Woe to he who comes to a sad end!
> The hall of Cynddylan has lost its splendour
> Now that his shield lies in the grave
> Once this roof was never open
> The hall of Cynddylan is dark-ceilinged
> Now that the Saxons have slaughtered Cynddylan
> And Elwyn of Powys

In a state of psychic dissociation engendered by extreme grief, Heledd sees visions of eagles feasting on the flesh of the slain:

> The Eagle of Eli screams loud.
> He is wet with men's blood,
> With the hearts' blood of Cynddylan the fair.
> The eagle of Eli guards the seas,
> The fishes no longer swim in the currents
> He howls to see the blood of men.
> The eagle of Eli wanders lonely in the forest.
> At first light he feeds from the victims of his tricks.
> The grey-beaked eagle of Pengwern
> Cries most piercingly,
> Greedy for the flesh of him I love...
> The eagle of Pengwern called afar tonight,
> He can be seen gorging the blood of men.
> Tren is too well named the deserted city.
> The churches of Bassa are in mourning tonight
> As they hold the remains of the pillars of battle
> Of the heart of the men of Argoed
> The churches of Bassa are in flames tonight,
> Very little remains of them.

John Morris was not the only one to see in this poetry a moment of transition, as the refugees from the Shropshire plain headed west, for the mountains of what would shortly become Wales. They left behind them a strange vacuum, the kind of atmosphere one experiences walking into an abandoned house, 'The Land of Lost Content' A. E Housman called it, and there are hints that he was aware of the *Canu Heledd* when he wrote:

> When Severn down to Buildwas ran
> Coloured with the death of man
> Couched upon her brother's grave
> The Saxon got me on the slave.
>
> The sound of fight is silent long
> That began the ancient wrong;
> Long the voice of tears is still
> That wept of old the endless ill.
>
> In my heart it has not died,
> The war that sleeps on Severn side;
> They cease not fighting east and west,
> On the marches of my breast.

For the few remaining pockets of Celtic speakers in the forests of Morfe and Kinver, life went on of course. The loss of their king and their tribal base had doomed them to accommodation with the Anglo-Saxon folk, but the sense of longing, or *hiraeth* – the desperate yearning for a homeland which no longer existed – never left them.

For over fifty years a Roman Catholic mission had maintained a precarious presence in Britain. Based initially in Kent, where the archbishop's original see was at Canterbury (it still remains there), its influence had spread to Northumbria, whose king, Edwin, had embraced the faith before he was killed at Haethfelth. When Edwin died his bishop of Northumbria had fled, as we saw, and it was only thanks to the diligence and compassion of the holy St Aedan, an Irish missionary Oswald had invited into Lindisfarne to become his new bishop that Christianity survived in Northumbria. By a supreme irony, Augustine, the envoy of Pope Gregory the Great, had landed in Kent in AD 597, the very same year that the founder of the Irish mission on Iona, which ultimately converted Northumbria, St Columba, had died. By the time Mercia regained its independence in AD 658 under Wulfhere, Penda's second son, nearly every Anglo-Saxon kingdom, with the exception of Sussex, had converted to Christianity. Wulfhere may not have been baptised for a while after he became king; there is a local folk tale in Staffordshire that he slew his own sons, Wulphad and Ruffius, because they had allowed themselves to be converted by St Chad. Eventually, however, he did relent but was careful to choose an Englishman, Trumhere, who he trusted implicitly as his own bishop of the Mercians. Now that Oswy had regained control of Northumbria, and was acknowledged as the *Bretwalda*, difficult and complex issues presented themselves, which, although they hinged primarily on what seem like petty disputes over the calculations for determining the date of Easter, or which style of tonsure was correct, were actually intensely political and strategic gambits to secure dominance over the island. In order to understand all this we must briefly outline the history of the relationship between the Celts and the Roman Catholic Church since Augustine arrived.

The story goes that as a young man Pope Gregory had become fascinated by a group of blonde blue-eyed children he had seen for sale in the slave market at Rome. He found out that they were from Deira, modern Yorkshire, of the people called Angles, but Gregory, in a revealing pun, replied that they looked to him more like 'Angels'. From that moment he was determined to convert these Anglo-Saxon people from heathenism and to bring them the light of Christ and when he became pope it at last lay within his power to send a mission to the island. The extraordinary irony was that the heathen Anglo-Saxons were viewed as 'noble savages' whose 'angelic' countenances revealed their natural affinity with the divine order. But the Britons and Irish, whose stubborn adherence to the Christian faith had survived all the ordeals and tribulations we have seen in the previous chapters, were regarded as anathema, schismatics or even heretics. This was particularly regrettable in the case of the Irish mission of Columba because it had been their protection of Oswald and Oswy that had ultimately saved Northumbria from complete apostasy. Aedan's diligence and humility had won the hearts of the people in their darkest hour, and was all the more remarkable because he could not speak English – Oswald acted as his interpreter. Aedan spoke by his actions, giving away rich gifts of fine clothes and silver plate to the poorest folk he could find. This simple, humble and extremely austere way of life had been Columba's way, and the monastery and cathedral of Lindisfarne achieved its extraordinary artistic splendour under a regime that continued the Irish traditions. But the Britons were regarded as having failed in their Christian duty by not evangelising the Anglo-Saxons. St Augustine was said to have prophesied 'in a threatening manner' that the Britons, for their 'perfidy' and their failure to bring the good news to 'the brethren', would one day 'suffer the vengeance of death' at the hands of the English. Bede thought the massacre of the poor British monks at the battle of Chester in AD 613 had been the divine outworking of this 'prophesy' (or was it a curse?). Yet Professor Patrick Sims-Williams in his *Religion and Literature in Western England, 600–800* (Cambridge, 2005) adduces powerful evidence that the English Hwicce tribe, or at least the portion of it settled west of the Severn, had been converted by a surviving British Church in the area at an early date. This may be an isolated case, but the survival in England of the British place names of Eccles, Eccleshall, and Eccleswall etc. reminds us that the British word for a church, *egles* (modern Welsh, *eglwys*) is derived from the Latin *ecclesia*.

The simple fact was that relations between the two peoples were so strained that there was a de facto 'apartheid'. The partiality of Rome towards the English, and the demonisation of the Celts as rustic simpletons, uncharitable, severe, and un-Christian, as well as clinging on to outdated and dubious practices, meant that the Anglo-Saxon kings had been given carte blanche to wage holy war against them by Rome. King Aethelberht of Kent had been baptised as early as AD 601 and he had facilitated a meeting between Augustine and seven bishops of the British Church somewhere on the borders between the Anglo-Saxons and the Britons (probably at Great Witley in Worcestershire, tellingly in the territory of the Hwicce, who had perhaps been partially converted by the latter). The tetchy and suspicious nature of the exchange tells us just how uncompromising both sides were. The Britons, for their part, had sought the advice of a *dyn hysbys* – a cunning man or wizard – and this perhaps shows us just how high the stakes were at the meeting. The hermit advised them that if Augustine rose from his episcopal chair to greet them, then he was a man who could be trusted, with whom they should cooperate, but if he remained seated, then he should be shunned. Augustine had sought the advice of Pope Gregory, who wrote back to him explicitly conferring his ultimate authority over the British Church and its bishops. The complex etiquette regarding who should remain standing or seated was actually of vital importance, and it was Augustine's decision to remain seated that doomed the negotiations. Pope Gregory's perceptions of Britain were coloured by what he knew of Gaul, and he imagined that the Britons lived a similar way of life to the Gauls. Gaul still had thriving cities and a reasonably functioning road system. Its inhabitants still spoke a language descended from Latin and the metropolitan sees governed huge diocesan tracts. But Britain had had a quite different experience. Its cities had been deliberately left in ruins by the Anglo-Saxons, and all Christian life in the areas they occupied had ceased for generations. A tiny mission such as Augustine's could not hope to make a sufficient impact on its own, and needed British help. He was, however, not entirely to blame. It was Gregory's decision to back the English against the Britons that consigned the latter to oblivion. Sixty years later it was Northumbria, whose king, Oswy, was a devotee of the Irish religion who was encouraging error. The key to winning him over to Rome was his Roman Catholic queen, Eanflaed, and his son, Alchfrith. Alchfrith had banished Irish monks from the monasteries he had endowed as early as 658, and replaced them with Roman clergy. Eanflaed ostentatiously celebrated Easter according to the Roman date (she was from Kent, which was Roman Catholic), which meant that as the royal household were feasting during the festival she was still fasting. Doubtless she remained celibate also and eventually Oswy convoked the famous

Synod of Whitby in AD 664 so that these irritating inconsistencies about Easter and the tonsure could be ironed out once and for all.

The synod was, in effect, a contest between the Irish/Celtic and Roman Catholic parties. The new Bishop of Lindisfarne, Colman, justified the Irish tradition by invoking the spirit of the saintly Columba. These were the ways of Iona, and perhaps Colman assumed too much when he appealed to the king's boyhood memories of that lonely isle, where he and his sainted brother had found refuge for so many years. There was little else to be said, but Colman's opponent in the debate, Wilfred, immediately demolished his arguments by denigrating Columba, whom he portrayed as a man whose 'rustic simplicity but pious intentions', though in some sense virtuous, were nevertheless aberrations, because they were at odds with the Roman Catholic faith: 'As for you and your companions, you certainly sin if, having heard the decrees of the Apostolic See and of the universal church you refuse to follow them.'

Summing up, Wilfred, the staunch advocate for Rome, pointed out that it had not been Columba who had been chosen as the head of Christ's Church but the 'most blessed prince of the apostles' – St Peter. The choice was clear, and Oswy made it. Smiling, he turned to Colman, and decided for Rome, lest when he approached the gates of heaven, he was barred on account of having offended the keeper of the keys – St Peter himself. Soon afterwards Oswy dictated a letter to the pope, in which he committed himself to asserting his authority over the entire island on behalf of Rome. In his response, Pope Vitalian was eager to encourage Oswy:

> We therefore desire your highness will hasten to dedicate all your island to Christ, establishing there the Catholic and Apostolic faith. Truly your highness seeks, and shall no doubt obtain, that all your islands shall be made subject to you, as is our wish and our desire.

This great divide in religion anathematised the Celtic population and legitimised English lordship over them. For Bede the divine displeasure shown towards the Britons, as a result of their manifold errors and sins, showed how God could intervene in the fates of nations, especially those who failed in their duty to spread the good news of the gospel. He had derived this superstition from Gildas, but his own history transmitted it down the centuries. It formed the basis of Archbishop Wulfstan's famous *Sermo Lupi ad Anglos* 'the Sermon of the Wolf to the English' in the eleventh century, for example. Bede is not, however, totally unsympathetic to the plight of the Britons. He thought God '...did not abandon His people whom He foreknew, but rather sent to them much more worthy heralds of truth.' But he wrote half a century and more after these events. At the time the cocksure Wilfred and his adherents used the decision at Whitby as an excuse to extirpate the Britons and Irish politically as well as theologically. This was what doomed the British Celts to centuries of unrelenting warfare and ruthless oppression. Their denunciation as heretics and the elevation of the Anglo-Saxon realms (in particular Oswy's Northumbria) as executors of a divine punishment on the Celts, explicitly sanctioned by the pontiff, condemned them to cultural and political oblivion – at the margins of Europe they were treated as a plague bacillus that might infect the rest of Christendom, rather like the Cathars in southern France.

Such ancient folk customs as the belief in a fairy otherworld, which we encountered earlier on, were now deliberately used as evidence of virtual paganism or witchcraft. There were immediate expulsions of the British and Irish clergy after Whitby, and probable seizure of their *parochiae*. British Christians were forbidden to visit *martyria* shrines to their local saints, many of whom would have been extensions of previous Celtic god forms. Wilfred kept a young British boy beside him at his great basilica at Ripon, to whom he gave an English name, Eodwald, known as 'the Son of the Bishop', and this seems analogous to the later renaming of black slaves in the eighteenth-century West Indies. In fact, Wilfred was the most controversial churchman of his age. He was exiled by the kings of Northumbria twice, and became embroiled in bitter disputes with two archbishops of Canterbury necessitating two visits to Rome to make appeals to the pontiff. It is true that Wilfred was exonerated and his titles and estates were restored to him, a measure perhaps, of his supreme intellect and his rhetorical powers. One of the most telling disputes concerned the holy St Chad. Chad had been a pupil of Aedan, and had become the Abbot of Lastingham in North Yorkshire. Oswy had decided to make Chad his new bishop of Northumbria. Unfortunately Wilfred had already been chosen as bishop of York and had gone abroad to be consecrated, at Compiegne, where the ceremony was performed by no less than twelve bishops. The elaborate ceremonies dragged on so long that by the time Wilfred returned, Chad was already consecrated, by a mere three bishops, and what was particularly galling to him was that two of these had been British bishops, heretics in Wilfred's eyes. This scandal infuriated Wilfred, who appealed to the pope's new Archbishop of Canterbury, an elderly Greek called Theodore of Tarsus. Theodore had arrived in Britain after travelling through Italy and France for over a year, in company with Hadrian 'the African', a Berber refugee from North Africa Pope Vitalian had sent to keep Theodore company (and also, perhaps, to ensure he did not introduce heretical ideas from the Eastern Church). Theodore, who was convinced that all Britons and Irish were heretics, upbraided Chad, only to receive the reply from the humble man that he was entirely willing to relinquish his role, for he had never considered himself worthy of such an honour. Chad returned to Lastingham, but his humility had so impressed Theodore that he compromised. Wilfred was restored at York, but Chad was chosen to become the bishop of the Mercians at Lichfield. Famously, Theodore bought a fine horse for Chad, having noted that he travelled everywhere on foot and even personally hoisted the bishop into the saddle, but at the first village he reached, Chad gave the animal away to a poor man. Chad died in AD 672 of the plague, only three years after he became bishop. He represented the religion of the past, whereas Wilfred, with all his ostentation and self-assurance, was a man of the future.

Theodore and Hadrian diligently reformed the Church in England and imposed a degree of uniformity over it at the Synod of Hertford in AD 673: 'the first constitutional measure of the collective English race' as William Stubbs called it. But Theodore's obvious affection for the humble Chad, despite his initial suspicion of him and prejudice towards him, showed that on contact with the Irish-trained clergy they were by no means the gloomy, bitter, uncharitable folk he had expected to meet. The alliance between English political expediency and Roman Catholic religion could not alter the facts. The Irish missionaries had penetrated the west of Britain as well as the north. They had sailed to Iceland, and legends that are not entirely incredible claim that St Brendan reached North America. They penetrated as far to the east as Prussia and Kiev in the Ukraine, and even the English missionaries who evangelised the Continental Germans had been influenced by Celtic Christianity. Willibrord had spent twelve years in an Irish monastery and Wynfrith, the great Apostle of the Germans, was born at Crediton in Devonshire, then very much a border realm with the Celts. The greatest imperial project since the fall of the Roman Empire, Charlemagne's empire with its capital at Aix-La-Chapelle, was administered by Alcuin of York, who had been educated by the Irish, and Dicuil, who was an Irishman. The Celts were resilient and they would not abandon their ancient traditions or surrender their remaining lands. The old struggle with the 'Saxons' (they called all Englishmen 'Saxons', whatever their actual ethnic origins) would continue and now an old ally was to become a formidable enemy – Mercia.

In AD 655, Mercia had suffered a humiliating reverse at Winwaed but we have seen before how fortunes could turn very quickly about. Peada had been eliminated, but his brothers, Wulfhere and Aethelred, survived him. Wulfhere remained in hiding close to the borders of western Mercia, probably in the remote forests like Kinver, whose church he later dedicated to the memory of his slain sons. Oswy was distracted by a war with the Picts in AD 658, and this was Wulfhere's moment to emerge from obscurity. A group of powerful nobles, Eadbert, Immin and Eafa, hailed Wulfhere as the new king of the Mercians. Acting with the same ruthless celerity as his father, Wulfhere chased out or killed the Northumbrian governors and their retinues. All Mercian fighting men were summoned to arms, and before Oswy could extricate himself from the far north the coup had achieved its goal of restoring Mercian independence. The Northumbrian raid on Llys Pengwern had opened up new opportunities in the west too, and Mercian settlers would not have been slow to advance towards the modern frontier with Wales. A place called 'Wulfhere's Ford' may mark the agreed boundary between the English and Welsh (as they were becoming by this stage). There may have been Mercian settlement in that area for some time. The place names of Pontesbury and Pontesford, nearby the Stiperstones in Shropshire, may derive from the Welsh name for Penda – Panta. There is a tradition in Wales that he took Heledd, the supposed author of the poem we have considered earlier, as his wife, though this seems unlikely. It is possible that another son of Penda, Merewalh, was set up by him as sub-king of the Magonsaetan people whose lands lay along the borders of the Britons in Herefordshire and south Shropshire. As his name tells us, this frontier zone was analogous to the 'Wild West', where ethnicity could become blurred. Merewalh means 'the famous Welshman'. The obvious obstacle we see to a marriage between Penda and Heledd is that he was, famously, a heathen while she would have been, presumably, Christian, but these were strange times – right at the interface with the first Christian missions to the Mercians, and also Mercia was, perhaps, a strange place. We know of Penda's devotion to Germanic Wodenism, but there may have been other pagan influences in the region. Stephen J. Yeates in his *The Tribe of Witches: The Religion of the Dobunni and Hwicce* (Oxford, 2008) adduces strong archaeological and place name evidence for the survival of a pagan nature cult in the area, which worshipped a goddess called Cuda, after whom the Cotswolds may be named. We know from later legends about 'Edric the Wild' in Shropshire, that he is supposed to have taken a fairy bride named Godda, and we have another case, perhaps, in the legend of 'Lady Godiva'. Shropshire was an ancient woodland zone, known to the Celts as Goddeu, which may recall the name of the goddess. Taliesin's '*Cad Goddeu*' or 'the Battle of the Trees' is one of the most enigmatic riddling poems in Welsh literature. Yeates speculates that the Hwicce were essentially a ruling aristocracy of Germanic origin, perhaps a branch of the Gewissae, overlying a population that retained the ancient nature religion, whose devotees principally worshipped rivers, springs and wells, but also gathered at 'high-places' amid groves and sacred enclosures called *nemetons*. In essence, what Yeates suggests is that the Hwicce adopted the ancient religion themselves and became, literally, 'witches'. Though this sounds controversial it is really no more so than another theory about the same region during the same period, namely that the Hwicce, or some portion of that tribe, were converted to Christianity by the native Britons, postulated by Professor Patrick Sims-Williams in his *Religion and Literature in Western England, 600–800* (Cambridge, 2005).

I point to these divergent theories only to emphasise how wide the possibilities are for innovative and unusual cultural interface at this time. There seems something about the eagerness with which Cynddylan responded to Penda's call for military assistance ('when the son of pyd [Penda] requested, he was so ready!'), which is more than a cold-blooded military arrangement. Penda may well have been a native of precisely the area where Yeates asserts that the ancient pagan cult was operating. His estates were on the Avon near Pebworth, and Pinvin outside Pershore in Wychavon (yet another survival of the name of the Hwicce tribe) probably means 'Penda's Fen'. If Penda had a British wife or concubine and proudly called a son 'Merewalh', this seems to me to indicate the possibility of a substantial cultural intermingling between the Mercians and Britons, which meant that in the pre-Christian phase of Mercian settlement, a truly Anglo-British culture existed in the borderlands. Only later, when the 'Welsh' had been anathematised as heretics, did 'the great divide' so ostentatiously represented by Offa's Dyke become desirable or necessary.

The long-established view that the word *walh* meant 'slave' as well as 'foreigner', and that the two were virtually synonymous in areas under English rule, was powerfully rejected by John Morris, but there was something deep in the collective Anglo-Saxon consciousness about the term. The very earliest Germanic contacts with Celts in Europe were with a tribe Caesar named the *Volcae*; it was from their name that the Germans developed the words *Walh* and *Waelisc* or 'Welsh', meaning, literally, 'foreigners' or 'strangers'. From that time all Celts were designated as Welsh. It is thought the word may be related to *gwalch*, the Welsh for a hawk, but another theory suggests that it meant wolf. The Celts, to the Germans, were the 'Wolf-People', because, like wolves, they lived in the dense forests and marshes – places that the Germans dreaded for fear of malign spirits. Like wolves, the Celts were also a threat, to be exterminated. These were, I believe, ancient and deep prejudices that the exigencies of frontier life, and the presence of a powerful common enemy in the shape of Northumbria, had combined to overcome. But as soon as Wulfhere became a Christian, and acknowledged the primacy of the Archbishop of Canterbury and the pope – and then the Northumbrian threat had been removed – the Britons were dehumanised, to become 'the Wolf People' or 'Hawk People' or 'Welsh' again, and worse, enemies of God. Under Wulfhere's rule, and then during his equally powerful and devout brother Aethelred's reign, Mercia became the strongest of the Anglo-Saxon kingdoms and the implacable enemy of the Britons. It was this enmity, indeed, that acted as a unifying force and created the opportunity for a united Celtic kingdom. It is noteworthy that Mercia, though it has not existed since AD 918, was instrumental in the formation of two modern nations: England and Wales.

Wulfhere's main objective was to dominate all of England south of the Humber, which he managed to achieve. After his death in AD 675, Aethelred, his younger brother, succeeded him. At the Battle of the River Trent in 679 Aethelred destroyed a Northumbrian army and killed the younger brother of the Northumbrian king. The compensation due for this to King Ecgfrith of Northumbria was negotiated by Archbishop Theodore of Tarsus, who arranged the terms to Mercia's advantage. This endorsement by the Church established Mercian supremacy in southern England for the next century and a half. In the west, however, the Celts were aware of the new dangers and were preparing themselves for a dogged resistance, ever watchful for encroachment on their traditional tribal lands. Near the modern border, just within England, at a place actually called 'the Bog', an old farmstead has a queer name, Squilver, which is derived from the Welsh *Disgwlfa* –'the place of observation' – from which the Britons watched for any hostile incursions. They were a hardy folk, bred to war from childhood, as Giraldus Cambrensis recounts:

> Not addicted to gluttony or drunkenness, they incur no expense in food or dress, and their minds are always bent on the defence of their country and on the means of plunder, and they are wholly employed in the care of their horses and their furnishings. They fast from morning till evening, and trusting to the care of providence they dedicate the whole day to business, and in the evening partake of a moderate meal – and if they miss this, they patiently wait until the next evening, and deterred neither by cold

or hunger watch through the dark and stormy nights for any hostile movements of their enemies.

This disciplined and austere, even Spartan devotion to their duty managed to halt Mercian expansion, and indeed wider Anglo-Saxon expansion seems to have run out of steam by AD 722 when they were defeated in three battles by the Celts. At Pencon, perhaps in Carmarthenshire, a Mercian army was beaten, at Hehill, probably Hayle in Cornwall, a West Saxon army met a similar fate, and another English army was beaten at a place called Garth Maelog. This looks like a concerted campaign by several Anglo-Saxon kingdoms, which failed miserably. So a new divide had been created, a dangerous and hostile frontier zone, where English settlers were never entirely safe. A memorial pillar to a King of Powys called Eliseg records that he 'seized the inheritance of the men of Powys by force from the power of the English'. The despised Welsh, it seems, could strike back, reoccupying lost territory. The powerful divisions of language and religion were too strong to resist, and the next century would shape nations.

10

A New Frontier

It has been noted (by Margaret Gelling in *The West Midlands* and by Anthony Lias in *Place-names of the Welsh Borderlands*) that there are more surviving place names of Celtic/Brythonic origin in Staffordshire than further west, in Shropshire. This anomaly may be explained. If there was a sudden catastrophe in the area that now comprises Shropshire, the former Dogfeiling or Pengwern, which meant that large estates were suddenly available to distribute as rewards for the nobles who had supported Wulfhere's coup. It is a possibility that Wulfhere was sheltered by his father's old ally in the debatable lands on the border of Pengwern, and perhaps the reason why Oswy was so incensed with the petty kingdom was because it had defied him in this way. Wulfhere would certainly have rewarded men whose loyalty to his cause had liberated his inheritance for him. Aethelbald, a later Mercian king, made grants of land on the borders of the Hwicce in north Worcestershire in AD 736 at a place called Stour-in-Ismere and at Wolverley nearby, to two 'companions' (meaning military comrades) called Cyneberht and Hwita. This was a few generations later, when literacy and Christianity were supporting a King of Mercia, who was also 'King of all the southern English' as the Ismere Diploma states. Wulfhere was still semi-pagan and so no such charters survive, but we may be quite sure that such arrangements of parcelling-out estates would have been practised in his day. Shropshire was a vacuum, as I have postulated, and so there was a sudden influx of English settlers in the central frontier zone, whereas to the north and the south the ethnic picture was much more mixed. Jean Markale, a Breton scholar, in *The Celts* (Paris, 1976), points out the very interesting fact that a proportion of the refugees from Pengwern possessed the necessary wherewithal to travel further afield than what is now Wales:

> It was at this point that several of the British peoples began to migrate. The Cornovii who had first settled on the Welsh borders were now in the Cornish peninsula, and some of them crossed the sea to find refuge in the Quimper region of Cornouaille in Brittany. The Dumnonii, who lived in Devon, also went to Brittany, to the area of St Malo and Dinan where they founded the kingdom of Donmonia; while some of the Welsh and Northern Britons found refuge in Finistere.

Such desperate measures betrayed the exhaustion of the Britons after their long struggles. A Welsh Triad states: 'Three things exhausted Lloegyr: resistance to the foreigners, delivering prisoners and the presence of the bald man.' The 'bald man' was St Augustine of Canterbury, who had supposedly prophesied their doom. But the impetus towards this overseas migration was in part so that they could practise their form of Christianity without fear of persecution, much like the later Pilgrim Fathers. The extraordinary favouritism shown by Rome to their national enemies caused the Britons to become demonstrative in their rejection of the English. When Britons went abroad on pilgrimages, the rule was that they would not stay under the same roof where an Englishman had slept, or eat food from tables which they had used. St Beuno famously fled from the Severn Valley all the way to Lleyn in north Wales after he heard men calling to their dogs across the river in English, rather than remain among 'heathens'. These petty and admittedly un-Christian gestures were noticed and condemned but the Britons would go to extraordinary lengths to be free from the oppressive presence of their enemies. The Britons in Brittany and Britonia in Galicia formed their own independent dioceses at the very edge of the known world. Their longing for the lonely windswept western shores was not simply about exile, or even the search for *diseartan* 'deserted places', such as Skellig Michael hermitage off the south-west coast of Ireland, or Dyzard in Cornwall. There was a deep-seated rejection of hierarchal authority and a suspicion of the pope. Dinoot, Abbot of Bangor, rejected papal authority, saying,

> I am prepared to show the Pope in Rome the affection and charity I owe to all Christian men, I owe nothing more to him whom you call the Pope and who unreasonably claims to be the father of fathers. We know no other leader than the Bishop of Caerleon. It is he whom God has set to watch over us.

This egalitarianism and the need for a common folk-bond ran very deep in the Celtic consciousness, and is perhaps a survival of that old heresy, Pelagianism. John Scotus, an Irish monk taught that since for God there was no sin, there could be no punishment for evil – it being itself a punishment, for by malefaction the sinner disbars him or herself from attaining the divine blessedness. This is, in effect, a restatement of Druidic ethics.

For those Celts who remained in Britain, however, a new way of life dominated by sharply defined frontiers with their enemies was to become the rule, exemplified by Offa's Dyke, but before we examine that structure it will be worthwhile to reacquaint ourselves with the political frontiers as they were by the mid-eighth century. The Welsh frontier lay more or less where the border is today, and although there were British speakers in the Severn Valley, along the Wye Valley and well into Cheshire, they would by this stage have been tenants of English lords. In Wessex there was a distinct Celtic population living alongside the English, and their paschal practices were tolerated by the West Saxon Church. By around AD 700 Devonshire had been annexed to Wessex, but Cornwall held out. These expeditions on the Celtic frontiers were now a tradition among the Anglo-Saxon frontier kingdoms. Young men who aspired to fame and glory – and of course land and treasure too – could make a name for themselves by banding together under some aristocrat or nobleman and raiding across the border. There was more or less constant warfare between the West Saxons and the Cornish from AD 722 until the end of the century, and occasionally West

Saxon and Mercian kings would combine against Cornwall. The campaigns were holy wars of course, blessed by the Church, and the terrible sufferings of the Cornish and Welsh were no more than a prelude to the later depredations of the Vikings; in 815 King Egberht of Wessex 'ravaged Cornwall from east to west', and although the peninsula remained nominally independent for a while longer it had been effectively subdued well before Alfred the Great came to the throne. The Cornish were forced to relent about the matter of Easter, and indeed Gwynedd, the most powerful kingdom of Wales, was forced to do the same eventually. To be a British Celt meant to be a second-class human being in one's own homeland. Ever since the recovery of Mercia under kings Wulfhere and Aethelred, the focus of Northumbria's military campaigns had shifted north, to campaigns against Alclud and the Picts. Aethelbald, the most powerful of the Mercian kings yet to have emerged, sacked York in the 740s and ravaged Northumbria. By the time he was eventually assassinated by his own bodyguards forty-one years into his reign, Mercia was becoming the most dominant English kingdom. Aethelbald's ambition was to reduce all the other Anglo-Saxon kingdoms to vassalage, but Wales was to be subjugated too.

Aethelbald's successor was a person called Beornred, who may have been behind Aethelbald's murder, but he was soon deposed to be succeeded by the man whose name was to be remembered for the earthwork he constructed along the Welsh border with England – with the most impressive sections in Shropshire, the newly acquired and heavily settled region along the central border. As we have seen, Eliseg (or Elisedd), a king of Powys, eventually drove out English settlers and reclaimed his inheritance. Welsh raiders must have intruded into the former region of Pengwern as far as the Severn, considering the land and the beasts on it to be rightfully theirs, and these incursions must have been a constant problem. In AD 760 a huge Welsh war-band ventured into Herefordshire but ran into Offa and his army. Both sides claimed victory, but the collision was ominous. Offa had his eye on Herefordshire, where he had a huge palace at Sutton Walls. As his power, wealth and ambitions grew to international proportions, and his generosity towards the Church increased, the time was approaching for the mighty king to settle the matter of the border once and for all. In AD 783, 'the Mercian incendiaries' under Offa marched on Dinefawr on the River Twyi, which was burned. After wasting the whole region during winter to ensure mass starvation there, Offa's employees set to work, parties of labourers summoned from the client kingdoms of Mercia, Mercia itself, and of course, Welsh prisoners of war and slaves. The greatest engineering project of the early Middle Ages had commenced.

The dyke is one of the most impressive and controversial structures of the entire Anglo-Saxon era (it should be noted that there are those who believe it to be a Roman construction, but as yet this theory is speculative). Nevertheless, there are a number of things that have been claimed about it that are not true. The man who fixed our concept of what the dyke is and who built it was Asser, the Welshman who was Alfred the Great's biographer:

> There was in Mercia in fairly recent times a certain vigorous king called Offa, who terrified all the neighbouring kings and provinces around him, and who had a great dyke built between Wales and Mercia from sea to sea.

The expression 'from sea to sea' is used by Gildas about the other frontier obstacle, Hadrian's Wall, and we must suspect that a Welsh monk, having read the works of Gildas, merely imitated his reference to that structure, thus embedding the idea of a continuous barrier – which it is not. To the north of Offa's Dyke there is another, probably earlier dyke, Wat's Dyke, which, while it was part of the same defensive line, was not built at the same time. The strongest section of the dyke is along the borders of Powys. It is constructed in such a way that any hills along the route lay to the east, giving commanding views over the territory of the perceived enemy, Powys. The defensive ditch and raised bank face in the same direction – west. The two dykes do not link up, so there is a gap, and Wat's Dyke did not quite reach the sea in the north, or indeed in the south where the southern sections are less impressive in design, scale and execution. In the days when the Britons and the Mercians had made common cause against the Northumbrians the borderlands had been a chessboard of British and Anglo-Saxon enclaves, probably demarcated by their own dykes. The *Canu Heledd* in lamenting Cynddylan states, 'The dykes endure. He who dug them is no more.' Offa seems to have taken a decision to clearly demarcate Welsh- and English-speaking areas, and to impose his authority over this landscape with its turbulent feuds. His was a centralised power, based in the middle of England, exerting its force over the kingdoms of the south, East Anglia, and its northern frontier. Campaigns into Wales were raids in force that devastated the small Welsh kingdoms and then withdrew, unable to remain for any length of time in a hostile country already wasted by their own depredations. As soon as the Mercians withdrew, retaliatory Welsh raids would inevitably follow into England and indeed areas of English settlement, which then extended well inside modern Wales. The defensive structure Offa built was targeted on this threat. Another function of the structure was that it contained the potential contagion of 'heresy' and defined Offa as a warrior of Christ, defending and upholding the will of Rome within all those lands of which he was the overlord. Offa was a parvenu and a bully but he liked to project a respectable image of himself to the papacy and was a most generous donor to the Church both in England and abroad. In fact, if we accept that Offa was responsible for the dyke, as I do, it seems reasonable to examine the character of the man, which may give clues about his intentions.

Offa was a descendent of Eowa, Penda's brother, and was a cousin of Aethelbald, whose assassination had precipitated a brief but bloody civil war in Mercia. It may well be that Offa's claim was spurious but he had been the victor in the civil war, and might was right. But, if his claim was weak, the name he bore was redolent of the most sacred Anglo-Saxon pedigree, for the Anglian kings claimed descent from Offa of Angeln, a mighty king of the area between Denmark and Germany. He was a putative descendent of Woden himself, and his deeds were still sung of by the *scops* in the mead halls: 'When he was but a youth he gained the greatest of kingdoms, none of his age achieved greater deeds of valour in battle; by his sword he fixed the boundary against the Myrgings of Fifledor.'

It could well be that the construction of the dyke was consciously recalling the deeds of this illustrious ancestor, a physical proof of his legitimacy as the Mercian king. Although he was not a loveable hero like the later Alfred, and was a man 'stained with blood' as Alcuin wrote, Offa was the most ambitious Anglo-Saxon king yet to have emerged. His achievements speak for themselves, and the dyke is just one among them. He was responsible for the standardisation of the English currency, which endured until 1971, based on a silver penny, examples of which are among the finest examples of numismatic craftsmanship in Europe at that time. It was his obsession with this very worthwhile project which may have reinforced his sanguinary reputation. King Aethelberht of East Anglia seems to have issued silver pennies bearing his own image. He was summoned to meet with Offa at his royal hall at Sutton Walls in Herefordshire – he did not return home. Offa ordered his executioner, Grimberht, to take the young man away and dispose of him. This regicide was an appalling crime, and betrays a paranoid, controlling, ruthless and cruel personality. Offa's military reputation and skill was remarked upon by Asser, and he was remembered with terror, a man not to be trifled with. Wales was attacked in 760, 778, 783-84, and in 796. Similar campaigns against Kent used the same incendiary and terrorist tactics on his English satellites.

Control of London yielded him vast wealth derived from port tolls, which he invested in massive rebuilding works in Mercia, including at Hereford and Tamworth. His 'micro-management' reveals a greedy character, prepared to assert his authority in respect of minor gifts of Church lands without his approval. He was too eager to impress, and overestimated his real status on the world stage. Offa liked to compare himself to Charlemagne, and when he insisted that his son marry the latter's favourite daughter, Bertha, the emperor was infuriated and imposed economic sanctions on English traders. Offa realised he had made a diplomatic blunder and began an expensive policy of endowing Frankish monasteries in an effort to ingratiate himself with Charlemagne. This succeeded, and the two became 'friends and brothers'; the emperor even sent Offa a fabulous Avar sabre he had captured on his campaigns as a gift. Trade with Francia increased, and an exchange of letters exists in which Charlemagne requests that English cloaks and blankets are restored to their former size – to which Offa willingly accedes, requesting Charlemagne to send more 'black stones' to England, for the revolutionary mills he was introducing. Charlemagne also had a grand engineering project – a canal between the Rhine and the Danube, but it was never completed. Perhaps Offa was trying to compete with the emperor, attempting to demonstrate his organisational genius and his undisputed power to summon work gangs from all the regions subordinate to him. The actual construction work may well have taken less than a year – a feat that would probably be beyond the powers of modern construction companies today.

Offa's supreme aim was to establish his precious son, Ecgfrith, as his heir, and again it was Charlemagne's model he sought to emulate. The emperor had had his two sons, Pippin and Louis, consecrated as his heirs during his own lifetime by the pope himself. Now Offa demanded that a new arch-bishopric be established at Lichfield, depriving Canterbury of much of its former influence. In 786, a papal legation visited England to facilitate this change, which was completed, though not without controversy. The achievement of his project was celebrated by a grand jubilee on the thirtieth anniversary of his accession, and an issue of magnificent coins depicting both Offa and his queen. Ecgfrith was anointed and crowned as king, only to die 141 days after Offa had in July 796. Pope Adrian thought that Offa had even tried to intrigue with Charlemagne to have him deposed and replaced by a Frankish alternative – this shows the sheer scope of Offa's ambitions and the extent of his meddling. For all his personal failings there can be no denying that he was a man who was powerful and ruthless enough to have commissioned the monument that still bears his name on both sides of the border, which it still largely defines. He was perhaps the most powerful individual ruler in Britain since the departure of the Romans, and the dyke consciously emulates their achievements. In the central section a ditch was dug 6 feet deep by 12 feet wide, with an earthen embankment up to 30 feet high in places, surmounted by a strong palisade of timber and stone revetments. There were watchtowers and beacons along the route, and the beacons could be lit to alert patrols who could concentrate strong forces within hours to any flashpoint. We still have much to learn about how the dyke developed, but it seems to me that Offa's reputation as the mind behind the project remains secure. The divide that had begun as a spiritual, theological dispute, had now assumed a physical form, and it remains to this day.

This demonstration of Mercian power was a sign that the individual Welsh kingdoms were not powerful enough in their own right to resist the Sais. Meredydd, king of the Demetae, died at the Battle of Rhuddlann in 795, the year before Offa died, but Meredydd's death was not in vain – Offa's forces were repulsed. In 798, Caradoc, King of Gwynedd, was taken as a hostage by the Mercians and later killed. After a lengthy series of civil wars, Hywel ap Caradoc succeeded to the throne of Gwynedd. The Welsh were now faced with a stark choice: ultimate subjugation of their kingdoms one by one, or unification under acknowledged kings whose power was sufficient to preserve Celtic independence.

It was in the ninth century that Wales as a defined nation began to emerge, a process that was also underway in England. The catalyst for state formation in both cases was the onset of extensive Viking raiding at the turn of the ninth century. I have examined the process in respect of England elsewhere. In the case of Wales, the process began when the ancient line of kings of Gwynedd, claiming descent from Cunedda, was replaced by a new line of kings from the Isle of Man, or Manaw. As a people who had committed themselves to the fortunes of the seaways, the Vikings were not limited by land borders; the scope for their ventures was unprecedented but also highly risky – the magnificent Polynesian navigators, skilled as they were, did not have to contend with the rough conditions the Vikings endured. We saw in an earlier chapter how a great channel existed from the Shetlands to the Breton peninsula, a highway for trade, and for a long period this channel was a Celtic lake. Now, with the appearance of the longships, all this was thrown into confusion. The Isle of Man was a key target for the Vikings because its position allowed whoever controlled it to control all the Mevanian Islands, including Anglesey, the coastlands of western Wales and all the eastern coast of Ireland – as well as Cumbria, the Hebrides and the west coast of Scotland. It seems that the Vikings drove out the King of Man, Merfyn

Frych, who escaped to Gwynedd where he somehow managed to establish himself as the king there. Merfyn Frych succeeded Hywel ap Rhodri in AD 825 and the line of kings descended from him, the Merfynion, endured until 1283. When he came to the throne all the Welsh kingdoms were in turmoil. Constant civil wars and fratricidal disputes had left the border vulnerable and the Mercians had virtually annexed Powys. The Viking raids were intensifying and the ancient line of kings that connected the Britons with the very hazy memories of Rome had been supplanted, but this end was a new beginning. Meanwhile, on the other side of Offa's Dyke, the English were embroiled in dramas of their own. In the same year, 825, that Merfyn came to the throne, the Mercian hegemony had been smashed at the Battle of Ellandun in Wiltshire, where the West Saxon king, Egberht, had defeated Beornwulf of Mercia. The domination of southern England by the Mercians, which had been uninterrupted since Wulfhere's day, was now replaced by that of Wessex and its kings.

In 830, Egberht invaded Wales and demanded the tributes that had hitherto been due to Mercia. Somehow Merfyn managed to maintain himself as King of Gwynedd, despite all these unrelenting external pressures, and he must have been cunning and ruthless to have secured the ancient kingdom in the first place. As with the case of King Offa, later pedigrees were intruded into Merfyn's family tree to legitimise his takeover. Genealogy was crucial to promoting Merfyn's project of asserting the dominance of Gwynedd over the other Welsh kingdoms. The uncomfortable fact that Merfyn was unrelated to the ancient line going back to Cunedda and a foreigner from Man was addressed by later redactions of his pedigree, in which he was a descendant of Llywarch Hen, a royal bard from Rheged who had found refuge in Powys. Thus his origins in Man could be replaced by ancestors from Mannau Goddodin – from whence Cunedda had set out to become the founder of the original dynasty. These illustrious ancestors were necessary for Merfyn's scheme of binding the separate kingdoms together under a dynasty of kings based in Gwynedd, through a system of marriage alliances. These were distant dreams for the moment. The grim reality was a bitter decline into austerity and warfare, the exhaustion of a people ground down by relentless misery. The bard Llywarch Hen 'the old' personified the groans of a powerless ancient folk, almost too careworn to go on:

> Before I bore crutches, I was eloquent at the feasting,
> I was honoured and little wonder
> For the men of Argoed always loved me.
> Before I bore crutches I was handsome,
> I was welcomed in the assemblies of Powys,
> That paradise of the Cymry.

Instead the old man sends forth his sons, twenty-four of them, to fight the enemy, only to lose them one by one:

> By Llawen Gwen kept watch last night.
> Never did he lack success.
> The battle swelled on the green banks
> His broad thigh open, Gwen kept watch that night
> Near the ford of Morlas.
> He was my son and did not flee
> Four and twenty sons had I
> Wearing the golden torc, leaders in battle,
> Gwen was the best of them...

But in these dark days a mighty new leader appeared, as has happened so often in Celtic history, Rhodri Mawr ('the Great') – the Welsh equivalent in some respects of Alfred 'the Great' of Wessex. He became king in 844 and was the most powerful Welsh king of the ninth century. He controlled Powys, which he annexed in 856, then Maelienydd, around modern Radnorshire, and Seisllwg (Ceredigion, Carmarthenshire and as far south as the Gower) followed in 871. He was known as 'King of the Britons' in Ireland and has been called a 'King of Wales', though this latter claim was only partially true. Nevertheless, in the face of continuous and ferocious attacks, new opportunities presented themselves under this formidable king.

The most ominous problem of his time, as for Alfred in Wessex, were the *Dub Gint*, or 'black gentiles', as the Vikings were known. The Danes formed the most numerous of the Viking raiders against England and they managed to occupy almost half of that country, but the Vikings who concentrated against the Celts seem to have come from further north, Norwegians. This geographical perspective is important because, from their point of view, the archipelago of Britain and Ireland and the islands offshore of the two were on the 'Whale's Road' – the channel to the south-west, which led on ultimately to Brittany, Spain and the Barbary Coast. Despite, to some extent, the recent rehabilitation of the Vikings' reputation, we should be in no doubt that a well thought-through strategy existed among the Viking *jarls* (admirals) – they were not just casual raiders or opportunist pirates. In the broad sweep of their push to the south-west plunder could be taken, but also slaves, in particular young women. Because of the high maternal mortality rate from childbirth complications a demand always existed for female domestic labour, a situation that persisted until quite recent times. The rulers of the Byzantine Empire were always interested in the, to their eyes, exotic attractions of women from the northern regions and, considering the vast network of trading routes open to them, it is interesting to consider just how far east some of these British, English and Irish women may have ultimately gone. The clearing port for such slaves was the Viking port of Dublin, and their bases were carefully selected to facilitate a continuous through-put of incoming and outgoing plunder and slaves, with the currency of silver in coin or hack-bar form as the medium of exchange. Of course, all this had to be fought for. No one, whether British, Irish or English, was going to allow these depredations to go unchallenged, but the Vikings were a very formidable force, perhaps the most ferocious and skilled warriors man-for-man in history. They were not cowards, far from it; they dreamed of a death in battle so that they may manfully show their wounds when they entered Valhalla, the extended chieftain's hall that formed their concept of heaven – a continuous round of drinking, whoring and feasting with the gods. This disdain for death made them oblivious to hardships that would overcome lesser men. So, now Wales was assailed not only from the landward side on the east by the Sais, but also from the sea, by the Dub Gint.

Despite this the Mercian threat, which had been a continuous oppressive force for over a century, was now much reduced due to the dominance of Wessex shifting the focus of English politics further south. Egberht's invasion in 830 was followed by a period of relative peace because the intensity of Viking raids gathered pace during the 850s until in 865 the *mycel heathen here*, as the Anglo-Saxons called it – meaning the 'great heathen army' – landed on the east coast of England. From that point on this collaborative piratical military venture concentrated on destroying the four English kingdoms. By 871 only Wessex remained unconquered (though West Mercia regained its independence) and the life or death struggle between Alfred and his descendants and the Viking hordes preoccupied the English, and gave the Welsh a temporary respite from their continuous aggression. This enabled Rhodri to consolidate his control of a large part of Wales. A Viking *jarl* called Orm was killed, his army defeated by the great Welsh king, but Orm's compatriots revenged him and compelled Rhodri to flee to Ireland. Although his exile was brief, Rhodri died fighting the English in 878. His sons, Cadell, Anarawd and Merfyn ('the three diademed kings of Britain') received Ceredigion, Gwynedd and Powys respectively, according to the principle of partible inheritance we have seen before. The eldest son, Gwryiad, died in battle beside his father. The enemy who had killed Rhodri and his son was Ceolwulf the 'foolish king's thegn' who the great heathen army had set up as their puppet king of Mercia. He was the last man to call himself King of Mercia (Aethelred II contented himself with the title of 'Lord') and this vigorous campaign showed that although the Vikings succeeded in capturing half of the Mercian realm, leaving only a rump state in West Mercia – they were still capable of inflicting grievous damage on Wales. Ceolwulf was succeeded in Mercia by Aethelred II, or 'Lord Aethelred' as he is known to history.

He had taken in marriage Alfred's formidable daughter, Aethelflaed, and had submitted to Alfred, agreeing to act as his viceroy in West Mercia. East Mercia, like East Anglia and Northumbria had fallen to the 'great army' and Alfred was forced to tolerate the predominance of their law and customs north of a line corresponding to the ancient Roman road of the Watling Street – a de facto partition. The decline of Mercian power left it with an influence much diminished, but it still continued to assert its dominance over Welsh affairs, and to demand tribute. In 881,

Aethelred attempted to compel the submission of Rhodri's sons but was defeated near Conwy. This was claimed, by the jubilant Welsh monks who recorded the victory, as a divine revenge on the English who had killed Rhodri. Anarawd, the brother who was probably the overall commander of the Welsh forces, continued the policy Merfyn Frych had begun – a gradual unification of the Welsh people under the royal dynasty of Gwynedd. Aethelred's failure at Conwy doomed any attempt by his military junta to revive Mercian fortunes and he was unable to secure control over Gwent and Glywysing, the two kingdoms of south Wales that had previously been most compliant. As Mercia lost influence in Wales, Alfred took his opportunity to extend West Saxon overlordship there. Not only did Gwent and Glywysing submit, but also kings Hyfaidd of Dyfed and Elise ap Tewdr of Brycheiniog. All these southern Welsh kingdoms feared Anarawd and his brothers more than the distant West Saxon king. Wales was far from being a united country, but the process by which Alfred and his son, daughter and grandson united England, was also evident there.

So, now that the kings of south Wales had pledged fealty to Alfred, Anarawd and his brothers had forged an alliance with the Viking kingdom of York, which also extended to Dublin, with which port city Gwynedd in particular had always retained strong links. However, in 892 a renegade force of Vikings from Ireland raided Gwynedd, so Anarawd seems to have switched his allegiance to Alfred. It was a crucial decision, because in that same year a huge fleet of Viking ships (more than 300 strong) arrived from France under the command of a notorious pirate called Haesten. The fleet split into two sections, one of which was brought to battle near Farnham by Edward, Alfred's son, and defeated. Undaunted, Haesten shut himself up at Benfleet in Essex but his ships were captured, along with Viking womenfolk and children the English held as hostages. Haesten struck out west and, in a brilliant forced march, led his army to the Welsh border country, where it was forced to take refuge from Lord Aethelred at Buttington on the Severn. The siege lasted so long that the Vikings were forced to eat their horses, and eventually, in desperation they broke through Aethelred's encirclement and escaped across the breadth of the country to Shoebury. The next year, Haesten's perambulations led his army into Wales, which was visited with the same devastation as in England (the English had adopted a scorched-earth policy to keep them on the move). In 895, Alfred was forced to deploy his army to protect the farm labourers as they gathered in the harvest and, foiled in his escape plan, Haesten repeated his cross-country marching and arrived with his army at Quatford near Bridgnorth where he over-wintered. It was this constant unrelenting pillaging which forced the English and Welsh rulers to grudgingly cooperate with one another. In 895, English troops, possibly West Saxon, but more likely Mercians, assisted Anarawd in his campaign to consolidate his grip on Ceredigion and Ystrad Tywi, which had the effect of confining further Viking raiding to south Wales in 896. For almost ten years Gwynedd was secure from Viking assault, but in 903 a Viking leader called Ingimund was expelled from Ireland and sailed to Anglesey, which he temporarily seized. Eventually Ingimund moved off to found a new Viking colony on the Wirral, but in the meantime the Merfynion had invaded Ceredigion, Dyfed and Ystrad Tywi. The latter two kingdoms were consolidated into a kingdom known as Deheubarth, ruled by Cadell ap Rhodri. The Merfynion brothers controlled most of Wales, Anarawd in the north and Cadell in the south.

When Anarawd died in 916 he was remembered by the bards as 'King of the Britons' – an ancient and august title exclusively reserved for the most revered of kings. The kings of Gwynedd, where the royal house had originated, were considered as pre-eminent, but in fact south and north Wales were developing into two distinct polities. A concept of a unified Welsh state had emerged from the ruins of Britain; a similar process was underway in England, where the mightiest king since the collapse of Rome was about to assert his authority, not only over his own people, but all the people of Britain, whether they were Anglo-Saxon, Scandinavian or Celtic.

11

Hegemony

Within a few years, the political situation in Britain was to be radically simplified, but at the outset of the tenth century the system of overlordship, exercised by Anglo-Saxon kings over the Welsh kingdoms, and the complex relations between Wessex and West Mercia and the Vikings of York, were so labyrinthine that it is worthwhile to begin this chapter by reviewing the political allegiances following the death of Lord Aethelred II of Mercia in 911. The most extraordinary consequence of his death was that he was succeeded by his widow, Lady Aethelflaed, as ruler of West Mercia. She was Alfred's eldest child and, although she was a West Saxon, her mother had been Mercian and she had acted as a deputy for Aethelred while he lay ill, possibly from wounds sustained at the Battle of Tettenhall outside Wolverhampton in 910. Aethelred had cooperated with the Merfynion dynasty when he had sought Welsh aid to contain the threat from Haesten's marauding Viking army and his widow sought to maintain her position as overlord of the Welsh territories they controlled. Gwent and Glywysing in the south-east, however, continued to acknowledge Edward 'the Elder' – Alfred's son and successor as King of Wessex – as their overlord. Therefore, when an emergency threatened in 914, it was to Edward that the southern Welsh looked for assistance. Two Viking *jarls* – Ottar and Harald – were baulked in their piratical raiding in Brittany where a plague was raging. Instead they crossed to Cornwall and ravaged there, before entering the Severn Estuary, where they pillaged south Wales, capturing Cyfeilliog, Bishop of

Ergyng or Archenfield, on the Welsh border with Herefordshire. Edward agreed to pay ransom for the bishop and, with West Saxon help, the Viking forces were contained and then expelled. This demonstration of West Saxon military power, perhaps combined with a natural reticence of the Welsh to acknowledge a woman as their overlord, caused a diplomatic spat in 916. Brycheiniog, one of the smaller Welsh kingdoms around modern Brecon, was the scene of the murder of Abbot Egberht and a party of his companions by Welsh malcontents. He was under the protection of Lady Aethelflaed and within three days she concentrated her forces on the border and marched directly to Lake Llangorse where the King of Brycheiniog, Tewdr, had constructed an ingenious crannog on a man-made island in the lake. The Mercians stormed the crannog and took Tewdr's queen and thirty-three members of the royal household as captives. Tewdr escaped by boat but was almost certainly forced to surrender, for he later attested charters in England.

As the penultimate ruler of an independent Mercia, Aethelflaed's schemes were mainly directed north against the Viking kings of York and the 'five boroughs' of Viking forts across the waist of England, but it was also essential that she stamp her authority on Wales. She had been forced to cede London and Oxford to her brother Edward, and the loss of revenues from that quarter made tributary payments from the Welsh essential for the success of her main military campaign. Another expense was entailed in her programme of construction of a network of *burhs* – fortified garrison towns. Many of these were located in the north-west to guard against the Norse colony established on the Wirral, such as Eddisbury, Weardbyrig, Runcorn, and refurbishment of the defences of Chester itself. Others were located along the Welsh border, at Chirbury, Bremesbyrig (probably Bromsberrow near Ledbury), and at Bridgnorth where a dominating fort now guarded the vital Severn crossing there. In Wales and in Ireland she was known as the 'Queen of the Mercians', but this was a title she relinquished in practice. In the space of a few years Aethelflaed completely turned Mercian fortunes around. Derby, one of the strongest Viking fortresses fell to her, and then in early 918 Leicester also surrendered (fearing the fate of their compatriots in Derby, which she had destroyed). Eventually the Northumbrian

Danes pledged to acknowledge her as their overlord in what would have been a remarkable coup against her brother, but on 12 June 918 she suddenly died at Tamworth. Her young daughter, Aelfwynn, was unanimously acknowledged as her successor by the Mercians but Edward acted swiftly. Aelfwynn, the last ruler of the mighty realm of Mercia, was deposed and taken to be immured in a convent in Shaftesbury. She never appeared in the historical record again, and this coup by Edward completely transfigured the political scene in Wales, as in England. There are good reasons for considering Edward as the first king of a united England, and the dominance of the West Saxon dynasty under him and then his illustrious son, Athelstan, meant that all lesser kings stood in danger of being crushed beneath the English juggernaut, whatever language they spoke.

Edward's reign was dominated by his attempts to secure his northern frontiers against any renewed Viking threat. He built a strong *burh* at Thelwall and seized Manchester (technically inside Northumbria), then fortified the town. Another *burh* was built in the Peak District at Bakewell and Nottingham was garrisoned with a mixture of Danish and English soldiers and a strong *burh*, with a bridge constructed to secure the crossing of the Trent. All this was designed to prevent any conjunction of the Vikings of York with their cousins in Dublin. The strategic centre of gravity had shifted to the Wirral, where this conjunction was most likely to occur, and it is unsurprising that Edward died at Farndon-on-Dee while patrolling this vital area in July 924. Meanwhile in Gwynedd a new king of the line of the Merfynion, Idwal Foel ('the bald') had succeeded Anarawd in 916. He was confronted in 925 with a prospect most dangerous to Welsh independence, namely the accession in England of Athelstan, Edward's eldest (but illegitimate) son. A year passed before Athelstan was crowned due to a power struggle with his legitimate half-brother Aelfweard. Athelstan had been brought up by his redoubtable aunt, Aethelflaed, and in him all the energy, ruthlessness, wisdom and military skill of his grandfather, father and aunt found their ultimate expression. Athelstan's objective was to set himself up as the undisputed 'emperor' of Britain. His unprecedented military power by land and sea, his vast wealth, and his powerful alliances with overseas monarchs made him the most formidable opponent either the Celts or the Vikings had yet faced. In 921, Ragnall, a pagan Viking chieftain of Dublin who had set himself up as King of York, died and was to be succeeded there by his brother Sihtric 'Caoch'. Athelstan invited him to Tamworth where a marriage alliance was struck whereby Sihtric would agree to baptism before marrying Athelstan's sister. Sihtric prevaricated and when he suddenly died Athelstan gathered a huge army and marched on York, which he occupied. Although the ancient defences were demolished, Athelstan prevented pillaging by his soldiers and churches were spared. During his brief stay Athelstan ordered the minting of coins in the city, depicting him as *Rex Totius Britanniae* or 'King of all Britain'. This was not an idle boast. To ensure that this unprecedented southern intrusion was remembered by the northern kings, on 12 July 927 a ritual submission was arranged at Eamont Bridge in Cumbria, whereby the Welsh kings already subservient to him (and on campaign in his army) joined the kings of Scotland and Strathclyde, Aeldred the English Lord of Bamburgh, and Owain King of Cumbria, in kneeling before Athelstan. Their titles and lands were abolished and annexed but immediately reinstated on condition that they swore fealty to him. All were forced to agree to renounce 'pagans and idolatry' (meaning the Vikings of Dublin) and Athelstan stood as godfather to the Scottish king Constantine's son. This was nothing less than a ritual humiliation of the entire Celtic and Viking population of Britain. The significance of this ceremony is that Athelstan is defined as a superior kind of king to these lesser men – in fact no less than an Anglo-Saxon emperor. From now on, the 'underkings' could not act except with Athelstan's permission. The resentment this caused may be imagined, and it led to a revival of the prophetic hopes and dreams that still lay sublimated in the consciousness of the Welsh people.

Within Wales there had been dramatic political developments. Since Merfyn Frych the dominant and exemplary kingdom of Wales was Gwynedd, but now the focus had switched south to Deheubarth and its shrewd King Hywel ap Cadell, later named Hywel Dda 'the good'. He had become the first Welsh king to make a pilgrimage to Rome and return from thence in 929. He calculated that his best policy was to assume an anglophile stance. He had willingly joined

Athelstan's campaign of 927. Hywel thought that English strength was too great to be successfully challenged, even by a grand coalition of all the non-English people of the island. Athelstan's backing could in fact be used to consolidate his own position as the dominant Welsh king, but these were not auspicious times for peaceful relations with the English. The bards of Wales were suddenly inflamed with the *awen* once more. A poem called '*Armes Prydein Vawr*' became popular, in which the reincarnated spirits of two Celtic heroes of yesteryear – Conan of Brittany and Cadwaladr son of Cadwallon – would appear to lead a great alliance of all the Celts and the Vikings to drive the English into the sea. Idwal of Gwynedd had rebelled against Athelstan in 927 but was forced into a humiliating surrender. Tribute payments were increased to levels that could not be met except by the expedient of enforcing crippling taxation on Church property. At Hereford, Athelstan held another durbar where the 'great king' received 20 pounds of gold, 300 pounds of silver, 25,000 oxen and his pick of the finest hunting hounds and falcons. Idwal remained king until 942, and while he lived Wales was divided between a militant anti-English faction in the north and Hywel's compliant regime in the south. The northern faction attributed the prophesy of *Armes Prydein* to Myrddin, in their eyes the supreme bard of all times. The Welsh Church, which was being reduced to penury by English taxes, naturally supported the bards and agitated against Hywel's wise policy of submission to the over-mighty English. Relations with Athelstan were so amicable that Hywel was allowed to have coins bearing his image manufactured at the English mint in Chester. Hywel was a regular visitor to Athelstan's court and spoke English fluently, he even gave one of his sons an English name, Edwin. Another king, however, was not content to subordinate himself, Constantine of Scotland. In 934, he broke his oath to Athelstan with results that must have sobered any Welsh malcontents on the verge of rebellion. Athelstan gathered his army at the end of May and marched north. Only ten days after leaving his capital of Winchester Athelstan reached Nottingham, where the Mercian and Welsh levies joined him. At Chester-Le-Street Athelstan visited the shrine of Saint Cuthbert, the saint who had visited his grandfather in a vision when Alfred had been trapped in the marshes of Somerset as a renegade. Perhaps

20,000 English (and Welsh) troops crossed the border and pillaged as far as Dunnottar, shadowed by an English fleet that hugged the coast as far north as Caithness. Constantine was forced into a humiliating climbdown and surrendered. Athelstan took him back to England as a virtual prisoner and in 935 the ritual humiliation at Eamont Bridge was repeated at Cirencester. Constantine and four other kings were in attendance, Hywel (of course), Owain of Cumbria, Morgan of Gwent and the recalcitrant Idwal Foel. The crucifying tributes were reducing Wales to destitution and the bards continued their agitation:

> There will be reconciliation between the Cymry and the men of
> Dublin,
> The Irish of Ireland and Anglesey and Scotland,
> The men of Cornwall and of Strathclyde will be made welcome
> Among us, the Men of the North will have the place of honour,
> The stewards of Cirencester will shed bitter tears
> When for their taxes we give them death.

Even Brittany, which had sought support against the Vikings from Athelstan, was invoked as a contributor to this imaginary alliance; 'a brave company' of Bretons were said to be on their way. Together this coalition would chase the *Iwys*, the West Saxons, as far as the Kent coast, where they would be driven from the 'Island of the Mighty' into the sea from whence they came. In a school exercise, a Welsh monk had his boys copy out lines that anticipated victory even before it had happened – news of a great battle won by the humble, pious Welsh against the proud English. The key to this alliance was Hywel. If he would join the rebels there was a prospect of success, but he was no fool. Not only did he keep out of the alliance, keeping faith with Athelstan, but there is good reason to think he passed on any information that came to him from Ireland of Viking progress there. On the other hand he offered no military assistance to the English, not that this was needed – Athelstan's army was so huge that he was forced to divide the command with his young brother, Edmund. In the event, only three of the allies conjoined: Constantine of Scotland; Olaf Guthfrithson the king of Dublin; and the kingdom of Strathclyde, which was by now a Scottish satellite. Sometime in the autumn of 937 these allies were confronted at a prepared redoubt called 'the hill of Wendun' at a place called Brunanburh, which may be Bromborough near Birkenhead on the Wirral. Athelstan's ferocious assault lasted all day; in the carnage, five allied kings and seven Viking *jarls* lost their lives, along with thousands of common soldiers whose bodies were left to decompose where they lay. Olaf and Constantine only just escaped with their lives. Olaf's fleet was reduced to a miserable remnant of 'only a few' ships, which returned to Dublin. Hywel's policy of loyalty to Athelstan had paid off. Within a few years he was able to achieve an objective using caution and shrewd diplomacy, which had eluded the Merfynion hitherto – namely the virtual unification of Wales – only Gwent and Glywysing remained outside Hywel's direct control.

English hegemony seemed complete but only two years after Brunanburh Athelstan died at Gloucester. He left no heirs, probably because an agreement had been made to pass the crown down to his brothers. His successor, Edmund I, was young and although he had fought in the battle two years earlier as a titular commander he was, as yet, inexperienced. This had the immediate effect of reviving Olaf's hopes, but it may also have encouraged a more distant relationship with the Welsh rulers, for they do not seem to have attested charters during his reign as had been expected during Athelstan's period on the throne. Constantine of Scotland failed to regain the confidence of the Scottish nobles and was forced to abdicate. With the active connivance of Archbishop Wulfstan of York, Olaf was encouraged to reinvade and take the throne as King of York (the Northumbrian churchmen and magnates were always prepared to accept Viking rulers rather than submit to the rule of southern English kings). Olaf received the submission of the Danish descended folk of the 'five boroughs' (Derby, Nottingham, Leicester, Stamford and Lincoln) but failed to capture the stronghold of Northampton. Instead he turned on the old Mercian capital, Tamworth, which eventually fell to him, yielding important hostages like Lady Wulfruna, the founder of Wolverhampton. Suddenly the achievements of Alfred, Edward, Aethelflaed and Athelstan seemed in jeopardy but fortunately for the English, Olaf was killed while leading a pillaging campaign in Bernicia. Just as the English hegemony was vulnerable, so too Hywel's proto-Welsh state was at the mercy of events. He is called Hywel Dda 'the good' because of his legendary interest in the reformation of the Welsh law codes. His conception of a fair-minded and merciful jurisdiction for all meant that he was remembered as a wise and just king, whose realistic appraisal of the power-politics of his time had meant that Wales prospered instead of being devastated by irresistible English armies. Unfortunately, as soon as Hywel died in 950 that ancient affliction of Celtic monarchy, partible inheritance, ensured that Wales was thrown into internal conflict. Idwal left five sons who had languished in exile during Hywel's reign but now they returned to claim their inheritance according to custom but they were so numerous that to meet these claims Hywel's own sons – Owain, Rhodri and Edwin – would necessarily be dispossessed of large domains, rendering them weak. The dispute could only end in war and the two sets of brothers met in battle at Carno where Idwal's sons were victorious.

A few years later, Idwal and Iago, two of Idwal's sons, won another battle against Deheubarth at Llanrwst. This marked an end to the dominance of Deheubarth and when Edwin died his brother Owain ap Hywel succeeded him in 954. Baulked in the north, Owain instead set his gaze on the kingdom of Gwent, the state in the south-east that was an effective client state of the West Saxon kings. All the efforts of the Merfynion seemed wasted, as Wales descended into petty civil wars and feuding. This was immediately noticed by the Dublin Vikings who descended on Gwynedd, raiding Caergybi (Holyhead) in 961, Lleyn in the same campaign, Penmon in 971 and Anglesey again the following year. These persistent raids preoccupied the northern branch of the Merfynion, but in the south Owain ap Hywel was intimidating Morgannwg. His son Einion annexed Gower to Deheubarth, and assumed command of Owain's soldiers, acting in effect as a co-ruler, perhaps because Owain had become infirm. Einion's expansionist aspirations led to a renewal of conflict with Gwynedd, and in 983 a large raid by Hywel ap Ieuaf of Gwynedd, in alliance with troops provided by Lord Aelfhere of Mercia – now the regent in England on behalf of the boy-king Ethelred 'the Unready' – was repulsed after striking deep into Brycheiniog and Morgannwg. Although Einion prevailed, he was so weakened that he was attacked by the Gwent nobles and killed. Owain's incapacity left another son, Maredudd, as the effective ruler in Deheubarth.

These turbulent times in the south had revived the expansionist hopes of Hywel of Gwynedd but his predatory ambitions were noted by the English, who contrived to have him killed in 985. The civil war between Hywel's brother Cadwallon and one of his cousins to inherit the kingdom resulted in victory for the former but other candidates emerged to issue their challenges. Maredudd, observing these bitter and costly disputes, decided to strike north and in 986 he overthrew Cadwallon and annexed Gwynedd, restoring to some extent Hywel Dda's power, and indeed under Maredudd the boundaries of the Wales Hywel had once ruled were restored, though the situation was always fluid. The Vikings backed Maredudd's rivals and attacked Gwynedd the year after Cadwallon was defeated, and then raided the coasts of central and south Wales too. Two thousand slaves were taken on Anglesey alone and many important monasteries were plundered. In 992, perhaps fearful of his growing power, the Mercians backed a rival to Maredudd with the English name of Edwin, Maredudd's own nephew, but with the help of Viking mercenaries Edwin and his English backers were repulsed. The unstable and frenetic situation in Wales was mirrored in England where the empire Athelstan had bequeathed to the West Saxon royal line was itself fracturing under relentless pressure from renewed Viking raiding. Indeed, within a few decades England would be conquered by the Danes and become part of a Scandinavian empire. This shifted the focus of the English towards the new threat, and away from Wales. Ethelred, the English king, had a reputation for vacillation, cowardice and perfidy, which precluded any consistent policy with regards to the Celtic frontier nations in any case. In 994, Maredudd was severely defeated by a revived challenge from the northern Merfynion. This eclipsed his power outside his own central kingdom of Deheubarth and he died in 999 leaving no surviving heir. These continuous enervating struggles between the northern and southern Merfynion had the effect of weakening both sides and as a new millennium dawned their power was receding, just as across the dyke, their old enemy England was approaching meltdown.

At the outset of the eleventh century, however, Wales was very much in the shadow of its larger neighbour, and there were good reasons to rely on English support when the Viking threat grew more serious. The patchwork of kingdoms that comprised Wales seemed doomed to interminable petty wars between their rulers, and England had not yet collapsed, but soon all this was to change radically. In November 1002, King Ethelred of England ordered a coordinated pogrom of Danes settled in the south of England – the St Brice's Day Massacre. Among those slain was the sister of the Danish king, Sweyn Forkbeard, who immediately made plans to revenge himself on Ethelred. This remarkable turning point in English history has been overshadowed by the later Norman Conquest, but it symbolised the beginning of the English collapse.

For the first time in centuries there was an opportunity for the Welsh to unite as a truly independent nation, taking advantage of England's apocalyptic adversities. In fact Ethelred's marked lack of military or political competence encouraged occasional campaigns against the Celts, perhaps because operations against the Danes were considered too risky. Cumbria was attacked in 1000 and in 1012 one of Ethelred's earls, Edric Streona, a nobleman from Shropshire, ravaged far into the south-west and sacked St Davids. This same Earl Edric was responsible, at least in part, for the English defeat at the battle of Assandun in October 918, which ensured Cnut's ultimate victory. A notorious traitor, assassin and dissembler we may presume that thievery was yet another of his vices, and the raid into Wales was probably for plunder. That Edric could penetrate so far into Wales suggests that the Welsh kings were by now so exhausted that they could not oppose him, and indeed the Welsh dynasties were undergoing a drastic change. In Gwynedd, a shadowy personage named Llywelyn ap Seisyll came to the throne. In the south, another equally mysterious individual turned up claiming to be the son of Maredudd, called Rhain 'the Irishman', and claimed the throne of Deheubarth. Llywelyn had claims by marriage to Deheubarth and he invaded, driving Rhain out. This seemingly minor feud produced a spectacular sea change for Wales. In 1023 Llywelyn died, exalted by the *Brut y Tywsogion* or 'Chronicle of the Princes' as the 'most noble King of the Britons'. Immediately, because his son was only an infant, the throne of Gwynedd passed to Iago ap Idwal ap Meurig, one of the Merfynion, but Gruffydd ap Llywelyn, Llywelyn's young son had a glorious future ahead of him.

It is possible that Llywelyn's ancestors came from Powys, which was at this time incorporated into Gwynedd. Angharad, his widow, remarried a powerful nobleman of that region, taking the infant Gruffydd with her. An illustrious ancestry was claimed for the boy: he was said to be the great-great grandson of Hywel Dda. But while he was in his minority the Merfynion royal line had been restored in the south, as well as the north, of Wales. Another 'mystery man', named Rhydderch ap Iestyn, with a spurious pedigree, came to the throne of Morgannwg and he managed to take control of virtually all of south Wales until his death in 1033. In that same year, Iago ap Idwal was killed in Gwynedd and the entire country reverted to monarchies ruled by the Merfynion. Then commenced the usual vicious infighting among the various sons, until in 1039 a dramatic event took place: 'Iago, king of Gwynedd, was killed. And in his place ruled Gruffydd ap Llywelyn ap Seisyll, and he, from beginning to end, pursued the Saxons and other foreigners and killed and destroyed them and defeated them in a great number of battles.'

How did this remarkable turnaround in Welsh fortunes come about? Firstly, we should recall that England had been conquered by the Danes in 1018 and now formed part of a wider Scandinavian empire ruled by King Cnut. He seems to have taken little interest in Welsh affairs, his focus was always on preventing secession by Norway and ensuring Denmark was safe, though he took a more active interest in Scotland. The sanguinary procession of Welsh kings and their intertribal wars becomes almost tedious in this period, but the constant warfare had bred a race absolutely inured to hardship, warfare and political machination – in short, very formidable opponents if they could but unite. When Cnut died in 1035 he was succeeded by his sons, Harald 'Harefoot' and Harthacnut, both of whom failed to live up to their father's illustrious deeds and reputation. In 1043, Edward 'the Confessor', indubitably of the West Saxon royal line (the so-called 'Cerdicings'), was crowned as the penultimate Anglo-Saxon King of England. By the time Edward became king, Gruffydd was already asserting himself against the English. In 1039 he had beaten an English army in battle at Rhyd y Groes in which many English noblemen were killed. Next, he drove out the King Hywel of Deheubarth, but encountered stern resistance from his namesake Gruffydd ap Rhydderch ap Iestyn and his brother Rhys. Constant feuding and banditry followed, of course, in which Viking mercenaries were often employed to augment the armies of the feuding sides. Gruffydd ap Llywelyn was temporarily taken hostage by them, and in 1049 the other Gruffydd allied with the Vikings to raid into England. In fact the final showdown between the two men named Gruffydd could not long be delayed. Carefully marshalling his strength Gruffydd ap Llywelyn invaded and killed his namesake in 1056. What had seemed an impossible dream had finally happened: all of Wales was now united under one king, who now set out to make war on the English.

Meanwhile, in England, King Edward was involved in a power struggle with his chief counsellor, Earl Godwin. He had been a commander in Cnut's reign and had risen to a position of unprecedented power, installing his five sons as earls in their own right and marrying his daughter off to the king. Gruffydd had enlisted the aid of the eldest son, a notorious braggart called Sweyn, in an invasion and plunder of south Wales. Sweyn's earldom was in Gloucestershire and Herefordshire, the border country with Wales. In 1051, Godwin was accused of insubordination and fell from power, along with his numerous sons, and Edward put away his queen, Edith, their sister. Godwin and his sons fled into exile and their earldoms were left vacant temporarily. This encouraged Gruffydd to make incursions into the borderlands; Leominster was sacked the following year, and this was in Sweyn's earldom (he had abducted the Abbess of the town and tried to marry her not long before). One bone of contention at this time may have been the installation by the English king of small garrisons of Norman knights in the area, under leaders like Richard Fitz Scrob and Osbern Pentecost. Edward had spent practically his entire adult life as an exile in Normandy and his favouritism towards Norman manners and Church rite, as well as his eagerness to introduce a potential counterweight to the Godwin clan, had extended to introducing these foreign soldiers and their new innovation – the castle. Ironically, the first Norman castles were built in the Welsh borderlands even before the Conquest. The Godwin tribe made their spectacular return in 1052 and the tables were turned on Edward and his Norman friends. Sweyn, Gruffydd's ally, was restored but, in a moment of contrition and thanksgiving, he elected to make a pilgrimage to Jerusalem but perished on the way. T. M Charles-Edwards doubts that the raiding in Herefordshire and the encounters with 'French' (Norman) troops was initiated by Gruffydd ap Llywelyn, suggesting that the culprit was the *other* Gruffydd ap Rhydderch; another scholar, David Moore, in his *The Welsh Wars of Independence* (Stroud, 2005) is equally sure that he was already dead by the time Hereford was attacked. Whoever it was, the clash was ominous, for these new foreigners were to become the most deadly enemy the Celts had yet faced.

When Earl Aelfgar of Mercia was deposed in 1053 he fled to Dublin and hired a small fleet. He then canvassed the support of Gruffydd ap Llywelyn, which he received. Gruffydd cemented the deal by marrying Aelfgar's daughter, Ealdgyth. The reason for Gruffydd's change of policy towards the Godwin family was the ascendancy of the eldest of the remaining sons, Harold. It was clear that he was the frontrunner to succeed Edward if, as seemed likely, he failed to leave an heir (he had abstained from sexual relations for alleged religious reasons). Harold was an enemy of Gruffydd and had sponsored a raid by the Bishop of Hereford into Welsh territory, which was repulsed with heavy losses on the English side. This entailed a very considerable loss of face for Harold as the bishop had been his own personal chaplain. Gruffydd and Aelfgar invaded into England and defeated the garrison of Hereford. The 'French' commander could not, allegedly, encourage his English troops to take to horseback and Ralph 'the Timid', as he was mockingly called by the English, was routed and the town and the cathedral were looted and set ablaze. Harold was the king's deputy and gathered an immense army. He marched north-west from Gloucester and eventually a peace was negotiated at Billingsley in Shropshire, but the conflict with the Godwin family had entered a decisive phase. Gruffydd had gone beyond the borders of Wales in his ambitions. Estates on the debatable frontier were being annexed back into Wales and a shrewd strategist such as Harold

Godwinson looked on nervously – an enemy very much to be feared, especially when Aelfgar was once more driven into exile to be replaced as Mercian earl by Harold's younger brother, Gyrth. Harold, however, was preoccupied by other important matters. Gruffydd remained loyal to Aelfgar, and again backed him with his own forces, showing just how powerful he had become, not only in Wales but in his influence on English affairs. This projection of Welsh power and influence outside its own borders was felt equally in Dublin, where Cynan ap Iago, Gruffydd's rival was in exile. To some extent the situation had resurrected the ancient alliance between the Britons and the Mercians that had once existed in Penda's day. No one resented this alliance more than Harold, and it was his trumped-up charges against Earl Aelfgar that probably led to his expulsion in the first place.

For many generations the border country around Hereford – Ergyng, known as 'Archenfield' by the English – had been settled by them, but now this border zone passed into Gruffydd's control. Aelfgar's death in 1062 marked an end to the Welsh renaissance. Harold took control of Hereford and a plan was made with his brother, Tostig, to eliminate the Welsh threat by striking down their powerful leader. During Christmastide 1063 Harold set out with a squad of assassins from Gloucester and within a few days they had ridden to Rhuddlan, where Harold's spies let it be known that Gruffydd was celebrating the festival. Like Alfred the Great at Chippenham centuries before, Gruffydd was warned in the nick of time and escaped by ship. With this attempt having been foiled, Harold upped the stakes. A few months later, in 1064, Harold sailed from Bristol and raided all along the coast before arriving at Anglesey. Simultaneously Tostig led an assault by land into north Wales, harrying burning and wasting as he came. The Godwin brothers were determined to end the Welsh resurgence, calculating that the Viking claimant to the English throne, Harald Hardrada of Norway, may use his influence with the Hibernian Vikings to threaten England from the west. The depredations visited upon the poor Welsh folk were accompanied by blandishments designed to entice them to betray their king. This latter policy bore fruit. Gruffydd's own household men turned on him and murdered him, sending his head and the figurehead of his ship (to prove he had not esacaped by sea) to Harold, who sent it on to the English king. There is every reason to think that this success led on to triumphalism from Harold, which eventually resulted in his downfall. He is supposed to have erected memorial stones throughout Wales bearing the legend *'Hic Fuit Victor Haraldus'* – 'here Harold was victorious'. A folk tale tells that Tostig was incensed by his brother's determination to take sole credit for the victory, to the extent that he disturbed a victory banquet Harold hosted for King Edward and massacred the cooks and servants. Harold decided to entertain the king at Portskewett at a huge hunting lodge he ordered to be built, which was located inside Wales itself. The builders were attacked and their materials seized by Caradog, son of Gruffydd ap Rhydderch, showing that Harold's much-vaunted power over Wales was illusory. In his desperation to capitalise on his victory and in order to ingratiate himself further with the ageing, ailing, and childless King Edward, Harold became a victim of his own propaganda, as well as alienating his very dangerous brother, Tostig. Harold's lightning attack on Gwynedd was repeated two years later at Stamford Bridge against Harald Hardrada of Norway, and his success there may have made him think himself invincible. While it is beyond dispute that Stamford Bridge was a spectacular English victory, Harold's efforts to repeat the same *Blitzkrieg* against William of Normandy a few weeks later failed, leading to the ultimate catastrophe for the Anglo-Saxons. In truth, Gruffydd's downfall had been induced by the treachery of his own people, not Harold's genius as was claimed. As the hegemony Gruffydd had exerted over Wales collapsed, so too, English hegemony, the domination of the island by the royal house of Wessex since Edward the Elder's day, was about to collapse, to be replaced by a new and potent enemy.

The greatest ever Welsh monarch in terms of his territorial reach was dead and Wales immediately disintegrated into the petty kingdoms and internal squabbling that had prevailed hitherto – but Gruffydd's achievements were not forgotten by his countrymen. His two sons were killed while attempting to claim their inheritance in 1069. Harold, on behalf of King Edward, had arranged to install two brothers as kings in north Wales – half-brothers of Gruffydd called Bleddyn ap Cynfyn in Gwynedd, and Rhiwallon in Powys – at the royal hall of Mathrafal near Llanfair Caereinion. Rhiwallon died in 1069, leaving Bleddyn as sole king of north Wales. He continued to honour the spirit of his submission to Harold even after the latter's death at the Battle of Hastings in 1066. Tribute arrangements, which had been suspended during Gruffydd's reign, were now reinstated. The Welsh were now, once again, under the heel of the English king. Thankfully for them, perhaps, Harold's reign only lasted for ten months during 1066. King William (as he became on Christmas Day of that fateful year) was very much preoccupied with the business of dividing out the land among his supporters and then, during 1069, in crushing nationwide rebellions. However, right from the outset his eye was on the troublesome Welsh border, which was already known to the Normans as a potential 'hotspot'. Bleddyn was well aware of the dangers the Normans presented for him and allied himself with an English resistance fighter, Edric 'the Wild' or 'the Forester', who had taken up arms against the Norman garrisons of Herefordshire and south Shropshire, fighting a desperate guerrilla war from the Forest of Clun and the hill country around the Stiperstones. He was a great-nephew of that infamous traitor during the reign of King Ethelred, Edric Streona, who had once been the Mercian earl – perhaps Bleddyn's strategy was to rebuild the old alliance between Gwynedd and Mercia. Welsh troops supported Edric and also the two brothers, Edwin and Morcar, earls of Mercia and Northumbria respectively, when they rebelled in 1069. The English rebellions, after inhuman and savage reprisals by William, were crushed, and within five years of the Conquest England was in an iron grip, garrisoned by hundreds of castles; the Welsh support for his enemies had been noted by him. As one ancient enemy lay prostrated, another presented itself – the Normans – and, across the sea to the west, the Vikings of Ireland were looking for fresh victims. A people long inured to conflict and struggle against the odds, must learn to endure yet more difficulties and challenges in the centuries that lay ahead.

12

The Matter of Britain

The ancient mythology of the Brythonic people had once again become a grim reality. A mysterious child had been born, Gruffydd, who had been taken into the care of a stepfather. He had emerged out of nowhere to seize power as a mighty and valiant king. He had striven to protect his people and extend his realm, initiating a golden age of Celtic unity – leading his armies to victory against the Saxon foe – only to be undone by the treachery of his own fellow countrymen. As soon as England had been finally secured, William turned his attention to Scotland and to Wales. We have seen already that Norman military garrisons had been established along the border of south Wales for many years. Edric 'the Wild' seems to have surrendered to William and joined his army on a campaign against the Scots. What became of him is a mystery, but local legend has it that he did return to his homeland, only to find that his manors had been seized by a 'French' knight, Sir Ralph Mortimer. The borderlands were too sensitive an area to be left under the control of a notorious guerrilla fighter, who had rebelled on two occasions already, plundering Herefordshire as far as the Lugg in his first foray and besieging the castle of Shrewsbury in 1069. His contrition and despair for having betrayed his countrymen by coming to terms with William was said to have driven him to take refuge in the fairy realm with his otherworldly bride, Lady Godda. As compensation for his failure he is allowed to ride out with the 'Wild Hunt' through the Shropshire Hills whenever foreign enemies threaten war against the English – the crazy spectacle was reported to have been seen in the days leading up to the First World War in 1914. Initially the Normans were viewed by the Welsh kings in the same way as the Anglo-Saxons and the Vikings. That they were a considerable threat was not in any doubt, but they could also prove useful. Norman mercenaries served in the army of Caradog ap Gruffydd ap Rhydderch at the Battle of Rhymni in 1072. When the Normans proved fractious, however, the same king had no hesitation in raiding over the border as far as Gloucestershire, so Welsh submissiveness could not be relied upon. Bleddyn was killed by his southern rival, Rhys ap Owain, but he left infant sons in Powys who founded a line of kings of that resurrected nation; Owain Glyndwr, perhaps the most famous Welshman in history, was a direct descendant of Bleddyn, who was remembered with affection and respect by the bards.

It is to these wandering poets and minstrels, perhaps, that we can attribute a process that was to have most profound cultural consequences. In his classic work *The White Goddess* (London, 1961 Edn) Robert Graves suggested:

These tales were told by a guild of Welsh minstrels whose status was not regulated by the Laws, who counted no bishops or ministers of State among their associates, and who were at liberty to use whatever diction, themes and metres they pleased. Very little is known about their organization or history, but since they were popularly credited with divinatory and prophetic gifts and the power of injurious satire it is likely that they were descended from the original Welsh master-poets who either refused or were refused court-patronage after the Cymric conquest of Wales. The Cymry, who we think of as the real Welsh, and from whom the proud court-bards were recruited were a tribal aristocracy of Brythonic origin holding down a serf-class that was a mixture of Goidels, Brythons, Bronze Age and New Stone Age peoples and aboriginals ... the non-Cymric minstrels went from village to village, or farm-house to farm-house, entertaining under the trees or in the chimney corner according to the season. It was they who kept alive an astonishingly ancient literary tradition, mainly in the form of popular tales which preserved fragments not only of pre-Cymric, but of pre-Goidelic myth, some of which goes back as far as the Stone Age. Their poetic principles are summed up in a Triad in the *Llyfr Coch Hergest* ('The Red Book of Hergest'):

> Three Things that enrich the poet:
> Myths, poetic power, a store of ancient verse...

This insight, obscure to the discipline of history, was more obvious to a poet such as Graves, and he developed the theme:

> However, in the thirteenth century the minstrels were taken up by the Norman-French invaders, apparently through the influence of Breton knights who could understand Welsh and who recognized some of the tales as better versions of those which they had heard at home. The troveres or finders, translated them into contemporary French and adopted them into the Provencal code of chivalry, and in their new dress, they conquered Europe.

The Norman warlords in their draughty castles were soon indoctrinated by these romantic tales, and especially by the allure of the mythic hero-king, Arthur. But of what did the magic consist? Lady Charlotte Guest, in her introduction to her translation of the *Mabinogion* (London, 1906) explains this revolution succinctly:

> In the twelfth and thirteenth centuries there arose into general notoriety in Europe, a body of 'Romance', which in various forms retained its popularity till the Reformation. In it the plot, the incidents, the characters, were almost wholly those of Chivalry, that bond which united the warriors of France, Spain, and Italy, with those of pure Teutonic descent, and embraced more or less firmly all the nations of Europe, excepting only the Slavonic races, not yet risen to power, and the Celts, who had fallen from it. It is not difficult to account for this latter omission. The Celts, driven from the plains into the mountains and islands, preserved their liberty, and hated their oppressors with fierce, and not causeless, hatred. A proud and free people, isolated both in country and language, were not likely to adopt customs which implied brotherhood with their foes.

This supreme irony, that the enemies of the Celts had appropriated their cultural traditions in order to use them as weapons *against* them, is one of the strangest stories in human history, but there were to be many more twists and turns along the way. The corpus of romantic tales and ancient chronicles of princes and kings stretching back to the legendary Brutus 'the Trojan', the putative ancestor of the British kings, became known as the 'Matter of Britain'. There were other so-called 'Matters', the 'Matter of France' was inspired by the epic wars of Charlemagne and the hero Roland, who had defeated the invading Muslim armies. The 'Matter of Rome' referred to all the tales of the classical Greek and Roman world and the legendary foundation of the city by descendants of Aeneas of Troy – two brothers called Romulus and Remus. The purpose of propogating these tales was to promulgate the notion that divine destiny had been involved in the establishment of the Roman Empire and, later on, of the empire built by Charlemagne, on whose august authority the sanctity of the French kingdom rested. The Normans, of course, were recent arrivals in England, so no such hallowed literary or historical proofs of *their* divine destiny to be rulers of England existed, and in fact they were parvenus, who until quite recent times had looked to the French king as their technical overlord. But now the case was altered. William and his heirs were no longer an aristocracy of a minor duchy in France, but kings in their own right, and what they desperately needed to legitimate themselves within the closed circle of the chivalric military elites of Europe, was a 'Matter' of their own. This was now conveniently supplied by the very people most likely to find this contentious – the Welsh. As their legends were bowdlerised and translated, declaimed in the courts from Byzantium to Iceland, they stuck rigidly to their own versions – for the Celts the poetic art was the most exemplary path a man could follow, far more than mere 'entertainment'. The tales of Merlin (the Norman translators changed the name to 'Merlin' instead of Myrddin – *merde* unfortunately meant 'shit' in French) and Taliesin were no child's game, but the culmination of generation upon generation of learning so recondite that it claimed it drew upon memories of the poets' previous incarnations. It was in an effort to preserve this 'Matter' (the genuine article) that the Welsh

1. Caer Caradoc, the hillfort near Knighton, which in folk tradition was the scene of the climactic battle against Rome that decided the fate of Britain. (Author)

2. The River Teme near Caer Caradoc, possibly the 'stream' mentioned by Cornelius Tacitus in his account of the battle. (Author)

3. Steep embankment between the Teme and the hillfort at Stowe village, possibly where the Britons erected a dry-stone wall as a defence against the advancing legions. (Author)

Left: 4. Romans this way! Signage at *Rigodunum*, the Roman fort at Castleshaw near Manchester where Caratacus was betrayed to the Romans. (Photograph courtesy of Simon Wheatley, Flickr/British Library)

Below: 5. The Menai Strait, across which the Romans launched their assault on the Druids in their holy sanctuary of Anglesey or Ynys Mon. (Photograph courtesy of Rebecca Boardman, Flickr/British Library)

6. Boudicca statue in London, the city which she ruthlessly destroyed. (Photograph courtesy of Massimillano Calamelli, Flickr/British Library)

7. The desolate north. Hadrian's Wall marked the northernmost limit of Roman imperial control. (Photograph courtesy of Magnus Hagdorn, Flickr/British Library)

8. Roman amphitheatre at Caerleon, South Wales. The ruins may have inspired the legend of King Arthur's 'Round Table'. (Photograph courtesy of Becks, Flickr/British Library)

9. Wroxeter Roman ruins, Shropshire. The city of *Viriconium Cornoviorum* was still a thriving urban centre well into the fifth century. (Photograph courtesy of Helen Simonsson, Flickr/British Library)

10. Portchester, one of the so-called 'Saxon Shore' forts, actually used as a defence against the legitimate imperial authorities by Carausius, the Roman admiral who seized control of Britain. (Photograph courtesy of Leimenide, Flickr/British Library)

11. 'Merlin's Cave', Tintagel, Cornwall, said to be the birthplace of Arthur in legend. (Photograph courtesy of Francois Schnell, Flickr/British Library)

12. South Cadbury Castle hillfort, traditionally the site of 'Camelot'. (Photograph by Hugh Llewelyn, Flickr/British Library)

Above left: 13. Celtic warriors of the fifth century. If Arthur's 'knights' really existed they would have looked something like these modern re-enactors. (Photograph courtesy of Shadowgate, Flickr/British Library)

Above right: 14. Arthur's grave at Glastonbury Abbey. The location was revealed to Henry II by a Welsh bard. (Photograph courtesy of Michael Gaylard, Flickr/British Library)

15. Shadow of the grove? Holy Innocents' church Tuck Hill, near to the ancient grove of *Onnenau Meigion*, or Six-Ashes between Kinver and Bridgnorth. The Merlinic Prophesies about the place exerted a powerful influence on Welsh national consciousness for hundreds of years. (Photograph courtesy of Dave Gardener)

16. Iona, the lonely island from which St Columba's missionaries set out to convert northern Britain to Christianity. (Photograph courtesy of Tim Regan, Flickr/British Library)

17. Lindisfarne, the island from which St Aedan set out to convert the devastated people of Northumbria. (Photograph courtesy of xlibber, Flickr/British Library)

18. Whitby Abbey, setting for the synod which condemned the Celtic Church to heretical status in the seventh century. (Photograph courtesy of Smabs Sputzer, Flickr/British Library)

19. Croagh Patrick, the Irish Holy Mountain, dedicated to the British St Patrick who converted the Irish to Christianity. (Photograph courtesy of Donna Marijne, Flickr/British Library)

20. St Davids, Pembrokeshire, ancient centre of Welsh Christianity. (Photograph courtesy of Phil Price, Flickr/ British Library)

21. The Great Divide. Offa's Dyke, the massive linear earthwork attributed to Offa the Great of Mercia, which formed a fixed frontier between English and Welsh territory. (Photograph courtesy of Chris Booth, Flickr/ British Library)

22. Bridgnorth Castle, Shropshire, stronghold of the infamous Robert de Belleme, third Earl of Shrewsbury. (Author)

23. Ludlow Castle, from which the Lords President of the Council of Wales and the Marches governed Wales in the fifteenth century. (Author)

24. Chepstow Castle. William the Conqueror moved incredibly quickly to build the fortification overlooking the key crossing point on the river Wye. The Great Tower was probably built as a show of strength, a reminder to the Welsh King of Deheubarth, Rhys Ap Tewdwr, of Norman dominance. (Courtesy of Stewart Black, Flickr/British Library)

25. Goodrich Castle, another fortification overlooking the Wye. It was certainly in existence at the beginning of the 12th century as an earth and timber construction. Who built the later stone keep is debated. (Courtesy of Hugh Llewelyn, Flickr/ British Library)

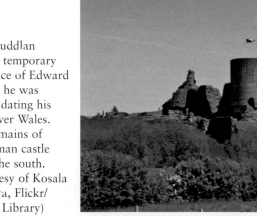

26. Rhuddlan Castle, temporary residence of Edward I when he was consolidating his hold over Wales. The remains of a Norman castle lie to the south. (Courtesy of Kosala Bandara, Flickr/ British Library)

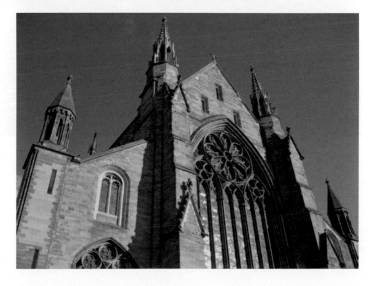

27. Worcester Cathedral, where Llywelyn ap Gruffydd finally married Eleanor de Montfort. (Author)

28. Caernarfon Castle, Gwynedd, one of the mighty fortresses Edward I constructed to subjugate the Welsh. (Photograph courtesy of Jim Linwood, Flickr/British Library)

29. William Wallace Memorial, overlooking the battlefield of Stirling Bridge, his famous victory. (Photograph courtesy of BusterBrownBB, Wikicommons)

30. Robert the Bruce, victor of Bannockburn. (Photograph courtesy of Derek Winterburn, Flickr/British Library)

31. Owain Glyndwr statue, Corwen. (Photograph courtesy of Steve Watkins, Flickr/British Library)

32. View over Edmund Mortimer's position at Pilleth. His army was drawn up approximately where the buildings in the foreground stand today. The attack up the steep hill against well-trained archers was suicidal. (Author)

33. Battlefield church near Shrewsbury, site of the Battle of Shrewsbury in 1403 in which Glyndwr's English ally, Henry Percy, known as 'Hotspur', was killed. (Photograph courtesy of Andrew, Flickr/British Library)

34. Harlech Castle, the powerful stronghold Glyndwr seized as his personal citadel. Edmund Mortimer held the castle on Glyndwr's behalf but in February 1409 the rebel forces were eventually starved into surrender. (Photograph courtesy of Nick, Flickr/British Library)

35. View from Woodbury Hill, Worcestershire, as far as Glyndwr got in his ill-fated invasion of England in 1405. (Photograph courtesy of Muffinn, Flickr/British Library)

36. St Ann's Head Pembrokeshire, where Henry Tudor landed on 7 August 1485. Henry claimed descent from Cadwaladr, the seventh-century King of Gwynedd. (Photograph courtesy of khrawlings, Flickr/British Library)

37. Primrose Hill, London, where Iolo Morganwg performed a neo-Druidic ceremony in the late eighteenth century. (Photograph courtesy of Andrew Crump, Flickr/British Library)

38. Glastonbury Tor, Somerset. Glastonbury has become the centre of the 'Arthurian' revival in recent years. (Photograph courtesy of Shrinkin' Violet, Flickr/British Library)

endured such bitter persecutions and deprivations, contemptuous of the phoney creature the Anglo-Norman 'King Arthur' had become. Nevertheless, the out-working of this unexpected cross-fertilisation of cultural ideas was to result in the creation of a global empire mightier than any before it, whose ambitions were predicated upon the original Welsh regnal lists and the ancient bardic lore.

All this lay in the future, but we must return to the Norman effort to subjugate the Welsh. William's most competent and calculating commander was his namesake, William Fitz-Osbern, the Earl of Hereford. He was a close personal friend of the king and when William took the gamble of crossing the sea to visit his queen the year after Hastings, it had been to Fitz-Osbern and his half-brother Odo that he entrusted the care of his kingdom. His strategy began with the construction of a screen of castles along the border with Wales, but his offensive thrust was designed to isolate the south-eastern part of the country and then to re-establish the control over it that the early West Saxon kings had exerted. Unfortunately, Fitz-Osbern's deputy commanders only managed a limited penetration before he was called away to fight on the Continent. The initiative passed to the central borderlands, the Severn Valley and the old heartland of Edric 'the Wild'. Just as Wulfhere had once divided up the area to distribute estates to his followers, now the new earl, Roger de Montgomery, parcelled out land to his soldiers. He established himself at Shrewsbury before building a castle near Forden Gaer, which he named in honour of his family home in Normandy, Montgomery, which became known as 'the key to Wales'. The location had been exploited by the Romans and Mercians before him, of course, and from this base Norman forays were launched into the Ceri Forest and beyond. The Norman commanders further north on the border of Cheshire, Hugh d'Avranches and Robert of Rhuddlan, penetrated the coastal region of north-east Wales and the latter established a strong castle at Rhuddlan, formerly the court of the mighty Gruffydd. Therefore, by the time Earl Roger died in 1094 the Normans had extended their control beyond Offa's Dyke into an intermediate zone that they called in Norman-French *marche* or 'borderlands', a word cognate with the English *Mierce*, which had given the Mercians their name. The Welsh March, as we know it, was divided into three 'Marcher' earldoms, which were the personal virtually independent fiefs of swashbuckling and treacherous men who operated in much the same way as the petty Welsh kings we have examined previously. They appropriated properties from both Englishmen and Welshmen, and their rapacity and ruthlessness was only matched by their energy and vision. Such men presented a threat not only to the Celts but to their own king, and it was probably in an effort to re-establish some sort of personal control that King William took it upon himself to mount a large campaign into Wales in 1081. The imperative for him by then was to annexe border areas and parcel them out to a new generation of young Norman knights greedy for land (by now the business of carving up England and allocating it to his followers was almost completed). It should be remembered that as this westwards expansion into Wales by the Normans was ongoing, at the same time there was relentless Viking raiding from Ireland, so the Welsh were beset from all directions at a time when savage and bloody internal conflicts were weakening them. By the 1090s, Gwent was firmly in Norman hands and they had pushed into Glamorgan. All of south-west Wales fell to them following landward and amphibious operations by the Normans who immediately set to work to build mighty castles in the area. By 1098, Gwynedd had fallen and its royal family had been driven overseas to exile in Ireland, and soon even that island, which even the Romans had decided to overlook, would fall within the ambit of Norman expansionism.

What manner of people were these Normans? They were, as Alistair Moffat the Celtic scholar remarked in his *The Sea Kingdoms: The History of Celtic Britain & Ireland* (Edinburgh, 2008) 'Natural colonizers'. In 1017, they had received a papal commission and enlisted in his service in southern Italy, where, with just a few hundred knights, they had conquered Apulia and Calabria and driven the Saracens out of Sicily, seizing that island and using it as a base for further operations, which culminated in the establishment of Christian colonies in the Holy Land itself. They intimidated the French and Scottish kings and had established total control over England within five years of Hastings. The complexities of inheritance laws meant that many landless young noblemen, indoctrinated by the cult of chivalry, were always eager to serve some powerful lord who could grant them land in exchange for military service. To maintain themselves as knights was extraordinarily expensive, since they needed to be able to provide themselves with weaponry and armour, as well as the squires, grooms and gleemen that accompanied them and their destriers (specialised warhorses). Their occupation was cruel and ruthless, both in England and in Wales. Forced labour was demanded for the construction of the castles, and sites deemed suitable for the construction of these were chosen without any regard whatever to local feeling or objections. Within the areas they had conquered inside Wales the common people rebelled against the 'laws, injustice and violence' of the 'French' just as they had in England in 1069, and Norman punishments were pitiless and harsh, with many empty sleeves and wooden legs and mutilations meted out to recalcitrant inhabitants of *commotes* where Normans had been ambushed. But, as the Normans began to patrol in the Irish Sea, they encountered the Norwegian fleet under King Magnus, and Hugh, earl of Shrewsbury was killed.

Three years later the third Earl of Shrewsbury, Robert de Belleme, and his brother, Arnulf, unsuccessfully rebelled against Henry I. Robert's cruelty and depravity was extraordinary; he was known as 'Robert the Devil'. The brothers' lands were forfeit and they were exiled and this gave the Welsh a desperately needed respite. The Anglo-Norman civil war of 1101 meant that at last the Welsh kings could exploit Norman divisions and gradually an accommodation was reached between the Welsh kings and princes and the Norman barons. Cadwgan, King of Powys and Ceredigion, who had returned from Ireland, provided Welsh troops to Robert de Belleme and attempted to support him at his great fortress of Bridgnorth Castle, which he had constructed against Henry's explicit instructions. Henry I swiftly marched on Bridgnorth and prevented this, promising Robert's lands in Wales to various Welsh princes in an effort to undermine him. However, Henry realised that Cadwgan was a considerable threat and also that the restored kingdom of Powys may eventually become a force that could destabilise the central Welsh March, just as it had done in Offa's day. Henry decided to consolidate control in Wales, where he had substantial personal fiefs, and to introduce Flemish immigrants to south-west Wales, in particular Rhos. By now it was clear that a long-term solution to the colonisation and control of Wales could not be secured by exclusively military means. Only in Dyfed had the Normans established a grip sufficient to displace the Welsh dynasties. Castles at Manorbier, Haverford and Carew protected the Flemish colonists and Pembroke became the administrative centre of an English-style shire. Henry gradually intruded his own placemen into positions of influence in areas under Norman control (Gerald of Wales called them his 'secret and principal advisors') – Miles of Gloucester, Payn Fitz-John and Brian Fitz-Count. They owed everything to the patronage of the king and their scrupulous loyalty was his price. In 1114 and 1121 the English king led invasions into Wales, designed to intimidate and terrify the Welsh just as the Mercian kings had done centuries before. The latter invasion was an attempt to cow Maredudd ap Bleddyn of Powys, who fell back, ordering his men to harass the royal army on its line of march with archery fire. King Henry was actually hit, but not seriously injured. He immediately requested a truce and a promise of fealty was given by Maredudd, enabling the shocked king to withdraw, no doubt with some sense of relief. By the time of his death in 1135, Henry had established control over Powys, which had descended into chaotic intra-dynastic feuding, and in the north-east Clwyd was under the heel of the Normans. The south-west and Ceredigion were firmly under Norman rule; only Gwynedd had managed to maintain a precarious independence. Gerald of Wales opined that Henry had finally succeeded in the subjugation of that country and the *Brut* called him 'the man against whom no-one could avail save God himself'. He had reserved the right to appoint Welsh bishops, arrogating to himself power over the spiritual as well as the secular realm. The men he had selected to do his bidding and administer his jurisdiction – those whom Orderic Vitalis says he 'raised from the dust' – had proven reliable. Whole districts of Wales were now subject to royal government and taxation, simulacrums of English shires, such as Carmarthenshire and Pembrokeshire. Soon after Henry's death, all this fell apart. There were risings all over south Wales. Richard Fitz-Gilbert the Norman lord of Ceredigion was killed in an ambuscade, and another marcher lord, Payn Fitz-John was lured to his death soon afterwards. Norman castles were taken and in 1136 the Normans and Flemings were beaten by the Welsh in open battle near Cardigan. As England descended into a protracted and bitter civil war, the years when 'the saints slept', the Norman momentum had faltered, and Welsh revival was, at last, possible.

The seemingly inexorable Norman advance was replaced by a delicate equipoise, but the civil war raging in England between Stephen, Henry's nephew, and Matilda, his daughter, sapped the energies of both sides and allowed a breathing space to the Welsh. Gradually the Welsh regained the initiative. Carmarthen fell in 1137, and areas right on the border with England were reoccupied – such as Oswestry in 1149. In the north-east, the Anglo-Normans were expelled between the Clwyd and the Dee. In 1137, Owain ap Gruffydd, known as Owain Mawr or 'the Great' succeeded to the throne of Gwynedd. He is known as Owain Gwynedd in order to distinguish him from Owain ap Gruffydd ap Maredudd, otherwise known as Owain Cyfeiliog. He immediately expanded into Ceredigion, seizing and burning castles and making gifts of estates to his brother and his son. That such a Welsh recovery could take place emphasises the collapse of consistent royal authority over Wales in this period, and a corresponding increase in the autonomy of the marcher lords. The investment in the development of castles and fortified towns had increased the population in the areas under Anglo-Norman governance and they were becoming more productive and lucrative, with a thriving local economy and infrastructure of their own. In order to retain their ultimate control of these powerful statelets and their potentially dangerous earls, the English kings were compelled to take a more than active interest in the region of the Welsh March, and to establish their authority there beyond question. This could not be practicably achieved *without* asserting a similar control over the independent Welsh rulers. The implication of this, of course, was that they must ultimately be eliminated, and so a military campaign to conquer Wales as a whole was inevitable. The key to this process was the castle; since these fortifications have been mentioned so often, and will be again, it seems remiss not to describe these revolutionary military installations in greater detail.

There had been castles in France from an early date. Charles the Bald prohibited their construction without his explicit permission in 864. The earliest castles in England had been simple earth-and-timber constructions. The strongest part of the castle was the keep, where the nobleman's family lived, and where his retainers served him in the hall – and to which everyone retired when the castle was under attack. It made sense to build the keep high, to overlook the attackers, and if possible to construct it from stone, but the earliest castles were almost invariably built from timber, and the keep was a mere hall atop a steep mound of earth called a motte. Surrounding the keep a palisade was constructed around a perimeter that was defended by a steep embankment and a deep ditch. Within this area, called the bailey, all the kitchens and stables and various other structures were built. The Normans were experts at selecting the most suitable dominating position for their castles, often places which the Celts or the Romans had already exploited before them. If any 'Englishry' or 'Welshry', as the subjugated people were known to the Normans, were already in situ then they were cleared and ordered to settle somewhere else. At first, it was not possible to expedite the construction of the massive stone castles we see around us today. The Normans were newcomers to a hostile land and their field of operations was limited – in fact it is astonishing to think that William's army was never larger than around 10,000 men. Together with Bretons, Flemings, and other Frenchmen, the entire colonialist population in Britain cannot have exceeded 50,000 at most. Most castles had only one gateway, which was heavily defended, but could also be used to launch sudden attacks on the besiegers from within. As time went on it became possible to flood the ditch and create a moat, which in turn necessitated a drawbridge.

The most obvious weakness of a timber-built castle was that it was vulnerable to fire. All that was required was an arrow with a rag doused in pitch attached and a castle could be set ablaze. It was absolutely essential for every castle to contain a well, not only for clean drinking water, but also so that fires could be extinguished quickly before they took hold. Gradually, as the Normans consolidated their hold on England and Wales, it became possible to build massive sophisticated structures in stone, and within a few decades hundreds of these castles were constructed. But they were not just fortresses – they were also homes. It was preferred if the hall, where the nobleman received his guests and took his meals, could be located on the first or second floor of the tower. The hall was always draughty because the door had to be slightly ajar to draw the fire, and the windows had to be kept open to allow in daylight – a major security hazard if English or Celtic archers were lurking nearby. Two storerooms adjoined the hall, called the pantry and the buttery, the former to store bread rounds and the latter to keep the bottles and casks of wine. The Normans could never acquire a taste for English or Welsh ale, and avoided places where the local populace drank. It was wiser to stick together and frequent only inns and taverns where wine was served (or cider, a Norman innovation). As castles grew more sophisticated indoor lavatories were built and also small chapels – the Normans were exceedingly devout, for all their ruthlessness and violence. Eventually some of these castles developed into something rather more than mere fortresses, as the threat of rebellion or civil war diminished. Some, like Stokesay outside Ludlow are not true castles at all, but fortified manor houses, but at Ludlow itself the castle became the seat of the Lords President of the Council of Wales and the Marches in 1472 – by which time the Edwardian Conquest of Wales had taken place. Not only was Ludlow the seat of government for the marcher region, but for the entire principality of Wales. In the twelfth century, however, Wales was very far from being a defeated nation, and the Welsh soon learned how to build their own castles. Wales contains some of the mightiest castles ever built, but that did not prevent the Celts from laying siege. Methods were developed to overcome the castles' strength: war engines, trebuchets, siege towers, battering rams, scaling ladders and parties of men who mined underneath the foundations so that the structures collapsed. Trapped inside, and often starving and demoralised, the defenders desperately threw down stones and fire pots full of pitch, or poured boiling oil or fat onto the attacking force. When we consider just how many castles there are in the Welsh countryside (over 600) and the incessant warfare that took place, we can perhaps imagine what turbulent and frightening times these must have been for the combatants on both sides. It is scarcely surprising that those who were confined within, with nothing but the fire-glow and the minstrel to soothe them, soon became obsessed by the tales of courtly love and gallant heroism depicted in the new 'Arthurian' ballads.

During the reign of Owain Gwynedd, a man called Geoffrey 'of Monmouth' wrote down a history, *Historia Regum Britanniae* purporting to be derived from a 'book in the British language' given to him by Archdeacon Walter of Oxford, where Geoffrey was a *magister*, or teacher. The book was surprisingly well received and Geoffrey followed it up with other works, whose principal character was 'Merlin', the *Vita Merlini* and the *Prophetia Merlini*. What was distilled from these legends came to form the basis of the cult of Arthur and his court at Camelot, with which most people are familiar, but they contained for the Welsh a kernel of hope. It was said in the Prophesies that the Britons (with whom the Welsh increasingly identified as they were separated by the passing centuries) would regain control of the 'Island of the Mighty'. The English name for it would pass away and it would be known by the name of its ancient Trojan founder-king, Brutus, or 'Britain'. As the Celts believed in the immortality of the human soul and the possibility of reincarnation, especially of semi-divine kings, it proved very difficult for the English to eradicate these beliefs. This was what lay behind the excavation of the supposed remains of Arthur at Glastonbury ordered by Henry II shortly before he died, and a similar public display of the head of Llywelyn 'the Last' was arranged later on to prove that he was, definitively, dead. Llywelyn ap Iorwerth was thought to be 'the man of courage' Myrddin had foreseen. So these seemingly harmless tales were a nexus for two related but divergent cultural forces, and while the Anglo-Norman version emphasised the updated corpus with its mystical questing and courtly love, the Welsh exegesis came to concentrate on their ancient connections with Britannia and Rome, and what they saw as their rightful entitlement to hold sovereignty by virtue of their kings' descent from the mythical Brutus. The scrupulous study of this ancient lore, poring over royal genealogies and traditions became known as *Brut*. The study of the *Brut* was not an exclusively Welsh phenomenon. Wace, a Jersey man and Layamon, from Worcestershire in England both wrote a *Brut*. There seems to be a tradition too, though this needs further study, of Anglo-Saxon intellectuals withdrawing to the banks of a river where they contemplated history. Aethelweard wrote down his *Chronicon* at Bridgnorth, Layamon his *Brut* at Arley Redstone, and we know that St Beuno, the seventh-century Welsh confessor, also dwelt on the banks of the Severn at one time. Despite his sobriquet, Geoffrey may not have been Welsh at all; Sir Frank Stenton thought he may have been of Breton stock and settled around Monmouth, and we have seen how it was precisely these incomers who were the first colonists to discover the Welsh Arthurian tales, which they then copied.

The ancient history commences with the flight of Brutus, great-grandson of Aeneas of Troy, who is directed by the goddess Diana to find a sacred island. He does so, and he and his retinue disembark at Totnes in Devonshire. Geoffrey lists shadowy monarchs who ruled before the coming of Caesar, then the long Roman occupation and the various usurper emperors, before the climax of the book – the reign of Arthur. Arthur holds a great court at Caerleon in South Wales (the ruins of the circular Roman amphitheatre there may have inspired the legend of the 'Round Table') and a gallant company of knights gather around him, who cannot enjoy the love of the womenfolk until they have triumphed many times in battle. Eventually Arthur clashes with Rome itself. Crossing the sea, he leads an army to attack the Eternal City but is foiled by rebellion at home and returns, to be mortally wounded by Medraut (or Mordred), his own nephew. According to Geoffrey, Arthur was borne away into Avalon in the year 542. This pseudo-history, written-up in scholarly Latin by an esteemed cleric (Geoffrey was appointed as Bishop of St Asaph in Wales, but never visited his see), gave the 'Matter of Britain' a credible historicity that it had not enjoyed before. Soon a Jersey man called Wace based his *Brut* on Geoffrey's work, and dedicated it to the formidable Queen Eleanor of Aquitaine, wife to Henry II. Sometime after 1155 but probably before 1200, a lay preacher at Arley Redstone in Worcestershire, Layamon, wrote a *Brut* of his own – a 16,000-line poem recapitulating Geoffrey and Wace, but containing new material, possibly derived from contact with Welsh-speaking drovers who waited to be blessed by Layamon as they boarded the Severn ferry. His translation was truly revolutionary, for it was in English, the then despised language of the 'Englishry' of the western Midlands. The momentum behind the lore was building, and by the end of the twelfth century it had completely captivated the Anglo-Norman monarchy.

In the occupied territories the Anglo-Norman population was by no means commingled with the natives. Welsh people were excluded within the English boroughs and their legal rights were curtailed. Layamon's work shows that the English had retained their language and culture and the aristocracy would one day have to come to terms and begin to speak English, though this lay some years in the future. In Wales, however, the Anglo-Normans were segregated, not just by virtue of status, but by the impenetrability of the Welsh language, and the divide between conquerors and conquered was more sharply defined even than in England. By 1154, the civil war that had raged for almost two decades in England was over, and a new and vigorous king came to the throne there, Henry II – or, to give him his full title, Henry, Count of Anjou and Maine, Duke of Normandy, Duke of Aquitaine, Count of Nantes, King of England and Lord of Ireland. In addition he claimed overlordship of Brittany, Scotland – and Wales. This empire, which stretched from Scotland in the north to the Pyrenees in the south, added a new dimension to the Anglo-Norman/Welsh conflict. Henry was the most powerful enemy the Celts had faced since the Roman legions left, and he used his military superiority against the Bretons, Irish, Scots and French as well as against the Welsh. In fact, although it was constantly riven by squabbling between Henry and his wife and sons, Henry succeeded in building an empire, the Angevin Empire. It was not long before the Welsh became a target for him. His first attempt was a naval operation in 1157 to attack Gwynedd from the rear by making a landing in Anglesey, but this failed miserably. Henry himself was ambushed by Welsh guerrillas and the peace he made with Owain Gwynedd was more a face-saving measure than a decisive imposition of his overlordship. A relationship that proved just as problematic was with 'the Lord Rhys' of Deheubarth in south-west Wales. When Henry sent his forces there, Rhys ushered his people 'with their wives and children and all their animals into the forest land of the Tywe, but the Anglo-Norman forces were not to be resisted and

Rhys was forced to give up Ceredigion to Henry. His forfeited lands passed to the control of the marcher lord, Walter de Clifford, and the resentment of this loss smouldered. Henry's empire was vast and he spent long periods overseas. Rhys exploited this by raiding into his former lands, but de Clifford retaliated by raiding the royal residence of Dinefwr, where the family of the Lord Rhys were undefended. In 1163, Henry was compelled to invade and Rhys was forced to surrender. He was taken as a virtual prisoner deep into England, to Woodstock, and here a ceremony took place that recalled the undisputed authority of King Athelstan: 'Rhys prince of the southern Welsh, Owain of the northern Welsh and five of the greater men from Wales did homage to the king of the English, and to Henry his son.' King Malcolm of Scotland was also required to abase himself, and the situation for Celtic Britain looked as ominous as in 937. The response of the Welsh on this occasion was more bellicose. The next year a generalised uprising took place and the Lord Rhys led a combined army of Welshmen to Corwen on the Dee. Henry also faced the threat of invasion from Scotland. However, it was the Welsh threat that was more serious because Rhys had achieved something truly remarkable – he had united the whole Welsh nation under arms:

> Owain Gwynedd and Cadwaladr sons of Gruffydd ap Cynan came to meet him and all the host of Gwynedd with them, and the Lord Rhys ap Gruffydd and all Deheubarth with him, and Owain Cyfeiliog and Iorwerth Goch ap Maredudd and the sons of Madog ap Maredudd and with them all Powys, and the sons of Madog ap Idnerth and all their strength with them.

Henry led his immense army into Wales, where, in the appalling summer weather, which occasionally grips that country, his troops laboured through the bleak Berwyn Mountains but Rhys fell back, enticing the English into even wilder country and harassing them in the usual way. Henry eventually had no choice but to retreat back into England, where, in the blind fury for which he is so remembered, he ordered his Welsh hostages to be tortured and mutilated as an act of spite. The most powerful soldier in Europe had been beaten by the Welsh – and their notorious weather. One of the poor souls who had their eyes gouged out was Maredudd, Rhys's son, but by 1171 Rhys 'made friends with the king'. Fourteen more high-ranking hostages were asked for, along with 4,000 oxen and 300 horses, but Henry contented himself with less onerous numbers in practice and freed Hywel, another of Rhys's sons he had taken as a hostage. The rapprochement was instigated in order to assist Henry's expedition in Ireland. In 1169, Diarmait Mac Murchada, King of Leinster, had invited Richard de Clare and a group of other powerful Norman noblemen settled in Wales to Ireland. Richard was married to the king's daughter and was heir to the kingdom. Rebellions in France, the controversy surrounding his archbishop of Canterbury, Thomas Becket, and a frenetic and infuriating family life, had all worn Henry down and the prospect of a powerful rival in Ireland could not be borne also. Rhys hated Richard and so it was in his interests to facilitate the king's countermeasures against him. Rhys, who had once been an outlaw and the leader of a national insurgency, was now an ally of the King of England. By 1177 Henry was in the comfortable position of summoning the *rex Nortwalliae* and *rex Swtwalliae,* the kings of north and south Wales, to Oxford, where they both paid him homage. Henry's more liberal attitude to Wales meant that he was prepared to be impartial in Welsh affairs. Even Roger Mortimer, the Earl of March, was imprisoned for raiding into Malienydd. Rhys had been appointed as the king's justiciar and he kept peace with him until Henry died in 1189. Unfortunately, the relationship with his eldest surviving son and successor, Richard I 'the Lionheart', was poor. Richard was preoccupied with his Continental domains and the Third Crusade and had little enough time for England, let alone Wales. Rhys resumed the war and built powerful castles. Prince John, Henry's son, negotiated a peace at Worcester but the war erupted again soon afterwards.

By the time Rhys died in 1197 he left behind him a much expanded Deheubarth. He was buried at St Davids and glorified as 'the noble diadem of Welsh grace' and the 'glory of Wales'. Considering the immense odds against them the resilience of the Welsh kings and the stubbornness of the Welsh people were truly remarkable. What was it that gave them this almost superhuman capacity to endure? I believe, and I am not alone in this view, that the answer is to be found in that ancient inheritance we have seen before – the legacy of Druidism, of Arthur, and of their designation as marginalised heretics. All this was contained in their history, which occupied a place in their culture more esteemed than, perhaps, any other nation on earth, material which came to make up the 'Matter of Britain'. Professor R. R. Davies sums this up neatly in his *The Age of Conquest: Wales 1063–1415* (Oxford, 1987):

> Central to this mythology was an intense pride in the past or rather in a particular interpretation of it. Two aspects of the past were especially emphasized. One was the unbroken link between the Old North – the kingdoms of North Britain of the fifth to seventh centuries – and the contemporary political order in Wales ... it was a mythical, validating past and, thereby, a potent, if gradually diluted part of the Welsh consciousness. The second point of reference in this native Welsh historical consciousness was a wistful memory of, and pride in, the Roman past of the country. This memory concentrated in particular on the legends which had encrusted around the figure of Magnus Maximus (d. 388), the Macsen Wledig of Welsh lore. Several Welsh dynasties in the medieval period traced their descent whether directly, in the male line or through marriage, to Macsen. He, thereby, served as a convenient bridge from native tradition to Roman glory and thence to Trojan origins; he also served to embody and to explain the transition from the Roman political order to the political dispensation of native Wales.

Professor Davies gives us a deep insight into the consequences of this reinterpretation of history for the Welsh:

> The Welsh were inordinately proud of their past; for them it was both the fount and mirror for the present. But their pride was balanced by a sense of loss and shame – the loss of the sovereignty of Britain and shame at the oppressions (W. *gormesoedd*) which the Island of the Mighty had suffered at the hands of alien races. Such a sense of deprivation often led to despair, to a deep conviction of the Britons' sinfulness and a sense of shameful contrition in the face of ineluctable divine retribution. Equally it

could and did beget a bitter resentment against those who had, willingly or otherwise, aided and abetted the Saxons to deprive the Britons of the sovereignty of Britain.

Among those who had aided and abetted the Sais were the legendary traitors Vortigern, Medraut/Mordred, Llovan Llawdivro and their ilk. For the 'children of Rhonwen' – the Sais – there could be nothing except eternal enmity; but there was a terrible cost to this gnawing, unending hatred, 'the endless ill' as A. E Housman called it. Indeed it could not be borne unless there were a compensatory myth, where 'all wrong would be made right'. This compensation myth, this promise of a future deliverance gave the Welsh a desperate sort of hope, underpinned by the magic of Merlinic prophecies: 'Hope was the great theme of the Merlinic prophesies – hope of delivery from, and extermination of, the Saxons, and hope of the advent of a messianic deliverer who would once more restore the Britons to their rightful control of the Island of Britain.'

Gerald of Wales said of his countrymen, 'they boast that in a short time their countrymen shall return to the island and, according to the Prophesies of Merlin, the nation of foreigners as well as its name shall be exterminated, and the Britons shall exult again in their old name and privilege in the island.' But when would their deliverer come?

13

'Mere Welshmen'

Henry II had set an important precedent. Increasingly he had invoked his superior authority and status in terms of legal statute rather than in military terms and it was this legalistic underpinning that Henry's descendants sought to extend. But the Welsh, inconveniently, had their own laws, those that had been reformed and codified by Hywel Dda. If the Welsh were to be subdued, it was imperative that their ancient laws be superseded by English law and that their ancient culture and illustrious history be eradicated. The ultimate objective was to reduce the Welsh people to a powerless and subservient class of serfs, 'mere Welshmen' or *forinseci*, 'foreigners' in their own land, almost subhumans. In time, no Welshman would have the right to prosecute a legal case against an Englishman. The consequences of such a change in a colonial society can be imagined. Englishmen were enabled to inflict the most iniquitous humiliations and get away with the theft of ancient Welsh lands, without the natives having any prospect of redress in the law courts. When Henry had appointed Rhys as his justiciar the principle had been set that the King of England exercised control of Welsh kings in the same way as over English lords and barons, and when Owain and Rhys had sworn homage and pledged fealty to the English king at Woodstock and at Oxford, this too set a precedent. Welsh kings could be summoned into England and required to renew their oaths, or face sequestration, imprisonment, mutilation or even death should they fail to oblige. In the year 1197 two important Welsh leaders died, the Lord Rhys in Deheubarth and Owain Cyfeiliog of Powys.

Llywelyn ap Iorwerth, prince of Gwynedd, made a new alliance with Gwenwynwyn ap Owain Cyfeiliog of Powys creating a strong bloc that constrained the territorial ambitions of the marcher lords. These lords were notoriously rapacious. Even their own chronicler, Orderic Vitalis, describes them as 'a warlike race, moved by fierce ambition to lord it over others' and describes the barons as 'men of extreme arrogance and presumption'. In 1199 a man of a similar stamp became the king of England – King John – perhaps the most notorious king in English history. During his reign he unleashed terror in Wales as well as in England and the miseries of the Welsh are described by Professor Davies:

> The aim of these warbands was brutally clear: to terrorize the country into subjection. They pillaged and plundered ruthlessly in north and south Wales alike: Llyn was said, doubtless with some exaggeration, to have been completely wasted in a week of relentless harrying … animals were driven away in large numbers, men and women were imprisoned and sold into captivity; large tracts of land, especially in north-east Wales were placed under forest law … one vile Norman lamented Rhigyfarch in the last decade of the eleventh century, 'intimidates a hundred natives with his command, and terrifies them with his look' … Gerald of Wales, no critic of the Normans, commented on 'the fear and terror' they had instilled into the bishop of St Davids, and how he had been 'intimidated by the hostile lances of the newcomers'.

By 1202 John was embroiled in wars in France and sought to secure his border with Wales by reaching a rapprochement with Llywelyn. In 1204 John promised his illegitimate daughter, Joan, in marriage to Llywelyn and the next year the marriage took place, Joan becoming known within Wales as 'Siwan'. She brought as her dowry the manor of Ellesmere, a former property of Dafydd ap Owain, which had fallen within the gift of the English king. From Llywelyn's perspective this marriage alliance was an enormous boost to his international status and prestige, for it was a de facto recognition of his status as prince of Gwynedd, the ancient country of Venedotia, of which he was, in effect, the king (he had already been declared as the first among his peers in Wales by the pope). In 1208, Gwenwynwyn of Powys was arrested and thrown into prison after a conference at Shrewsbury, which Llywelyn used as an excuse to seize control of large parts of Powys. Ceredigion followed and John thought it expedient to compel Llywelyn to accompany him on an invasion of Scotland the following year so as to keep him close. In 1210, John asserted his authority over the de Lacey and de Braose families in an invasion of Ireland. To check Llywelyn's growing ambitions, John supported his enemies and reinstated Gwenwynwyn as prince of Powys. Llywelyn immediately reacted to these hostile signals, leading a sporadic raiding campaign in the Welsh Marches.

John, despite his appalling character, tempestuous moods, and disregard for the prevailing religious mores of his time, had inherited his father's keen intelligence and possessed undoubted organisational abilities in the military sphere. Moreover, unlike his Norman predecessors, he was familiar with his English and Welsh possessions and even knew some English speech. Few kings have been more marked by infamy. He swore and cursed and flew into blind rages, frothing at the mouth and gnawing on cushions and rugs. He hired *routiers*, mercenary cut-throats, to do much of his fighting and Brabancons and Aragonese, men from foreign countries who had no interest in the countryside they ravaged, who mocked Christ as they sacked churches and monasteries and defiled holy shrines – the scum of Europe. It is perhaps interesting that such men were often shocked by John's almost satanic lust for destruction; he would arrive at the manors of noblemen, seduce their wives and daughters, and then personally set fire to the house before he progressed on his grim itinerary. He feared neither man nor God and was content for his entire kingdom to suffer under the papal interdict by the terms of which churches were closed for many years. In fact, John offered to convert his domains to Islam in order to borrow sums of monies from the Islamic Caliphate, and may have been something more sinister than a non-Christian. In short, he was not a man to provoke. The crime for which he is most notorious, the murder of his nephew, Arthur of Brittany – some say he personally strangled the lad – seemed to the Celts a sort of deicide. Some thought Arthur to be the reincarnation of his namesake.

John was familiar with Wales. After the loss of Normandy in 1204 John was confined to his insular realms and he became a peripatetic monarch constantly travelling around the country with a vast wagon-train and a huge retinue. He spent much time on the Welsh borders, especially in Worcestershire. He also spent a lot of time in Worcestershire, where he is buried in the cathedral, and Staffordshire, where Stourton Castle was one of many royal hunting lodges. John was obsessed with hunting and hawking – his greatest love was his favourite falcon called 'Gibbun'. The campaign against Ireland had been launched from south Wales and for five years running he progressed through the border area, traversing it from south to north. In 1211, John resolved to 'dispossess Llywelyn and destroy him utterly'. At first John's troops could not make progress, but he reinforced them and returned later in the summer, sacking and burning Bangor and penetrating even the mountains of Snowdonia. Llywelyn had no choice but to send his wife to plead for peace terms with her father. John took a perverse pleasure in reducing Llywelyn to a prince of a minor, much reduced Gwynedd, a virtual pauper. There was no choice but to break the treaty and in 1212 he regained control of the lands of which he had been deprived, and renounced his homage to John. The English king was by now excommunicated, and the pope lifted the interdict in Llywelyn's territory – a signal of tacit support for a wider rebellion. In fact John's own Norman barons were now agitating against his cruel misrule, and this gave Llywelyn the opportunity to make an alliance against the king. In 1215 John affixed his seal to the momentous Magna Carta, and in that document John was forced to accede to major concessions to the Welsh. Hostages, many of whom had been tortured, maimed, starved to death, roasted alive on gridirons and hanged at his command in the past, were to be freed. Lands that had been disseised illegally were restored to the rightful owners, and the option to transact litigation under native law was acknowledged. These concessions, wrung out of a king of England temporarily powerless, enabled Llywelyn to prosecute the campaign to bring all Wales under his rule, and when England once more fell into the grip of civil war, the English were distracted from events in Wales. In 1216, Llywelyn invaded Powys and expelled Gwenwynwyn, who died in England, and Llywelyn took custody of Powys until his sons were of an age to inherit. In October 1216 John died, probably by poison, at Newark Castle in Nottinghamshire aged forty-nine. His son, Henry, was a minor, which gave the Welsh an opportunity to do what had been done under Gruffydd – the chance to unite and assert their independence from English domination and control.

The new détente in Wales masked deep resentments, particularly among marcher lords who had lost lands to the Welsh, such as Hugh Mortimer and William Marshal. Llywelyn realised this and sought to make marriage alliances with powerful marcher families and potentates such as the marriage of Gladys, his daughter, to Reginald de Braose, and another daughter, Marared, to John, Reginald's nephew. His marriage to Joan had been made with an explicit assurance that only sons born to her would be eligible to succeed. This was a problem, because Llywelyn had mistresses, concubines and illegitimate sons – who were, under native law, eligible to inherit under the ancient system of partible inheritance wc have seen before. In fact, Llywelyn already had an illegitimate son, Gruffydd, when he married Joan and his legitimate son by her, Dafydd, was technically next in line to his older brother under Welsh law. Llywelyn, however, decided to try to prevent the catastrophic infighting after his death with which the reader will be so familiar – by recognising Dafydd as his undisputed legal heir. The marriages to powerful Norman barons wcre designed as security for Dafydd against a threat from his brother. To confirm the arrangement in English law, Llywelyn presented himself to the King of England at Worcester and had it ratified by him, as additional security. The boy, was of course, a relation of the English monarch and so could expect the favour of the king there. The pope was also solicited for his blessing and in 1226 all the leading nobles of native Wales were forced to swear an oath to promote Dafydd's succession. Gruffydd was understandably resentful and in 1228 he was thrown into prison at Degannwy, where he remained for six years. Llywelyn's positioning within Wales and the pledges exacted on behalf of his son did not pass unnoticed in England. At the mighty castle of Montgomery, Henry established Hubert de Burgh as a counterweight to Llywelyn. Hubert's construction parties trespassed onto Welsh lands in the Forest of Ceri, quite by accident.

Two massive castles had been re-established at Painscastle and Montgomery, built at vast expense to the English Crown. Miners were enlisted from as far away as the Forest of Dean to sink a deep well at the latter. They bored hundreds of feet down through the solid rock. The skirmishes around 'Hubert's folly', a castle de Burgh attempted to construct inside Welsh territory, led to a full-blown siege of Montgomery Castle. Unable to break in, the Welsh set fire to the adjoining town, whose taxes supported the fortress. During the fighting Llywelyn had taken an important prisoner of war, William de Braose. William was eventually released, and an alliance proposed. Frequent contact between the two men continued, but in 1230 there was an incident in which William was discovered to be having an affair with Joan, Llywelyn's queen. This peccadillo had dramatic consequences. William was hanged and Joan, a blood relative of the English king, was exiled from the court of Gwynedd.

Joan was imprisoned for a year, but then reinstated. The English king refrained from exacting punishment on Llywelyn (perhaps William's action was considered unchivalrous, as well as immoral). In 1221, Llywelyn attacked Montgomery Castle and led raiding parties into Radnorshire, Hay and Brecknockshire. Cardigan was taken by him, and while a baronial rebellion took place in England, Llywelyn skilfully expanded his influence in contested territory. By 1234 he felt secure enough to release his illegitimate son, Gruffydd. His focus on assuring the succession for Dafydd was paramount for him, however, and he tried to arrange for him to be legally recognised by the English king as *princeps de Abbefrau et dominus de Snaudonia* – 'prince of Abberfraw and Lord of Snowdon'. This title carried with it an ancient right to be acknowledged as pre-eminent among all the Welsh kings. At the Peace of Middle, a village in Shropshire, hostilities were again suspended. In 1237, Llywelyn's unfaithful queen died and he suffered a stroke. Henry proved intransigent about favouring Dafydd as his heir and Llywelyn's last years were troubled and uncertain. Gruffydd was now in a position to assert his claim, and the ailing Llywelyn sought English royal protection against him. Dafydd forestalled the danger by imprisoning his brother at Cricieth after luring him to parley under false pretences. Shortly afterwards, worn out with cares, Llywelyn ap Iorwerth or 'the Great' died on 11 April 1240 at

Aberconwy. His dream of leaving a united Wales to a son with an undisputed legal title died with him. The longed for title his father had so coveted was substituted for the inferior sounding 'son of Llywelyn, sometime prince of Aberffraw and lord of Snowdon' a mere feudal vassal of the English monarchy. The English king was now in the happy position of being able to exploit the divisions between the two Welsh brothers. In 1241 he gave his explicit backing to Gruffydd and ordered Dafydd to release him. When Dafydd refused these demands Henry immediately invaded and compelled Dafydd's submission before a week was out. What seemed like the prelude to English domination followed, a humiliating settlement that reduced Dafydd to the status of a petty princeling and also to penury by making him liable for the expense Henry had incurred in his invasion, a colossal sum. Dafydd was forced to agree that if he died without heirs, his lands would be forfeited to the king in perpetuity, and also that he and his heirs would be faithful men of the King of England and his heirs. As one more security against rebellion, Gruffydd was confined in the Tower of London from whence he could be released at any time should his brother renege on his pledges. All that Llywelyn had built up over so many years was dissipated by his sons. On 1 March 1244 Gruffydd made an escape attempt from his prison in the Tower, tormented by another long incarceration, but the improvised rope he had made from his bed linen gave way and he fell to his death, on the very feast day of the patron saint of his country. Lack of exercise had caused him to become overweight. The high window from which he made the attempt was ordered to be bricked up, and is still visible. Two years later Dafydd himself died, leaving behind no heirs. This technically entitled Henry to take Gwynedd for himself, under the terms of the treaty with Dafydd. Gruffydd, however, left four living sons, the second eldest of which, Llywelyn ap Gruffydd, was at large in Gwynedd itself. His elder brother Owain was confined in England but escaped to join his brother in Wales. In 1247, at the Treaty of Woodstock, the two brothers were recognised as co-heirs to the kingdom of Gwynedd. By 1247 Matthew Paris could comment on the lamentable state of the country, 'Wales was brought to nought at this time'. An ancient and proud nation seemed almost on the verge of extinction, but it is at precisely such times that the Celts are at their most dangerous. Gerald of Wales was clear about the motivations of the two adversaries: 'the English are striving for power, the Welsh for freedom; the English are fighting for material gain, the Welsh to preserve themselves from disaster; the English soldiers are hired mercenaries, the Welsh are defending their homeland.'

The sons of Gruffydd immediately commenced the usual internecine squabbling, but this was decisively resolved at the Battle of Bryn Derwin in the summer of 1250. Llywelyn was the victor, defeating Owain and Dafydd. In 1256 he seized control of the Perfeddwlad or 'middle-land' where there were long established English colonies. These were driven out, and this was a flagrant violation of the terms of the Treaty of Woodstock. Other English settlements were repatriated, and Meirionydd, Ceredigion and Gwerthrynion. Within a few years Llywelyn was positioning himself to be proclaimed 'Prince of Wales' and in 1258 he officially adopted the style. Negotiations were opened with an anti-English faction in Scotland that was attempting to overthrow Alexander III, adding a new international, pan-Celtic dimension to the intrigues against the English Crown. The proximate cause for this resurgence of Celtic self-confidence was, of course, the weakness of England, whose king, Henry III, had been faced with the same militancy among his feudatory lords and barons that had brought his father to Runnymede in 1215. Henry reigned for fifty-six years and he was a devout and godly man, meek and easily intimidated – though he was by no means foolish or simple-minded. The most powerful of the barons, and the man of whom Henry was most terrified, was Simon de Montfort. There could be no compromise of the positions of either side, and so the issue was sent for arbitration to the most respected monarch in Europe at that time, St Louis, the French king. Louis immediately saw that Henry had been intimidated into large concessions under threat of armed rebellion, a situation no sane monarch could endorse, and at a Court of Arbitration at Amiens, he found in Henry's favour. The hapless fellow was actually at the court in person, but by the time he returned to England de Montfort had already mobilised. He was a messianic personality, confident of his divine selection to overthrow the discredited and weak regime personified for him in the shape of Henry, who quaked in fear in his presence. A religious fanatic with what we would now call a 'death wish', Simon was popular among the growing urban population in England, those of the 'lower orders', who were gripped by xenophobia towards 'foreigners', Savoyard and Poitevin courtiers among them, which Henry had imported; in many ways the conflict that followed was a rehearsal for the English Civil War of the seventeenth century. So, once again, civil war in England gave opportunities for Welsh and Scottish resurgence, but eventually the bloody conflict would throw up a personality who would prove the nemesis of both nations – Edward, Henry's capable heir.

Confident in his considerable achievements, Llywelyn now sought to buy peace from Henry in return for his recognition of him as prince, but Henry was intelligent enough to realise that any such concession would be another drain on his precarious authority, and consequently prevaricated. By 1260 Llywelyn was in a position to attack Builth, and by 1261 he was intruding along the borders of the middle-March, and once again the marcher lord who was his target, Roger Mortimer, lost important castles including at Cefnllys, which the Welsh destroyed. As the civil war in England developed Llywelyn finally abandoned the project of seeking Henry's approbation. Henry had already signalled his true intentions by dispatching his son, Edward, with a force whose mission was to relieve besieged English garrisons, but this had failed. Llywelyn decided to ally himself with de Montfort against the king and sent troops to assist the rebels in the siege of Bridgnorth Castle. In May 1264, de Montfort decisively defeated the royal army at Lewes in Sussex with horrendous slaughter – Henry's position seemed hopeless. Many powerful Marcher lords had sided with Simon, including John Fitz-Alan, John Giffard and Roger Clifford, and Llywelyn supported their claims in order to consolidate his position within Wales. He anticipated a new settlement with the de facto 'king' of England, who was now Simon de Montfort. Simon had managed to capture both Henry and Edward after the battle of Lewes and on 14 May 1264 he began to issue writs in Henry's name. In 1265, Simon was concerned enough about the situation in the Welsh marches to visit the area with Henry and Edward with him, as effective prisoners; however, on 28 May 1265 Edward made a daring escape bid at Tillington in Herefordshire while out hunting. His confederates had arranged for him to be conveyed with all haste to Wigmore Castle, which was a garrison of the Loyalist Mortimer family, and in the morning he rode to Ludlow where a meeting with the Earl of Gloucester – hitherto Simon's principal ally and the commander of a large military force – had been pre-arranged.

Suddenly Simon was confronted with a very dangerous situation in the shape of Edward, an opponent whose military acumen was equal to his own, and, moreover, at Hereford he was quite exposed to sudden attacks, which could secure vital river crossings and box him in beyond the Severn. Therefore, he acted swiftly to negotiate favourable terms with the Welsh in order to secure his rear for the forthcoming campaign. Then, to quote Professor R. R. Davies, Llywelyyn 'turned the discomfiture of the English to his own ends' and received concessions that acknowledged his many conquests in north Wales. On 19 June 1265, with the war developing not necessarily in his favour, Simon officially recognised Llywelyn as 'Prince of Wales' at Pipton-on-Wye. But Simon was, as he had always suspected, doomed. Edward had seized Gloucester and had blockaded him west of the Severn. Simon attempted a break out at Kempsey just below Worcester, with King Henry as his prisoner for a bargaining counter. Edward was at Worcester itself and appeared to withdraw to Bridgnorth, but according to Hilaire Belloc in his *Warfare in England* he skilfully forded the Severn near Grimley by night, and then marched across country to Evesham. According to other sources Edward had sallied out to Kenilworth Castle, Simon's family stronghold, which was under the command of his son, also called Simon, then doubled back after defeating him, using his captured banners to delude the elder Simon into thinking his son had come to conjoin with him. Such ruses were quite typical of Edward's subsequent career, but whichever route his army took to Evesham, on the morning of 4 August 1265, Edward stood with an army of 10,000 men barring Simon's way to Alcester. By sunrise, his forces, though no doubt exhausted, had managed to take the high ground outside the town. When Simon saw Edward's standards he is said to have exclaimed, 'May the Lord have mercy on our souls, for our bodies are Prince Edward's.' Even Henry, a prisoner in his enemies' camp, was almost slain in the pitiless slaughter, but at the crucial moment cried out to his assailants, 'Slay me not! I am Henry of Winchester, your king!' Only the Welshmen among Simon's force managed to escape by swimming the river while their English comrades-in-arms were brutally massacred almost to the last man. The restored King Henry needed time to repair the disarray into which his kingdom had fallen, but on 29 September 1267, at the ford of Rhyd Chwima outside Montgomery, the Prince of Wales met Henry, did homage and he was formally recognised as Prince of Wales in exchange for certain concessions and payments, particularly in relation to reparations to the Mortimers and his brother, Dafydd. The title of prince was to pass down to his heirs, which was a considerable coup. In fact, when we consider how parlous a situation he had inherited, Llywelyn's achievements are remarkable and this was not just because the English were weakened but because his own forces had shown that skilful mastery of guerrilla warfare, targeted raiding and cunning use of the terrain, which had characterised their tactics since the days of Caratacus. There was deep hatred of the English and growing Welsh patriotic fervour, as well as a firm resolution to throw off English rule, sentiments that Llywelyn exploited to the full. Some proclaimed that they 'preferred to be slain in war for their liberty than to suffer themselves to be unrighteously trampled on by foreigners', a pithy summary of their war aims as noble as the famous Declaration of Arbroath. The man who had achieved so much for Wales was truly what he claimed: a prince among his people and 'No Welshman is his peer' according to the bards. But there was another prince, one whose career was to have an even greater influence on Wales – Prince Edward of England.

Edward had joined the crusade and had been badly wounded when, as he was making his return to England in 1272, he heard of his father's death. Curiously, Edward, who was to be remembered as one of the most ruthless and cold-blooded warriors in British history, was stricken with grief. His affection for his father was genuine. He is said to have remarked that, 'the loss of sons is easy to bear since more of them can be produced any day, but there is no remedy for the death of parents, who are irreplaceable.' He made his way home in stages and was not finally crowned king until 19 August 1274. Pointedly, Llywelyn did not attend his coronation ceremony. Edward had been thoroughly indoctrinated with the Arthurian legends of the Matter of Britain and the cult of knighthood. This obsession enabled him to convince himself that he, rather than their natural prince, Llywelyn, was the heir to Wales and the embodiment of the Merlinic Prophesies, and at Nefyn, the coastal village where the prophesies had been written down, he later held a grand tournament replete with Arthurian references. A chance to make good Llywelyn's breach of etiquette about the coronation, as well as his delay in paying homage and fealty to the new King of England, went begging, and in 1274 a palace plot was discovered in which Llywelyn's brother Dafydd was accused of attempting to murder the prince. Dafydd and his co-conspirator Gruffydd ap Gwenwynwyn rode for protection to the English king, who immediately supported their raiding into Wales. Knowing that Llywelyn must either backdown or fight, Edward summoned Llywelyn to Chester but the prince did not attend, and neither did he respond to further summonses. A stand-off had developed, which only required an incident to initiate a conflagration and, in the traditions of courtly love, this was provided by the frustration of a royal love affair.

Llywelyn had been betrothed to Eleanor de Montfort, Simon's daughter, who was now in exile. The two were married by proxy and she set sail from France to Wales. Unlike many such marriages of this period this was a genuine romance – the two were deeply in love. Edward had a personal grudge against the de Montfort family. His cousin had been murdered by Simon's sons during a parley in a church. Edward arranged for a pirate vessel from Bristol to intercept Eleanor's ship as it was making its way to Welsh waters. She was conveyed to Windsor where she was confined at Edward's pleasure. Llywelyn appealed to the pope but this got him nowhere. Edward was already deploying troops to the borders and last-minute appeals to the Archbishop of Canterbury also proved futile. Llywelyn, whose wife (they were married, even though the union had not been consummated) was languishing in prison, was understandably reticent about presenting himself in England, and demanded Eleanor's release and high-ranking hostages before he would meet the king. Edward had never truly desired peace, he was pre-eminently a man of war; on 12 November 1276 he declared Llywelyn to be a rebel. Hostilities immediately commenced, and indeed there had been continual skirmishing throughout the year. Edward was a military commander with a ruthless, calculating well-organised turn of mind, whose victory at Evesham and experience in the crusade had given him supreme confidence. Llywelyn was also a man of destiny, hailed by the bards as 'the governor of the Welsh host', 'true king of Wales' and 'defender of Deheubarth and Powys and upholder of Glamorgan, lion of Gwynedd'. Despite the inestimable odds against him, Llywelyn stood guard over his ancient inheritance, last of a line stretching back to 'Camber, son of Brutus' as he declaimed in a defiant speech, refusing to yield. He was indeed the true heir to Caratacus, Boudicca, Urien, Arthur and Cadwallon – and so the Edwardian expedition commenced, a battle to decide the fate of Britain, the 'Island of the Mighty'.

Edward's advance was inexorable and Llywelyn, abandoned by his allies, was forced to take refuge in Snowdonia. Eventually he was forced to capitulate, and to submit to humiliating terms, at the Treaty of Aberconwy on 9 November 1277, yielding up all the gains he had made at the Treaty of Montgomery, leaving him with a mere rump-state of Gwynedd and a few minor lordships. The work of thirty years had been squandered but this was inevitable; Edward's force was immense, over 15,000 strong with specialised mercenaries such as Gascon cross-bowmen and a huge commissariat of wagons, carts and pack-ponies, supported by strong marine forces. Nothing had been seen like it in Wales since the days of the legions. Another army of labourers and camp followers followed this host, well fed and equipped, ready to construct new fortifications. Llywelyn was now a prince only in name, growing older, brooding on his downfall. He began conspiring to retrieve his position within a year. Eleanor had finally been released and he was allowed to marry her in Worcester with the approval of the king, giving him hopes of an heir. Llywelyn soon began to complain of bias shown in favour of persons with whom he was in legal disputes, claiming his ancient right for the cases to be heard according to Welsh law, and appealing the matter to Edward. The English king, by now contemptuous of Wales and its prince, dithered and procrastinated, but this was interpreted, probably rightly, as a prelude to the establishment of royal English law within Wales, fuelling popular resentment. By 1282 the mood for a popular uprising could no longer be contained. 'Mere Welshmen' all over Wales rose in arms, at Hawarden, Rhuddlan, Flint, and in Powys, Carmarthenshire and Ceredigion. Aberystwyth fell to the insurgents and there was a popular demand for Llywelyn to lead a national insurrection. But, Llywelyn was middle-aged and at last had found some happiness with his wife, on whom he doted and who was now expecting a child, perhaps, God-willing, a son and heir. Notwithstanding all these powerful reasons to collaborate with Edward, Llywelyn knew that Wales must fight, and that he must lead his compatriots, even if it ended in his destruction – and so the climax approached.

In point of fact the rebellion had been started not by Llywelyn, but by his brother Dafydd. Unfortunately he did not take care to coordinate his actions with those of his brother, or may even have acted without his knowledge. Edward delegated command in the south to Gilbert de Clare, the so-called 'Red Earl' who led an army of Welsh mercenaries he had hired for the princely sum of a penny a day against their fellow countrymen. On 17 June 1282 de Clare was ambushed at Llandeilo Fawr and his force of 2,000 men all but destroyed. De Clare was dismissed but Edward responded in August 1282 with an army composed of Gascons, Picards, Basques and various other contingents of specialist troops. His initial progress was steady, but then faltered. Finally an abortive assault on Gwynedd made Edward offer a final deal to Llywelyn, in which he would become a royal pensioner with an estate in England. Dafydd was offered a financial sum to quit the island and join the crusade – virtual banishment. The children of both men were to be surrendered to him as hostages (Llywelyn had just become father of a little princess, but his dear Eleanor had died delivering her). These derisory terms were treated with the contempt they merited, and utterly rejected out of hand. The Welsh council advised Edward that they, 'would rather die than live' and that irrespective of the fate of their prince they would, 'refuse to do homage to any stranger of whose language, manners and laws (they) are entirely ignorant'. There was rejoicing in Welsh hearts when a treacherous attack during the peace negotiations by the English (though possibly not authorised by Edward) failed. Unable to capitulate with honour intact Llywelyn, in desperate hopes of support, set out towards the south. Emmisaries arrived from various marcher lords, notably the Mortimers and the Giffards, indicating that they were prepared to negotiate with him. Llywelyn was still at the head of an army of almost 8,000 men but, on 10 December 1282, he and a group of about eighteen loyal retainers and his squire became detached from his main force at Cilmeri. The eighteen were left to guard a ford while Llywelyn, with just his young squire, set off to meet a young noblewoman – the contact who would lead them to the proposed rendezvous. This lady failed to appear and immediately the pair were ambushed, but managed to escape and take refuge in a cave. After some time they emerged and were able to ford the river to scramble back to their comrades. On 11 December the eighteen gallant heroes guarded the ford and allowed Llywelyn and his young squire to make a desperate bid to rejoin the Welsh army. All fell in the attempt. Llywelyn and his squire were discovered staggering along a wooded track in the snow. The lad was killed, and then Llywelyn was mortally wounded, possibly by one Stephen de Frankton and a retainer of Roger Lestrange called Robert Body. Llywelyn was wearing no armour. There are conflicting accounts of what happened. The *Brut y Tywysogion*, the chronicle of the Kings of the Britons since Brutus and Camber should perhaps have the final word about the circumstances of the death of Llywelyn 'the Last': 'And then Roger Mortimer and Gruffydd ap Gwenwynwyn and with them the king's host came upon them without warning, and then Llywelyn and his foremost men were slain'.

At first it was not realised that the man killed was Llywelyn, but the royal seal was found on him and a priest came forward who had heard his last confession, who confirmed his identity. Robert Body decapitated Llywelyn and washed the head in a nearby well. The seal, along with his head, were sent to London, where Llywelyn's head was decorated with an ivy wreath to symbolise his outlawry and set up on display at the Tower, in a mocking allusion to the Welsh prophesy that a Welsh prince would one day be 'crowned king in London'. It remained there for fifteen years, but the rest of his body was, eventually, given Christian burial. The Welsh army, completely unaware of the fate of their prince, were surprised shortly afterwards and almost annihilated. Dafydd survived him, but his desultory war fizzled out and all castles loyal to him fell. On 2 October 1283 he was hanged drawn and quartered, and his head taken to be set up next to his brother's. The ultimate catastrophe had finally been visited upon the desolated Welsh people. Their bards knew it well enough. One of them, Gruffydd ap yr Ynad Coch put it thus:

> Do you not see the path of the wind and the rain?
> Do you not see the oaks beating together?
> Do you not see the sea scourging the land?
> Do you not see the truth preparing itself?
> Do you not see the sun sailing the heavens?
> Do you not see the stars fallen?
> Do you not believe in God, simple men?
> Do you not see that the world has ended?

This apocalyptic moment, the end of liberty and the extirpation of the long and noble line of warriors and kings, stretching back into a distant, half-mythical past, was an ineluctable fact. However the Celtic resistance was far from over.

For Edward, the triumph in Wales was personal. The great castles that most symbolise Wales in our day – Harlech, Caernarfon, Beaumaris and the rest – were constructed by the most pre-eminent designers in Europe, principally Master James of St Georges, a Savoyard. Conwy and Harlech were both completed soon after the Conquest; the idea of the fortresses was that they could be supplied by sea, so that the long supply trains winding over the mountain passes, vulnerable to ambush and enfilade, were no longer essential to maintain large garrisons. An iron grip had been established and a ring of mighty fortresses, unsurpassed even by the crusader castles of the Holy Land, isolated Gwynedd, heartland of the culture that was now to be eradicated. The consequences of the defeat were cataclysmic. Llywelyn's baby daughter, Gwenllian, was immured in a nunnery at Sempringham in England where she remained for over fifty years until she died. The native Gilbertine order built high walls around their priories so this prevented either her escape or contact with the outside world. Even if her countrymen had managed to make contact she could speak no Welsh, not even knowing how to pronounce her own name correctly. Edward reminded the pope of the (paltry) financial cost of keeping the girl as a prisoner, almost complaining about this, the consequence of his own directive. In latter years a memorial has been put up at Sempringham, and another lonelier memorial stands on the summit of Snowdon to this Welsh princess who knew nothing of her native land. Dafydd's son, Owain, was simply thrown into a dungeon and forgotten about and his daughters also shut away in nunneries. The lesser kings of Wales, most of whom had supported the rebellion, were punished and their inheritances made forfeit to the Crown – they were, after all, 'contumacious vassals'. All regalia and emblems of the Welsh nation were removed and taken to London, including the crown jewels and the *Croes Naid*, which was said to contain a fragment of the True Cross. Edward enjoyed the humiliation of the Welsh and arranged a grand tournament at Nefyn, where he flaunted his armed might and mimed Arthurian themes. The army of occupation were taunting the subjugated Celts and using their own folk-myths – perhaps one of the cruellest jokes in history. A crown had been taken, indeed, which was said to have belonged to Arthur himself. The Merlinic prophesies were invoked to glorify Edward by Pierre de Langtoft, an English canon, who compares Edward's conquests to the glories of Arthur:

> Ah God! How often Merlin said truth
> In his prophesies if you read them!
> Now are the two waters united in one,
> Which have been separated by great mountains;
> And one realm made of two different kingdoms
> Which used to be governed by two kings.
> Now are all the islanders all joined together,
> And Albany reunited to the royalties
> Of which King Edward is proclaimed lord.
> Cornwall and Wales are in his power,
> And Ireland the great at his will.
> There is neither king nor prince of all the countries
> Except King Edward, who has thus united them;
> Arthur never held the fiefs so fully.

All references to the Welsh 'nation' or the Welsh 'people' were strictly forbidden. Henceforth, it was merely *terra Walliae* 'the Land of Wales', and in it Edward's word was law; no appeal to native law or custom was permitted. For over a year Edward remained in Wales, personally supervising the imposition of the new order. He mobilised the resources of the entire English kingdom, monies, labourers and craftsmen, the most ingenious designers and master masons of Europe, and set to work to interpenetrate Wales with a network of castles unprecedented for a country of its size, a project that almost bankrupted the English treasury.

At Caernarfon, the extent of Edward's obsession with the ancient Welsh mythology and the links to ancient Rome were revealed. The place had been Segontium, a Roman fort that had legendary connections to the Emperor Constantine and 'Macsen', or Magnus Maximus. Edward claimed to have discovered what were claimed to be his remains, which he had reburied there (he had done the same thing with the putative remains of 'King Arthur' which had been discovered at Glastonbury). The polygonal towers and variegated stone walls were in deliberate imitation of the Theodosian wall of Constantinople, one of the most remarkable fortresses anywhere in the world at the time. Surmounted by statues of imperial eagles, this was to be the centre of the new regime. The whole country was interpenetrated by a network of English boroughs, with English burgesses – no Welshman could live in them, and they were excluded from the civic organisations within them. Perhaps most pointedly, the Welsh stopped composing poetry – the royal Welsh patrons who supported the bards were now impoverished and enfeebled, where these had survived. In all likelihood, even that most enduring Welsh diversion, song, was driven to the verge of extinction. Welsh farmers were driven off the most fertile land to be replaced by retainers of the English incomers – two cooks who had served in the Earl of Lincoln's support-train were given estates in Clwyd as a reward. The entire country became a cash cow for England. Edward's conquest was absolute and the Statute of Rhuddlan in 1284 spelt out the abject nature of Welsh subjection:

The land of Wales is annexed and united ... unto our crown of the aforesaid realm as a member of the same body ... we have caused to be rehearsed before us the laws and customs of those parts ... which being diligently heard and fully understood ... we have abolished certain of them, some thereof we have allowed, and some we have corrected.

In 1294, Madog ap Llywelyn called himself 'Prince of Wales' and led an abortive rebellion, but now Wales was truly conquered and the castles prevented a united insurgency across the entire country. Edward seemed triumphant, but his Celtic wars had only just begun.

14

The Wider Celtic Struggle

My rationale for concentrating in particular on the *Brythoniaid*, the Britons who had been the pre-Anglo-Saxon inhabitants of the island, who gradually morphed into the Welsh, Cumbrians and Cornish, is that it was they who were most exposed to the successive invasions of Britain by various peoples, until their penultimate independent prince and his people were eventually compressed into a final redoubt in Gwynedd. It was this element of the Celtic population that had preserved a quasi-historical lineage connecting them with the kingdoms of North Britain, and to the Roman Empire – the foundations of the mythical lore known as the Matter of Britain. The evolution of this mythology became a legitimating cover story for what was, in effect, a rehearsal for global imperial expansionism from the sixteenth century onwards and, indeed, Edward's campaigns were the first step on the road to the 'British Empire'. Notwithstanding this deliberately narrow focus, it is time now to consider the fate of the other Celtic nations, for they too became victims of English and French expansionism. Related to the insular Britons and emanating from Britain originally, the Bretons had strong ties to their Celtic cousins, in particular with the Cornish. Hazy memories preserved a tradition that the Roman usurper emperor Magnus Maximus, or 'Macsen', had established the first British colonies in Armorica (Brittany) even before the barbarian threat had grown serious in the fifth century. Another Western Emperor, Anthemius, had summoned a British leader called Riothamus or 'John Reith' to help him repel the barbarian Visigoths. This was in AD 469 or thereabouts; Riothamus commanded 12,000 men, a very considerable force – the equivalent of two Roman legions. These troops could not have come from Britain at this time, for the legions had been withdrawn over half a century before. What we must surmise is that the cadres for this army were drawn from Bretons living in Armorica, and to provide such a large number of fighting men suggests that the Bretons were populous, well organised and capable of mounting large military operations planned and executed by their own kings (the historian Jordanes called Riothamus a *rex*). Unfortunately Riothamus and his army were decisively defeated by the Visigoths at Deols in central France. Nevertheless, this ambitious campaign demonstrates that the Britons had arrived in the peninsula in large numbers and with an organised military and almost certainly they would have had to fight the indigenous Celtic people who were already in situ to establish their colonies, just as the Anglo-Saxons did in Britain. Soon almost all of the northern and western part of the peninsula was controlled by the incomers, who seem to have set up small regional dioceses whose names recalled the kingdoms they had abandoned, such as Domnonia (Dumnonia) and Cornouaille (Cornovia) or Kerneo, analogous to Kernow or Cornwall, with which people they traded. There was a constant interchange of cultural and especially religious ideas between the peninsulas and many of the Celtic saints of Brittany came from Britain.

The Bretons were one of the last Celtic people to relinquish their independence, and it was not until 1532 that they agreed to be, 'united under certain conditions with the kingdom of France but not subject to it', at Vannes. Their battle to preserve their freedom was truly heroic and only the very briefest outline can be given here, but it followed a pattern quite similar to the gradual encroachment on its autonomy by its larger neighbour we have followed in Wales. From the earliest times it was known as 'Britannia' and was fiercely protective of its Celtic Christian inheritance. One of their kings, Waroch II – ruler of the Vannetais or Gwened (these people may have originated in Venedotia or Gwynedd) – was attacked by King Chilperic of the Franks in 578 and the Bretons fought bravely, especially on account of the fact that Chilperic had employed Saxon allies in his army against them. Waroch eventually came to terms. Each independent canton or diocese had its own petty ruler, as in Wales. French kings attempted to extract tribute from the Bretons, usually without success until the reign of the mighty Charlemagne. He sent his most famous warrior, Roland, to be the marcher lord on the borders around Nantes and Rennes. The Bretons responded in exactly the same way as their Celtic cousins in Wales – raids over the border. Louis the Pious pushed deep into Brittany and sent envoys to demand that the Bretons capitulate. Their leader, Leiz-Breiz, or Morvan, sent the reply,

> Go with all speed to your lord with this reply: I do not till his land and I do not want his laws. Let him reign over the Franks, I Morvan, will reign over the Bretons. It is my right as it is his. If the Franks want war let there be war. There is still strength in my right arm.

These brave words could not prevail against the power of Louis. Morvan was forced to back down. Louis faced continual rebellion, however, and in 824 he installed Nominoe, a loyal subordinate as duke of Brittany in hopes of bringing order there. The plan spectacularly backfired. Nominoe managed to unite the separate cantons under his leadership as Gruffydd and Llywelyn had done in Wales, with exactly the same result: Erispoe, his son, was murdered by a jealous cousin called Salaun and the Celts resumed their traditional squabbling. Salaun was himself assassinated by rebellious subjects in 874. He had allied himself to the Vikings. Their brutal and destructive raiding along the Breton coast made them hated and they vented their fury on their king. In 890 at Questembert Alain, the Count of Vannes defeated the Vikings, for which achievement he gained the sobriquet 'Alain the Great'. Thanks to that ancient Celtic curse, partible inheritance, it was impossible for the Bretons to maintain a national unity for any length of time, and when Charles 'the Simple' of France ceded large adjacent territories to the Vikings they were confronted with a dangerous enemy on their frontiers. Their only hope was an appeal to the mighty English king Athelstan, and with his financial and military aid the Vikings were driven back. The situation in Brittany resembled the ravaged kingdom of Wessex, with many churches and monasteries destroyed, and the clergy slaughtered or driven into exile. More seriously, perhaps, the Breton population halved in this period, a sign of the devastation the Vikings had wreaked there.

The year 1066 is as momentous in Breton history as it is in English, for in that year Conan II their King died, and Duke William of Normandy summoned thousands of Bretons into his army for his expedition against England. A third of the 'Norman' army (it was in fact a heterogeneous force composed of Normans, French, Flemings, Bretons and others) was Breton, and in the land-grab in England that followed Hastings they were amply rewarded with estates on the western frontiers such as Devon and Cornwall and the area around Monmouthshire. They had the natural advantage of being conversant with the native language, which was virtually identical to Breton. This 'homecoming' was the key to the extraordinary reinvention of the Arthurian tales, which we have seen previously, and while it is true that they originated in Britain, it was the Breton versions that influenced medieval culture more widely. This led to a tragic incident, in which history and myth coalesced. To legitimate the claims of Henry II of England in Brittany and other French regions the Arthurian myth had been subtly doctored, to make Arthur a King of *Lloegyr* corresponding to England, and also of large parts of western Gaul, including Brittany. Conan IV of Brittany had made an alliance with Henry by marrying his daughter to Henry's son, Geoffrey. Geoffrey succeeded to the Duchy of Brittany and immediately used this as an opportunity to cut off ties with his father and negotiate with the French king (the Plantagenet family was notorious for its internal intrigues). Geoffrey's schemes were foiled when he died before his father, and Henry perished soon afterwards in 1189. But Geoffrey had left an heir, born posthumously, who was deliberately given the name Arthur. The boy was used as a pawn by King Philip of France, who invested him as Duke of Brittany when he made war on King John of England. The creation of a powerful leader called Arthur raised Celtic hopes, but these were dashed. Arthur was taken prisoner by his uncle, John, who either arranged or actually committed the murder of the sixteen-year-old boy at Rouen on 3 April 1203. The Bretons managed to survive as an independent duchy and their politics and the military campaigns against them were along very similar lines to the Welsh resistance, but eventually Francois I of France arranged events in such a way, using shrewd financial inducements, that the Bretons requested a union with France in 1532. It became very much like Wales, an economic backwater, the butt of sneering and mockery. Like their Welsh cousins who were punished at school with the infamous 'Welsh Not', a signboard that they were forced to wear to discourage use of their native tongue; Breton children were also subjected to these vile injustices. In recent times a cultural revival has taken place and Breton is still spoken widely and, like Wales, although it has eventually become subsumed, it retains its own distinctive Celtic identity.

Language and culture are the keys to survival, and God-willing, resurgence, as is demonstrated in the case of another Celtic nation, Ireland. As I have indicated in the introduction, the long and complex story of Ireland is beyond my scope in this brief work, but I am permitted to involve it insofar as it affects the wider story. In brief, Henry II of England invoked the *laudabiliter* – a papal bull authorising him to collect 'Peter's Penny' in Ireland and to institute reforms in its Church. The warring Celtic chieftains actually welcomed him, but soon had cause to regret the arrival of a new Anglo-Norman noble class, who were as rapacious and brutal as they were in England and Wales. In time they were absorbed by the native culture, even adopting Gaelic variants on their names. The Irish became the most abused of all the colonies of the British Empire, and its ruling elite suffered the mass starvation and emigration which followed the Great Irish Famine in the mid-nineteenth century to continue, until millions had died or sought exile in 'coffin-ships' to North America. On 24 April 1916, however, there was an unusual disturbance in Dublin, 'a row in the town'. Writing in the centenary year of these events, I will intentionally divert and mark them, because they stand, as it were, as a vignette of all that had gone so badly wrong with British rule over so many centuries.

On Easter Monday 1916 a group of Irish revolutionaries about 1,500 strong converged on Dublin, and occupied key strategic buildings, the Four Courts, Jacob's biscuit factory, St Stephen's

Green, the South Dublin Union Hospital, Westland Row Station, City Hall and the General Post Office on the (then) Sackville Street. Many of the 'Irish Republican Brotherhood' or I. R. B had ridden in on bicycles. Another group 'Plunkett's Own', as they called their ramshackle unit, crammed aboard a tram and struggled to find enough change to pay the tuppence fares. Joseph Plunkett, their eponymous leader, had been appointed as their 'general' on the dubious basis that he had owned a set of toy soldiers as a schoolboy. At the General Post Office a British officer was posting a letter to his aunt when he was astonished to find himself the first prisoner of war taken during the insurrection. The Union Flag was taken down, and a new one hoisted in its stead – the green and gold flag of the Irish Republic. The bemused Dubliners looked on as Padraic Pearse emerged to read the proclamation of a new, but also very ancient, nation:

> Irishmen and Irishwomen: in the name of God and of the dead generations from which she receives her old tradition of nationhood, Ireland, through us, summons her children to her flag and strikes for her freedom. Having organised and trained her manhood through her secret revolutionary organisation, the Irish Republican Brotherhood, and through her military organisations the Irish Volunteers and the Irish Citizen Army, having patiently perfected her discipline, having resolutely waited for the right moment to reveal itself, she now seizes that moment, and supported by her exiled children in America, and by gallant allies in Europe, but relying in the first on her own strength, she strikes in full confidence of victory ... the Republic guarantees religious and civil liberty, equal rights and equal opportunities to all its citizens, and declares its resolve to pursue the happiness and prosperity of all its parts, cherishing all the children of the nation equally, and oblivious of the differences carefully fostered by an alien government which have divided a minority from the majority in the past ... we place the cause of the Irish Republic under the protection of the most high God whose blessing we invoke upon our arms, and we pray that no-one who serves the cause will dishonour it by cowardice, inhumanity or rapine. In this supreme hour the Irish nation must, by its valour and discipline,

and by the readiness of its children to sacrifice themselves for the
common good, prove itself worthy of the august destiny to which
it is called.

It is perhaps the most eloquent suicide note in history, for the
rebels were quite serious. The symbolism of Easter, of death and
resurrection, must, they knew, find its mark in the psyche of this
most religious of peoples. They must have known that Britain, at
the height of its effort on the Western Front in the First World War
(1914–1918) would react with brutal celerity and so it proved.
There were 5,000 British troops around Dublin and these were
quickly reinforced by the North Midland Division, which was
dispatched from Liverpool. When they disembarked, many of
them assumed they were in France and greeted the local Irish girls
with ribald comments in French. The Dubliners had taken the
opportunity to commit mass looting of shops and the British troops
moved in. The IRB had already fired on the looters but suddenly a
British gunboat, the *Helga* opened fire from the Liffey and the empty
Liberty Hall was shelled. The British declared a state of martial law
and a Captain Bowen-Colthurst shot a young lad in front of an
adult witness, Sheehy Skeffington, who protested. He and three
other complainants were also taken away and executed on the spot.
On North King Street soldiers bayoneted civilian bystanders. As the
British troops arrived and artillery was brought into play Dublin
became a desperate battleground. Countess Marcievicz and her
volunteers at St Stephen's Green were forced to flee to the shelter of
the College of Surgeons. All week the savage battle raged on, until
finally, exhausted and out of ammunition, the rebels surrendered
at Tom Clarke's shop on Parnell Street. There was much anger
and resentment among Dubliners towards the rebels but this soon
changed when the British began executing the revolutionary leaders
who had been taken as prisoners. Theirs had truly been a brave
and noble sacrifice, to stand beside any of the other gallant Celtic
fighters in this story. Their sacrifice was not in vain. Within a few
years a free Irish nation was established in most of the island of
Ireland, the only independent Celtic nation at the time of writing.
The British hold on most of Ireland was always tenuous and the
callousness and brutality that characterised their custody of Ireland

could not fail to turn the hearts and minds of a proud and ancient nation against them. It was in its oldest colony, Ireland, ironically, that the fracture and disintegration of the British Empire began. The final nation we must consider briefly is Scotland, and we can at this point take up the story of Edward I and his wars, for having subjugated Wales at last, he now turned his gaze upon that second Celtic nation.

Rebelliousness against tyranny was not a peculiarly Irish or Welsh trait, but seems to be a characteristic of the Celts. The English thought that the Welsh predilection for insurrection was due to something 'in the air' and that they became 'light-headed' and susceptible to impulsive phantasy. The Celts have certainly produced their fair share of rebels and even 'Che' Guevara had Irish ancestors, so it is time to consider the career of another archetypal Celtic outlaw, William Wallace. This famous Scottish figure, the hero of an extravagant cinematic production of recent times, had other Celtic connections. He spelt his name 'Walays', which is derived from the English word *Walh* we have examined in a previous chapter – the Latin form is *Wallensis*, 'the Welshman'. William's ancestors had served the Fitz-Alan family, who were Breton marcher lords from Clun, and with such a name they must have been indigenous. The Fitz-Alans and their retainers, such as Richard le Walays, had been given a considerable land grant in Ayrshire and would eventually become kings. They became 'stewards' of the Scottish royalty, which name they changed to Stuart, the dynasty that eventually ruled over Scotland, Ireland and England. Wallace, however, was of lowlier stock, minor yeomanry, though by no means the rogue and thief portrayed in English propaganda about him after his death. In all likelihood he would have remained obscure had it not been for the time in which he lived. A brief introduction to the political background will elucidate this. Edward I of England had taken advantage of disputes between various cousins and their factions about the Scottish succession and had agreed to act as a broker there, in exchange for their recognition of him as 'Lord Superior of Scotland'. The reader will be familiar with Edward's character and will not be surprised to learn that conflict was in the air. When John Balliol came to the throne of Scotland in 1292 Edward bullied and intimidated him as if Scotland were a mere vassal state, and demanded troops for a campaign against France. There remained the alternative course – an alliance with France – and the Scots cemented 'the auld alliance' with Edward's enemy instead of responding to his commands. In 1296, King John of Scotland suffered the same fate as the Welsh and was forced into a humiliating climbdown. The emblems of Scottish royalty, its crown jewels and seals of office, were taken into England in a repeat of the Welsh humiliation. Even the Stone of Scone on which the Scottish kings were crowned was taken away by Edward, along with the hapless King John as his prisoner. In fact, in every way Edward simply repeated the process he had enforced on Wales and treated Scotland as a conquered 'land', not, mind you, a 'nation' any longer – Scotland had ceased to exist in his mind. Earl Warenne, the commander who had served Edward so well during his campaign, was rewarded with the dubious honour of the governorship of the 'conquered' territory. Edward dismissed the country as he left Warenne in charge: '*Bon bosoigne fait qy de merde se deliver*' or 'it does a man good to rid himself of shit'. This contemptuous attitude, the arrogance of a man whose entire experience had been predicated on a belief in his divine selection to become the embodiment of the Arthurian traditions, percolated down through the ranks of the occupying English garrisons. Warenne soon tired of the country and returned to his estates in England, leaving Scotland to a deputy, Hugh Cressingham, his treasurer (the Scots called him a 'treacherer'). This left Hugh and his accomplice, Chief Justice William Ormsby, in a powerful position to line their own pockets at the expense of the Scots, which they duly did – by manipulating the oath of allegiance that every Scotsman was required to swear, and charging them for the privilege. To refuse the oath meant instant outlaw status. Many people, of course, avoided the oath, or were content to be outlawed. There were many such renegades, but in 1297 one of them slew the Sheriff of Lanark. His assailant was our hero, William Wallace. He was later the subject of vituperative propaganda by the English – he was called 'a bloody man', 'a thief', and 'a leader of brigands'. It may well be true that his initial skirmishes with the authorities were minor affairs but, like so many other Celtic rebellions, his insurgency flared into a full-scale war and a savage revenge on those who had trampled on Scotland's honour.

The immediate cause of the rebellion was that ancient Celtic controversy – land entitlement. Wallace's brother Andrew had died at the hands of the English, and his estates, which should have passed to Wallace, had been sequestered by one William Hazelrig, the Sheriff of Lanark. Wallace, presumably already an outlaw, had forfeited his rights so attacked with a small band of followers and broke in on Hazelrig, overwhelming his small bodyguard. The hapless sheriff was stripped naked and cut into pieces, which were sent far and wide as proof of the seriousness of rebel intent to other Scottish renegades. Soon hundreds of outlaws flocked to join the rebellion, but among them there were true patriots whose motivation was revenge on the hated English. Galloway was attacked and at Ayr a night attack burned 300 sleeping English soldiers in their billets. These grim exploits soon earned Wallace fame, but a more effective ploy was the simple expedient of spreading rumours to the effect that the Scottish yeomanry class was to be resettled by Edward, and their lands appropriated. The Scottish Kirk also harboured deep unease about Edward's intentions and Bishop Robert Wishart had his priests promulgate the notion that the English king intended to make the Church an extension of royal power in Scotland. James 'the Stewart', Wallace's technical landlord took no active measures against him, and this amounted to collusion with the rebels. Other local risings followed in the remoter regions in 1297 but as yet there was no truly national support. To take things to a new level a spectacular raid was required, and Wallace attracted the backing of a nobleman, Sir William Douglas, for his next scheme. The plan was to strike nearly 100 miles across country and eliminate the hated Chief Justice Ormsby in a repeat of the Hazelrig affair. Ormsby managed a narrow escape but when it was known that Wallace was in Perthshire a fresh host of recruits joined the rebels. Their numbers were now in the thousands and they proceeded to vent their anger on any Englishmen they could find:

> They even dragged English monks violently from monasteries and made a spectacle and sport of them ... they took old men, priests and women of the English nation (who they had kept specially alive for the purpose) to bridges over rivers: when they had tied

their hands together, so they could not swim they pushed or threw them into the water, laughing and jeering as they went under...

Not even their cloth or the sanctuary of Holy Church could save the English now and it was necessary to dispatch a relieving force led by two English lords to intimidate the rebels. Many of Wallace's fresh recruits abandoned the cause and went home with their booty. The convulsion was not sufficiently appreciated by Edward, despite frantic pleas from Cressingham, whose revenues from taxation had ceased. Henry Percy and Robert Clifford, the lords sent to interdict the rebels, were quite convinced they had crushed the rebellion, but Wallace was still in arms, and while he lived trouble could flare up anywhere and at any time. This was exactly what happened, for Wallace left his refuge in the Selkirk Forest and marched to conjoin with Andrew Moray to besiege Dunbar. The Earl of Warenne, after much delay, was leading an English army to finally destroy Wallace, and his project was to link up with the English garrison of Stirling Castle, which guarded the Forth Bridge below. The Scottish rebel army were on the opposite side of the river and a parley took place, delaying the vital river crossing to the English. In fact many of the vanguard were Welshmen serving in the English army and they did cross but were recalled because their commander was still asleep. Eventually, a second crossing was made, but again aborted for envoys from Wallace finally arrived, and it was assumed they had come to surrender. They came with less welcome tidings, Wallace intended to stand and fight. Two friars were sent urgently to find out if this was really true, and to ask him to make peace but they were rebuffed with these words from Wallace, 'Go back and tell your people that we have not come here for peace: we are ready, rather, to fight to avenge ourselves and to free our country. Let them come up to us as soon as they like, and they will find us prepared to prove the same in their beards.' These were defiant words, spoken by a determined and confident man, for 20,000 Scotsmen stood with Wallace, and in him they had chosen a ruthless and cunning commander.

Wallace knew that the English could only cross the bridge two abreast and that when they did cross they would be funnelled into a narrow causeway between areas of boggy low-lying ground.

The main Scottish army blocked the English advance from high ground called Abbey Crag, but another force was dispatched to seize the rebel side of the bridge once a sizeable proportion of the English had crossed, but before the main army came over. The English vanguard, over 5,000 men, which included the portly figure of the hated 'Treacherer', Cressingham, found it was cut off and they either jumped into the Forth where they drowned, or were hacked to pieces by howling mobs of blood-crazed Scotsmen. In Cressingham's case, he was flayed and pieces of his skin handed out as trophies, Wallace made a sword-belt out of his portion. Five thousand English (and Welsh) soldiers were wiped out in a frenzied bloodlust. Warenne, who was by now well and truly awake, hurriedly called for the bridge to be destroyed before galloping 100 miles to refuge in Berwick Castle. It was no use appealing to Edward, for he was in Flanders, and the Battle of Stirling Bridge gave Scotland a unique opportunity to regain its national liberty. What had been a mere local rebellion had now become a matter of the utmost importance for King Edward, 'the Hammer of the Scots', but for the time being it was Wallace's moment, and he was duly rewarded by his people. There was now nothing to stop him and during winter he harried into England where his army took much booty from the terrified folk of Northumberland and Cumbria. When he heard of these outrages Edward was apoplectic. Stories were widely circulating of Scottish atrocities, the slaughter of babies and so forth, which were always told in the aftermath of Scottish incursions, but they spread panic. It was time for Edward to respond personally in his own inimitable style.

Wallace, inconveniently, was not of royal blood, but he was knighted and elected as the 'Guardian of the Kingdom of Scotland'. He must have known that Edward would strike hard and soon with a professional army composed of specialists of all arms. Such an army could not be resisted by half-trained militias, and he needed officers of noble rank to whom the rank-and-file looked for inspiration. If the nobles failed in their duty, or worse, if they were actively hostile to Wallace personally (many resented being subordinated to a commoner), the Scottish nation would simply collapse. Therefore, Wallace appealed over their heads, and ordered a national conscription of every able-bodied fighting man, a truly national army. This was inculcated into every common soldier, that it was his patriotic duty to defend his hearth and home, and Wallace exhorted the men to choose death, rather than subjugation. Command status was accorded to men of ability whatever their rank and strict discipline enforced. These men would need 'brave hearts' indeed, for the Edwardian war machine was in preparation. In summer 1298, King Edward led an army of 2,500 heavy cavalry, 13,000 archers (of which 10,500 were Welshmen), and supporting men-at-arms into Scotland. Wallace fell back and burned the countryside as the great English force came on, leaving them no provisions. The Welshmen became restless, and when a cargo of wine was intercepted they became so roaring drunk that they turned on their English allies and slew a number of them. The riot was quelled but the surly Welshmen muttered threats that they would join Wallace to fight the Sais. The strategy of scorched earth seemed to be reaping its reward but suddenly a report came in that the Scottish army was at Falkirk, only a day's march away. The king ordered his men to get to sleep but during the night he was kicked by his own horse, breaking his ribs; the tough sexagenarian immediately mounted and led his forces out in the morning. On the mass of St Mary Magdalene, 22 July 1298, Edward's army sighted the Scots. Wallace had taken the courageous decision to confront the mightiest warrior in Europe. His army were drawn up in formations called *scheltrouns* or 'hedgehogs', with tightly-packed bodies of spearmen holding their long spears at an oblique angle to repel cavalry. In addition stakes had been driven into the ground and ropes attached in a sort of fence, which the men thought looked like the 'rings' at country fayres and dances. Wallace then appeared and, contrary to the cinematic oratory, he just made a simple joke to his men about this: 'I have brought you to the ring, now let's see you dance.' Wallace's men awaited the onslaught and as soon as the heavy cavalry came on, the Scottish cavalry, many of them noblemen, spurred their horses in the opposite direction. This was fatal, because the most dangerous part of Edward's army, his archers, could now deploy forwards unopposed. The cavalry could not penetrate the Scottish 'hedgehog' formations. Edward ordered forward his Welsh archers, but at first they hung back, still sulking about the earlier incident, but Edward was not a man to cross. Soon they were unleashing a literal rain of arrows and crossbow bolts – 100,000 per minute – into the Scottish positions. They fell where they stood, unable to escape for fear of the English horsemen, until 'their bodies covered the ground as thickly as the snow in winter.' Over 10,000 brave Scotsmen fell that day; English losses were light. The devastated common people blamed their nobles who had betrayed their hero, and Wallace survived the battle to fight another day. But for all that, Falkirk was a crushing and brutal defeat, supervised by a ruthless and vengeful King Edward, who was now determined to impose himself on the rest of the country. As he marched north, Wallace ensured only smoking ruins were left for him, and this policy succeeded, for Edward's starving army was forced to withdraw. Edward was content to let the Scottish nobles decide Wallace's fate, knowing full well he was doomed.

John Comyn and Robert Bruce soon replaced Wallace as 'guardians' of Scotland and the latter was forced to find refuge among the common people for whom he was still a folk hero. He continued to wage his own personal war on the hated English even travelling abroad to canvass the support of foreign monarchs, but his stock was now too low for any hope of success. By 1301 he was at large in Scotland again and this was enough to require a fresh invasion by Edward, and once more the Scottish nobility chose capitulation. Edward put up a reward of the then vast sum of £200 for Wallace's head. Edward's stratagems extended to more cunning methods. A prisoner whose family had served Wallace in the rebellion of 1297, Ralph Haliburton, was released, and knowing his hiding places he infiltrated himself into Wallace's inner circle. Wallace was taken 'in bed with his whore', according to one source, at Robroyston on 5 August 1305. He was placed under arrest by Sir John Stewart, the local sheriff and conveyed south to London. By 22 August, baying mobs had gathered in the streets of London to see the manacled captive paraded, to be pelted with rotten vegetables and eggs. The next day Wallace was arraigned, and a laurel crown placed upon his head in mockery. There was no trial. Wallace was a known public enemy, but when the charges were read to him Wallace cried out that he could not be guilty of treason for he was not a subject of the Crown, but he was guilty as charged for the rest. Then he was dragged away behind horses naked all the way from Westminster Hall to Aldgate wrapped in a bull hide. At Smithfield he was hanged, then cut down alive before being disembowelled. Then his 'privy parts' were cut off. His liver, heart and lungs were torn out before, finally, he was beheaded (the head was later stuck on a spike on London Bridge). His organs were then burned, from which the poison of rebellion had proceeded, and the body hacked into four quarters, which were preserved in tar barrels to be sent for public display – one each in Berwick, Newcastle, Stirling and Perth. It was a terrible end, but Wallace's revolt and his brief rule had awakened a new, popular, consciousness in Scotland, and we must concur with the cinematic version in one respect – Wallace did indeed lay the foundation for Scottish liberty, the noble cause for which he had sacrificed so much, indeed, the utmost any man can give.

By 1307 Scotland was flexing its muscles once more under Robert the Bruce. Edward was now sixty-eight but set off to Scotland with his army as he had done on countless other such campaigns, but died before he reached the border. He was succeeded by his son, also called Edward II but he was a man of a very different stamp from his austere forbidding father. He was effeminate, and had a passion for play acting and dancing, with male partners. He openly promoted his most favoured friend, Piers Gaveston, and antagonised his chief councillors and major grandees. What was worse, he had absolutely no military skills. Robert the Bruce took swift advantage of this and by 1314 only one lonely English garrison at Stirling Castle remained. It was imperative to relieve the fortress and so an army of 25,000 men was assembled, which Edward led into Scotland with the intention of breaking through by Midsummer's Day, 24 June. Over a quarter of the English army were Welsh foot soldiers. The garrison at Stirling had made it clear that without reinforcement by that day they would capitulate. Edward's troops came in sight of the castle on 23 June, just in time, but the Bruce was waiting there. He left behind a small force to besiege the castle, but prepared to meet the main English army on carefully chosen ground at Bannockburn nearby. The Scots were outnumbered by over two to one, but they had learned their lessons from Wallace well. On either flank of his position, the

Bruce had protected his flanks by utilising a ridge above an area of bog called the Carse of Stirling. In front of him a stream, the Bannock Burn, provided an obstacle, and to his rear dense woods enabled swift retirement if necessary, but a natural obstacle to cavalry pursuit. Entrenchments and pits were excavated along his front, hidden by bracken, within which sharpened stakes had been driven. In short, a killing ground had been cunningly prepared, as at Stirling Bridge, and the Scottish troops were confident with high morale. King Edward did not think so. When the Scottish army were observed to kneel to say Mass he exclaimed, 'See! They kneel to beg for our mercy!' but he received a chilling reply from a Scottish mercenary serving in his ranks, 'Aye, but not from you. They kneel to ask it from God, and now you must either win here, or see your army perish!'

The Bruce almost came to grief before proper battle was joined. Henry de Bohun, an English knight, blundered into the Bruce as he was inspecting his lines and promptly charged him, but the Bruce deftly side-stepped on his little grey palfrey and parried with a blow from an axe, which cleaved Sir Henry's skull. This was observed by the Scots with great merriment – a good omen. Unlike Falkirk, where the Scottish cavalry had fled the field, as soon as Edward's archers came on they met an immediate response, which was crucial. Edward ordered forward his own heavy cavalry to drive them off but they careered into the concealed pits and were impaled. Wave upon wave of English infantry were building up behind the stricken men and horses who could barely manoeuvre, but eventually some of Edward's archers found their aim. Sensing that the English effort was faltering the Bruce ordered a general advance and the English front line broke. The Scottish camp-followers, even the womenfolk, now saw the powerless mass of suffocating Englishmen and they too joined in the slaughter with cooking knives, screaming, 'They fail! On them! Slay, slay, slay!' Edward had observed this new mass of Scots entering the fray and concluded that they must be some strategic reserve the Bruce had concealed. He immediately took flight and tried desperately to seek refuge in Stirling Castle but its disgusted garrison refused to let him in. He made his way to Dunbar and was eventually taken off by ship, deeply traumatised. The Scots had won a great victory and with it their precious liberty, which they retained precariously until the Acts of Union in 1706 and 1707 by which they united with England. So the Celts of Brittany, Ireland and Scotland, had known sanguinary struggles of their own against their larger neighbours, and it was not until the birth of the modern era that they were incorporated. Only humble Wales had been truly conquered, and during the fourteenth century its archers were at the core of the English army in the Hundred Years War with the House of Valois in France. The entire island was devastated by the Black Death, a pernicious plague that wiped out between a third and a half of the population. Here was one Celtic land at least where the English could be secure in the knowledge that the 'Red Dragon of Cadwaladr', the mythical beast that symbolised Welsh nationhood, had breathed its last fire. The bards could only lament, '*Gwae ni ein geni yn gaeth*' 'woe unto us, born to slavery.' But, just a few miles across Offa's Dyke in rural Wales, a child had been born. Strange omens accompanied his birth, as Shakespeare has him relate:

At my birth ... the frame and huge foundations of the earth shaked like a coward ... the goats ran down the mountains and the herds were strangely clamorous to the frightened fields, and all the courses of my life do show ... I am not in the roll of common men.

The *Mab Darogan* or 'Son of Prophesy', the long-awaited messiah of the British Celts, had entered into earthly manifestation. He bore the name Owain, as had been prophesied.

15

The Son of Prophesy

Wales did not formally unite with England until 1536 (around the same time the Bretons united with France) but by 1400 it was very heavily anglicised. The slow process of cultural assimilation meant the tense coexistence of both communities was only precariously maintained, but the devastating consequences of the Black Death preoccupied the minds of both Welshmen and Englishmen. In England there had been a popular uprising in 1381, the so-called Peasants' Revolt. Tensions had built up following the plague years, which manifested themselves in a new confident spirit among the yeomanry class, the men who formed the backbone of the English archers during the Hundred Years War. Such men often returned from the wars and failed to readjust to civilian life, using their deadly skills as outlaws and brigands. As the year 1400 approached there was a millenarian expectancy, and a rumour of a golden age that would soon be established where there would be peace, health and plentiful food, dancing and frolicking in 'the land of Cockayne', where hard labour would be unnecessary. The Peasants' Revolt had been brutally crushed, but the boy-king who had heroically disarmed the rebels became a brutal tyrant – Richard II. In 1399, Henry Bolingbroke, a son of John of Gaunt, the third son of Edward III, deposed Richard who was imprisoned and died shortly afterwards, probably of deliberate starvation. Bolingbroke thus became the new King of England, Henry IV. To have served the previous regime under Richard was consequently viewed with suspicion by Henry and his faction, and one of the Welsh nobles who had served Richard was a down-at-heel ex-lawyer turned small farmer named Owain ap Gruffudd Fychan, whose family estate was at Glyndyfrdwy in Merionethshire. Lord Reginald de Grey of Ruthin, Owain's neighbour, had seized common land at Croesau nearby. Owain Glyndwr, as he became known, had ancient grazing rights on the common and he knew his law. He took the case through the courts, then to Parliament itself, but he received no redress. De Grey was a personal friend of the new king and he intercepted a royal summons enlisting Glyndwr for military service. Craftily he then told the king that Glyndwr had failed to fulfil his obligation, the inference being that he was a disaffected partisan of the former regime and, by implication, a traitor. At his family home at Sycharth, Owain was seething with resentment and he was a man not to meddle with because although to Englishmen he seemed like a failing country gentleman (if a 'mere Welshman' merited the name of a 'gentleman'), in Welsh eyes he was something entirely different – the culmination, in one man, of all their long and illustrious history, all their hopes and dreams, the '*Mab Darogan*'.

Glyndwr had an illustrious pedigree and a propitious name. The Merlinic prophesies anticipated the incarnation of a glorious leader named Owain. He would be the last in a series of five Brythonic heroes; his predecessors had been Arthur, Cadwaladr, Cynan and Hiriell, an early King of Gwynedd. One of Llywelyn the Great's descendants had been named Owain Lawgoch, who, in the 1370s, obtained monies and a fleet from the French and made abortive attempts to instigate uprisings in Wales. Many had thought him to be the 'Owain' prophesied, but he was assassinated by agents of John of Gaunt, King Henry's father. So another candidate was eagerly sought, and a Welsh bard, Iolo Goch, 'a great teacher and minstrel', became convinced that he had found the very man. For a start, he was of royal blood, descended in the male line from the kings of Powys, and his mother was descended from that mighty Welsh hero the Lord Rhys. As Alex Gibbon points out in his *The Mystery of Jack of Kent & The Fate of Owain Glyndwr* (Stroud, 2004), the Lord Rhys was in turn descended from that mighty Celtic hero, Urien of Rheged, whose court bard was the famous Taliesin.

Gibbon postulates that Iolo Goch incited his patron into the rebellion having identified him as the promised redeemer at an early age. The formula of the particular emotional atmosphere appertaining to the promised deliverer was indicated to the bards by certain signs and portents, but the man himself remained in ignorance. His was a life of relative comfort and ease, though he would have been troubled with the usual cares of a country farmer, but life was good. Iolo describes Owain's hall at Sycharth:

> The court of a baron, a place of courtesy
> Where many bards come, a place of the good life
> Orchard, vineyard, white fortress
> Ploughs and strong steeds of great frame
> The deer park within that field
> A fine mill on a smooth-flowing stream
> Dovecote, a bright stone tower
> A fish pond, enclosed and deep
> His land a board where birds dwell
> Peacocks, high-stepping herons
> His servants do their work
> Bringing Shrewsbury's finest beer
> Whisky, the first-brewed bragget
> All drinks, fine white bread and wine
> His meat, and fire for the kitchen
> His children come in two-by-two
> A pretty nest of princes...

Would Glyndwr really have thrown all this away on account of some obscure prophesies? I think this ancient lore certainly played its part in stoking the fires of rebellion, but the fuel for the insurgency was something more, the *gormesoedd*, the afflictions, injustices, privations and oppression inflicted upon the Welsh by the English. The cursing hatred towards the Sais or *glam dicin* was evoked with renewed venom and it was a truly national feeling. Even Welsh scholars at the universities of Oxford and Cambridge abandoned their studies and returned to their native land to join in the rising. Gibbon is probably correct to assert that the bardic propaganda masked a deeper mystical tendency inherited from Druidic times.

The Celtic obsession with the number three gave the formula for the prophesied redeemer kings. First had come Owain of Rheged, then Owain Gwynedd, the redoubtable opponent of Henry II, and now another Owain – the culmination of the previous incarnations, a man of royal blood with a strong claim to the ancient kingdom of Gwynedd through his paternal descent from Bleddyn, had arrived to claim his inheritance. On 16 September 1400 Glyndwr was proclaimed Prince of Wales on his family estate with a few family retainers and relatives present to witness the event. To the English it probably seemed a minor farce, suitable for the 'bare footed clowns' and ragamuffins of rural Wales. Little did they realise the incredible convulsion that was about to befall them, for the rising took on an avenging fury of its own, until the whole of Wales was in flames, its soil bathed in blood.

On the very night Owain was born his father had been forced to wade through blood to tend his horses who were whinnying in panic in their stables, a strange enough omen in itself, but as the sullen boy grew he could not be comforted unless a weapon was put into his grasp. These were the signs that, 'have marked me extraordinary ... I am not in the roll of common men.' Alex Gibbon surmises that Owain was an adept, and could summon evil weather against his enemies, interpret the song and flight patterns of birds and other specialised faculties inherited through his bloodline. These are matters for the reader to judge, but we may concur that Glyndwr was a most extraordinary fellow. Two days after his investiture he rode out at the head of a motley collection of a few hundred of his local retainers. They cunningly infiltrated themselves into the market place of the Anglo-Norman borough of Ruthin, the stronghold of Glyndwr's enemy, de Grey. Suddenly producing concealed weapons, they proceeded to ransack the whole town; only a handful of buildings and the castle escaped the flames. New recruits flocked in and with lightning speed the rebels marched on Denbigh, Flint, Rhuddlan, Hawarden, all of them English boroughs, and burned them too. The conflagration soon spread to Welshpool, Oswestry and Holt before at last, on 24 September, English troops arrived. They routed the rebels who, sensing the tide was spent, returned home with their spoils, just as Wallace's supporters had once done in

Scotland. But like Wallace, Glyndwr was still at large, and he retired with his core retainers and much plunder into the Welsh mountains.

The revolt spread, to that ancient hotbed of Druidism, Ynys Mon or Anglesey, led by Glyndwr's cousins Rhys and Gwillym ap Tudur. During Easter 1401 they managed to capture the mighty Conwy castle by ingeniously disguising themselves as workmen. Their comrades then captured the town and held out there for a few months with a small garrison. They were forced to surrender the fortress in exchange for an amnesty from the English king but their audacious tactics inspired fresh recruits to the patriotic cause. In fact their exploits were more spectacular than Owain's so he intensified his campaign, determined to make it clear that this was a truly national war of liberation. He besieged the mighty Harlech Castle, then Caernarfon. Inevitably the English king was forced to muster an army and lead an invasion, and in October another English force snaked over the mountain passes exactly a year after Henry led his first desultory expedition against the rebellion. Glyndwr's guerrillas observed every movement of Henry's army, but fell back and took evasive action until the English were exhausted from tramping from one town to the next. They burned and looted everything in their path, in the time-honoured way, but Glyndwr simply evaporated, and his irregular troops melted into the eerie terrain like ghosts. An exasperated Henry secured six key garrisons at strategic locations and returned to Shrewsbury. In truth he had only made matters worse, because the infuriated Welsh peasantry flocked to Owain, who had now proclaimed himself as prince of Gwynedd. Envoys, if not ambassadors, were sent out to request recognition of Owain's status by the King of Scotland. Although these were rather quaint overtures they make plain that Glyndwr had a well thought-through programme which entirely depended upon his absolute belief in his personal destiny, and it was a Welsh Nationalist programme first and foremost, whose aim was to restore the past glories of Wales and annihilate its hereditary enemy, the English. Glyndwr was explicit in letters he wrote to various monarchs that he saw the war as a crusade, a Holy War. Such fanaticism was not peculiar to the Anglo-Welsh conflicts, but in this war there was a new, keener, sense of hatred and bitterness about the injustices against them felt by the common folk of Wales, a morbid xenophobia towards English people, a mood ugly and barbaric, yet strangely exhilarating. But in the snow-capped mountains of Snowdonia, where Owain was in hiding, the mood must have been mixed, because the splendours of Sycharth were now long gone. Support still came in from far and wide though, and the Welsh Oxbridge scholars arrived, as well as many Welsh journeymen, drovers and farm labourers who had absconded from England. There were many Welshmen who, for various reasons, but predominantly socio-economic ones, refused to back the insurgency, just as many Scottish nobles had opposed Wallace. Ultimately Glyndwr's appeal was rooted in the rural peasantry of Wales, and if he was to stand any chance of success they had to be firmly behind him, and now the English Parliament did Glyndwr a huge favour.

In March 1401 a series of oppressive and discriminatory measures were enacted against the Welsh, along similar lines to English policies in the West of Ireland. The Welsh, as an entire nation, were made liable for reparations and damages the rebels had caused. All public meetings, public fairs, private gatherings at households and conclaves of bards were prohibited. Weapons were to be turned over to the justices and fortified manors were ordered to dismantle their defences. No Welshman was to hold any position of authority or distinction. No Welshman could bring litigation against an Englishman unless it was heard in a court using English law. Plans were drawn up to make speaking the Welsh language a crime. Convicted Welsh felons, however minor their offence, were executed and city and borough ordinances made it an offence for a Welshman to remain within the town limits after dusk. In Bishops Castle a Welshman could be shot with a longbow after dusk, and in Chester he could expect to be beheaded. Englishmen were deprived of their legal rights if they married a Welsh woman. This early experiment in apartheid – and it amounted to institutionalised racism as wicked as any before or since – plunged Wales into chaos because the infuriated peasants, inspired by their bards and their priests, wound their way over the mountain tracks to join the rising. Now south Wales exploded and Abergavenny was attacked.

Owain was soon powerful enough and possessed such charisma that he could attempt to win over the crucial yeomanry class. In a letter to Henry Dwn, Glyndwr revealed how he had conflated the destiny of the country, with his own personal fate:

> We inform you that we hope to be able, by God's help and yours, to deliver the Welsh people from the captivity of our English enemies who, for a long time elapsed, have oppressed us and our ancestors. And now you may know from your own perception that their time draws close and because, according to God's ordinances from the beginning, success turns towards us, no one need doubt that a good issue will result, unless it be lost through sloth or strife.

Men like Henry Dwn had much to lose and they made their calculations with careful deliberation, but for the 'bare-footed rascals' the Welsh peasants, it was the Merlinic prophesies and portents that mattered most. It was supposed that a sign would be set in the heavens, the same star that had appeared over Bethlehem at Christ's birth would announce the liberation of the *Cymry* and when, in 1402, an exceptionally bright comet appeared they were no longer in any doubt – their prince was indeed the expected one.

The vaticination of the bards won over the peasantry, but it was to the Welsh Church that Glyndwr looked to gain influence with the nobles and middling landowners. John Trefor, bishop of St Asaph, and Lewis ap Ieuan (or Byford) prelate of Bangor both went over to the rebellion in 1404, when Owain was at the height of his fame. But in June 1401 he was still a mere renegade, and the process by which he established his mastery in Wales had been truly spectacular. Henry decided to trap Glyndwr by sending three strong detachments. The northern section was under the command of his dashing young son, Prince Hal, and from the east Lord Charlton approached. Another force was marching from Dyfed, where the English garrisons had held firm. Glyndwr was leading a small raiding party through the mountains only 120 men strong when he blundered into the 2,000-strong force from Dyfed, just as reports reached him that Prince Hal's force was nearby. Using the cover of the mountain mists Glyndwr retired into the barren country around Pumlumon or Plynlimon, 'the five peaks', and harried the Anglo-Flemish force as it followed. As they tramped through the bogland near to where the Severn rises near Hyddgen, 'Stag's Mountain', they grew weary, weighed down by armour and other encumbrances. They were, for the most part, foot soldiers. Glyndwr's men were lightly-armed archers, mounted on tough little hobblers, mountain ponies famed for their strength and endurance. After some hours, Owain gathered his forces and counter-attacked, slaying 200 men in a few minutes and taking many prisoners despite being vastly outnumbered and holding lower ground. The rest of the Anglo-Flemish force fled for their lives, and indeed the latter were mercenaries who had little patriotic motive for their military service. For the Welsh side this was a signal victory, and within weeks thousands of Welshmen joined the rebellion in mid-Wales and the south-west. With this new army Glyndwr switched his activities to the borderlands. Welshpool, Montgomery and Bishops Castle were burned before the rebels arrived at Radnor, where they destroyed the town and stormed the castle, slaughtering its garrison. The rebellion was now the longest-lasting in Welsh history, and the most successful, Henry was forced to dismiss his army at Worcester and prepare for another campaign, but his bungling in Wales had been noticed by predatory noblemen in England, as well as the kings of France and Scotland, and powerful Irish and Breton lords always on the lookout for profitable mercenary ventures.

The ancient lore that underpinned Owain's newfound status as prince, the *Canu Darogan* or *Cywyd-dau Brud*, which had captured the loyalties of the Welsh peasantry was now used in a diplomatic initiative to the King of Scots, Robert III. Glyndwr wrote to him, explaining the ancient ties between the two countries:

Brutus, your most noble ancestor and mine, was the first crowned king in the realm of England, formerly called Great Britain. Brutus begat three sons, Albanactus, Locrinus, and Camber. You are descended in a direct line from Albanactus. The descendants of Camber reigned as kings until Cadwaladr, and the Merlinic prophesy says that I will be delivered from my oppressors and bondages with your aid.

Similar appeals were addressed to the Irish and the Bretons, and a desperate delegation sent to solicit French support but, ironically, it was not from the Celtic nations that Glyndwr was to obtain the crucial external support he needed – but from within England itself. At Ludlow, Edmund Mortimer, exasperated at continual harassing raids over the border by Welsh insurgents and reliably informed that Glyndwr was near to Knighton, gathered a force of 3,000 well-armed troops against him, many of whom were Welshmen from the Mortimer fiefs in the Marches. On 22 June 1402 Owain's force was sighted on top of a steep hill called Bryn Glas known to the English as Pilleth. Edmund's troops sweated uphill in their padded tunics and heavy armour until Edmund's archers closed range on the rebel archers, who had the advantage of high ground. They could not respond in kind until they gained height. Glyndwr's army was apparently quite small, just over 1,000 men, and as soon as the English men-at-arms came to grips the lightly armed Welshmen would be routed. But Glyndwr had concealed a strategic reserve of about 700 men in a narrow defile hidden by woods, and these now smashed into Edmund's flank. The English panicked, and to add to the confusion the Welsh archers in their own ranks now turned their coats and began loosing arrows at Edmund's troops. Glyndwr's archers loosed a final volley and then charged, dispatching hundreds of Englishmen with halberds, bill-hooks, and long knives. A horrific slaughter ensued and it was later claimed that Welsh women emerged to roam the battlefield, where they cut throats, mutilating and emasculating dying Englishmen. This is often dismissed as English propaganda, but I see no reason why it should not be true. The previous year, Henry had permitted his troops to perpetrate acts of rape and beastliness throughout Wales and over 1,000 Welsh children had been taken as prisoners into England to become slaves. The girls were brutally mutilated with facial disfigurements and the boys castrated to prevent the reproduction of future rebels. Small wonder then, that local Welsh women vented their hatred on the suddenly stricken Englishmen, if indeed this atrocity was perpetrated by them. The English bodies were left to rot where they lay, and in the summer heat the stench was so overpowering that local people avoided the area, though the bones were eventually interred in a cemetery near St Mary's Church, which still exists. Human remains are still unearthed from time to time. This was a straightforward victory against a strong English army, against numerical odds, in open battle – but there was a greater prize taken at Pilleth. Edmund Mortimer, one of the most powerful nobles in England, had been captured. This meant that Glyndwr now had two prestigious English captives, Edmund, and Reginald de Grey, the man whose dispute with Glyndwr had sparked the original rebellion. De Grey was ransomed, but Henry dragged his feet about Edmund. It was known that elements of his army had defected to Glyndwr during the battle and despite the fact that this was a common feature of late medieval warfare, Henry chose to doubt Edmund's loyalty. What was more, Edmund had received minor wounds in the battle, which were tended by Owain's charming and beautiful eldest daughter, Catrin (or Catherine). He soon succumbed to her charms and the two were married in November. Edmund, with his powerful contacts and traditional feudatory authority over the middle-march, had defected to Glyndwr, and declared himself a rebel against a usurper King of England, Henry, stating that if Richard II, Owain's former master still lived, that he should be reinstated, but that if he were proven dead, that his own namesake, his nephew, Edmund, was the rightful English king.

Glyndwr had cunningly spread Henry's Welsh imbroglio into the heart of England itself, and soon his new son-in-law involved his brother-in-law, Henry Percy, known as 'Hotspur' because of his impetuous bravery in war, and his uncle Thomas Percy, in a joint rebellion. It was eagerly anticipated that Hotspur's father, also called Henry, the Earl of Northumberland, would join the campaign to overthrow Bolingbroke. The confederacy was joined by Archibald Douglas who had been taken prisoner the previous year at the Battle of Hallidown Hill. He was freed on condition that he returned to Scotland to recruit the most select warriors there for the enterprise. Hotspur and Douglas with a large army set off south without the Earl of Northumberland who was sick at Berwick. They aimed to march through Cheshire to Shrewsbury where Glyndwr's forces would conjoin, their object being to impress the county gentry and their forces into their army, Cheshire was still loyal to the former king, Richard II. Unfortunately for them, Glyndwr had troubles of his own. Lord Carew of Narberth had managed to raise a substantial force against the rebels just as they were heading towards Kidwelly to besiege and destroy the castle there, and Carew's well-equipped troops were approaching Carmarthen. Glyndwr was so disconcerted by this unexpected development that he consulted a *dyn hysbys*, or seer, named Hopcyn ap Thomas, who advised him that he would be defeated and captured if he continued his march on Kidwelly. He therefore aborted the mission and turned his army around for the proposed conjunction with Percy and Douglas at Shrewsbury. But time was of the utmost essence because King Henry was gathering his own army, at least 20,000 strong, which was at Burton-upon-Trent. He left Burton on 16 July 1403 and by the next day he had reached Lichfield, which lay on the old Roman road to Wales – Watling Street. Making all speed, the royal army reached Shrewsbury just a few hours before Hotspur on 19 July. The frantic effort to gain the town before Glyndwr could capture it, and thereby combine with his allies, was in fact unnecessary, because Glyndwr was nowhere near. Some local Welsh rebels did manage to reach Percy, but their numbers were not great and they were mainly light troops. Percy observed the royal standard flying over the castle, and immediately knew he was at a major disadvantage. The Abbot of Shrewsbury was sent to mediate, to avoid unnecessary bloodshed, but his efforts failed. Henry, although he outnumbered the rebel army, had every reason to fear battle. Hotspur was one of the most renowned soldiers of the day. There now followed one of the bloodiest struggles ever fought on British soil, at a place known ever since as Battlefield, just over 3 miles north-west of Shrewsbury.

On 21 July Henry and his gallant son Prince Hal (later Henry V) marched out to meet Hotspur. He had perhaps 20,000 men against Percy's 15,000 and the two armies confronted each other on a dusty field on which peas were being grown. A persistent and deadly exchange of archery followed, and Hotspur, seeing his men were getting the worst of it, resolved to decide the issue by leading a charge against the king himself. They hacked their way through to the royal standard, but Henry had expediently retired to the rear. Henry's standard was cast down and many hundreds of his elite troops were slain. The young Prince Hal was seriously wounded in the face by an arrow but refused to withdraw from the fight. In fact he redoubled his efforts and King Henry was encouraged to re-enter the fray and, smiting down his enemies right and left, managed to encourage his men to further efforts. Meanwhile, Hal had wheeled his troops around Percy's exposed flank and they began to roll up the rebel army and compress it in a killing-ground between his force and the main royal army. Percy was still acquitting himself manfully but was hit by an arrow that pierced his helmet and entered his brain. After three hours of bloody slaughter, which could be seen from the walls of Shrewsbury as a vast dust-cloud, the rebel army broke and ran. Over 7,000 men had been killed – three-quarters of them of the rebel army – and many more were grievously wounded. In thanks to God Henry erected a church on the site, called Battlefield. This decisive victory was a disaster for his enemies and most notably for Glyndwr. While he had managed to spread his revolt to all parts of Wales, this stood no chance of ultimate success unless he could coordinate his policy with Henry's English opponents, who were for the time being cowed and powerless.

Despite this famous victory, Glyndwr was still in a secure position in Wales. In August an English force was destroyed with great slaughter at Stalling Down outside Cardiff. Lord Carew responded by ravaging the country around Caerphilly. Glyndwr's forces managed to break in to Abergavenny and burn it when an accomplice opened a gate to them. His forces were so threatening to the citizens of Hereford that a delegation was sent to Owain offering large sums for him to desist from his border-raiding. By September King Henry had arrived at Hereford and once more led his forces into south Wales. With his English allies temporarily incapacitated, Glyndwr had intensified his campaign to obtain material help from the French and Breton mercenaries, and at last a small fleet arrived in his support. With his allies Owain once more attempted to capture Kidwelly Castle but was again repulsed. At last, in November, a French admiral named Jean d'Espagne arrived with a larger fleet and cut-off seaborne resupply to Caernarfon Castle and Beaumaris Castle, King Edward's mighty legacies. Two other mighty castles were put under siege, at Aberystwyth and Harlech, which both fell to Owain's forces in the spring of 1404.

Glyndwr installed himself with his family at Harlech and soon afterwards the Welsh rebels took Caerphilly Castle, which was partly demolished. Next, Cardiff was attacked and burned and its castle ruined before Glyndwr, flushed with these major successes, convoked a Welsh Parliament or Welsh National Assembly at Machynlleth, where envoys from France, Scotland, Brittany and Spain bore witness to the rebirth of the ancient Welsh nation. Resplendent in royal regalia which included a crown, orb and sceptre, Glyndwr took the title of *Owynnus Dei Gratia Princeps Wallie* 'Owain by the grace of God Prince of Wales'. On May 10 an embassy was dispatched to the French court requesting a formal alliance against Henry, and the treaty was ratified on 14 July. By the terms of the treaty, Glyndwr would receive the assistance of a large French fleet and a considerable force of heavy cavalry as well as vital siege equipment. As the year ended, Glyndwr, now comfortably ensconced at Harlech Castle, involved himself in an infamous intrigue, which reveals a great deal about his national vision for Wales and his devotion to the ancient traditions of the *Canu Darogan*, a document known as the 'Tripartite Indenture' which was drawn-up at the end of February 1405. Glyndwr, Edmund Mortimer and Henry Percy the Earl of Northumberland agreed that as soon as Henry was deposed his domains would be apportioned between the three. Edmund would receive the south of England, Percy the north of England, and Glyndwr's portion was to be Wales – but not the Wales we are familiar with in our time. The new Welsh border was to lie somewhat east of the Severn, and the boundary was set at Onnenau Meigion (Six-Ashes) between Bridgnorth and Kinver, the very place where I postulate that Cadwallon and Penda had conjoined to drive the Northumbrians out of Gwynedd in the seventh century. This was the place where 'a great eagle' would summon a Celtic army to reclaim Britain in the prophesies of Merlin. From the Severn Estuary, the border ran north to Worcester, and from the north gate of that city to Onnenau Meigion so that the course of the sacred river would henceforth lie entirely within Wales. Professor R. R. Davies remarks that such grandiose territorial ambitions indicate that Glyndwr (and indeed his co-conspirators) were 'losing touch with political reality', but this is to underestimate the extent to which Glyndwr had become deluded by his absolute faith in the ancient lore. When we consider how much he had achieved, from nothing, in the space of five brief but glorious years, perhaps we can understand how such visionary notions gripped his imagination, particularly as he had become an iconic hero of the Brythonic resistance. His recreated Welsh state, though it was not universally supported, restored Celtic pride. As David Moore remarks, 'Glyndwr did for the Welsh what Wallace and Bruce had done for the Scots, what Jeanne d'Arc did for the French, and what Jan Huss did for the Bohemians – he gave them respect, belief and an acute sense of who they were. In that sense, he succeeded.'

In August the promised French fleet arrived and anchored in Milford Haven. Unfortunately their crossing had become becalmed and all the vital destriers (warhorses) died of thirst. Nevertheless, the foot soldiers, with their sophisticated siege equipment, marched to Haverfordwest and Carmarthen. The size of the expeditionary force is not accurately known but was probably around 3,000 strong. They combined with Glyndwr's army and marched through Gwent to Caerleon, but Henry's army had so thoroughly devastated the area that the presence of another 'foreign' army frightened the poor inhabitants, who retired into hiding. Despite these less than encouraging omens Glyndwr now commenced the climactic endeavour of his career – the invasion of England. As at Shrewsbury, King Henry was not slow to respond. He arrived at Worcester on 19 August 1405, just in time to prevent the Franco-Welsh army from entering the city. Glyndwr and his allies retired around 9 miles to the north-west of Worcester, to the Abberley Hills, where Glyndwr's forces fortified themselves against Henry on Woodbury Hill. Henry marched out to meet them, as at Shrewsbury just over two years before, but no similar slaughter followed. The two armies were so evenly matched that neither side wished to be the one to initiate offensive action. On a hill at Great Witley, Henry's army encamped in full view of the Franco-Welsh army and negotiators were sent to break the deadlock. Owain was not minded to back down and so challenges were issued: great jousts took place on the open ground between the hills, in which 400 men were slain. The stand-off lasted all week, before Henry began to sense the demoralisation in the rebel camp. They were starving and deep inside England they could obtain no food supplies for 10,000 hungry Welshmen, and more poignantly, Frenchmen. The rebels and their allies found other comforts apparently: many local people claim descent from liaisons between the invaders and local girls to this day. Henry had no such difficulties and after a week he turned his army around and marched away, gaining a bloodless victory. The frustrated Welshmen harried his baggage train and wreaked havoc, but it was a pointless exercise. Glyndwr's invasion had failed miserably, and he turned his army northwards towards Bridgnorth, from whence its tired demoralised soldiers made their way back to their own country. The great liberation of Lloegyr had proven to be a damp squib. From that moment Glyndwr's rebellion was doomed, but the struggle was by no means at an end.

Early in 1406 Henry decided to press home the initiative he had gained from Glyndwr's abortive invasion of England by attacking Anglesey with a fleet supported by the English garrison of Caernarfon Castle, despite his crippling financial problems. The early enthusiasm for the rebellion was dissipating as the population was ground down by constant invasions by the English, but equally by fugitive Welsh war-bands who seized their diminishing food stocks. Glyndwr knew that he needed to offer a fresh vision for an independent Wales, underpinned by a Welsh Church independent of Canterbury with a Welsh archbishopric at St David's. This new archbishopric extended well into central and south-western England in the same way Glyndwr envisaged future Welsh control of the western Midland counties under the terms specified in the Tripartite Indenture. There was at this time a schism within the Roman Catholic Church, and there were two rival popes – one at Rome and the other at Avignon. The rival pope at Avignon agreed to recognise Welsh ecclesiastical independence, and exclusively Welsh-speaking priests in exchange for Welsh recognition of his legitimacy. Radical Church reform was then one plank of Glyndwr's programme, but another was the establishment of two universities – one in north Wales and the other in south Wales. This is a poignant demonstration of the primacy for Celtic people of a culture of learning and, although these were pious hopes then, in time Glyndwr's vision of prestigious universities for his country was eventually realised. None of this could change the stark fact that the rebellion had peaked. The only hope for Wales was further naval support from France, and Owain was convinced that this would soon be forthcoming. A French fleet did arrive, but it came to evacuate the men who had campaigned the previous year, not with new troops. A few Scottish and English renegades from the force who had come to grief at Shrewsbury arrived, but they were, as Professor R. R Davies remarks, 'broken reeds' – more hungry mouths to feed who were now mere felons on the run from royal English justice. Many parts of Wales now submitted to the English in their desperation for peace. By the close of 1406, Anglesey, the bread basket of Wales, had finally fallen. As Welsh hopes diminished, the mood towards Owain among some sections of the Welsh nobility soured, and those who knew their history recalled the fate of Gruffydd ap Llywelyn, Glyndwr's predecessor as prince, and plots were made to assassinate Owain. His own cousin, Hywel, tried to stab him but Glyndwr's breastplate saved him. Another scheme involved Dafydd Gam, later Henry V's master of archers at Agincourt. As punishment for his treachery, Hywel was entombed alive in the hollow of an enormous oak tree, at least according to folklore extant shortly after the events.

These desperate attempts to eliminate Glyndwr were the prelude to the expected English invasion and Henry hoped that another expensive operation could be avoided. In the summer of 1407, the vast English army brought up siege engines and artillery to attack Aberystwyth Castle, which was under the command of one of Glyndwr's most trusted lieutenants, Rhys Ddu. Despite constant bombardment and an effective blockade by land and sea, the Welshmen held stubbornly on to the castle all through the summer. Rhys and his tiny garrison could not hold out indefinitely and so he entered into negotiations to surrender but was overruled by Glyndwr, who took personal command of the defence of Aberystwyth in the autumn. The prince was obdurate that there must be no surrender or negotiations with the English. By early 1408 the situation was desperate, Owain had been abandoned by his French allies, and in February Lord Bardolf and the Earl of Northumberland were killed at the battle of Bramham Moor in Yorkshire, shattering the power of the Percy clan for good. The remaining Welsh rebels and their prince were on their own.

Desperate entreaties were sent to France and Scotland, but with the mighty Harlech Castle, Glyndwr's personal royal citadel, under siege the denouement was in sight. The two great castles hung grimly on, despite desperate privations and the harshest winter weather for a century. Edmund Mortimer perished of hunger and his widow, Catrin, and their children (Glyndwr's grandchildren) must surely follow unless surrender terms were sought. Harlech finally fell in February 1409, and Catrin and the four children were taken away to incarceration in the Tower of London where Glyndwr's relatives were slowly starved until they died. Somehow Glyndwr himself had slipped the net and had evaded capture. A small band of French and Scottish supporters managed to land on the north Wales coast and assisted Owain in reprisal raiding in Clwyd and along the English border. In late summer, the last faithful band of Glyndwr's hard-core followers, Rhys Ddu and his cousin Rhys ap Tudur among them, assembled a small mobile force and rode out on a death-or-glory mission into England, with the object of burning and pillaging Shrewsbury. Just as their ancestors, the Gododdin and Cynddylan, had done all those centuries before, they resolved to die rather than to live in slavery and dishonour. Owain's comrades were all slain and his surviving lieutenants were captured, to be publicly hung, drawn and quartered. Glyndwr was not among them, he had escaped yet again, but there could be no prospect of a comeback now. All he could do was to become an outlaw, emerging with a small gang of followers to burn the homes of men who had betrayed the cause, and to ambush English outriders in the wild mountain terrain of north Wales. Owain knew of the incarceration of his daughter and grandchildren of course, but in 1411 came the dreaded news that his precious son, Gruffydd, who had been made a prisoner of war, had died of the plague in his dungeon. These were the wretched personal costs of rebellion, and all across Wales folk both humble and well-to-do were grieving for their lost sons and daughters, grandchildren and cousins – and for their burned homes, ruined farms and their slaughtered livestock. For all its heroism the rebellion was a catastrophe for Wales, and now, with the energetic Prince Hal acting as regent in England, the Crown was to demand punitive reparations from the stricken country. In 1413 came the bitterest blow of all, when Catrin and two of her children expired from starvation. There was one last victory Glyndwr could hope for against the English – he could deny them the satisfaction of allowing himself to be captured. He would sedulously avoid Wallace's grim fate, for he was never found, and despite generous financial inducements at a time of substantial impoverishment, indeed famine, the Welsh people never betrayed him and he failed to respond to many offers of an amnesty. In 1415, he disappeared from the historical record. What became of the *Mab Darogan* has never been established with absolute confidence, but Welsh people, as ever, said that he did not die, and is living yet, like the glorious Arthur before him. Ramblers on the 'Glyndwr Way' a trail through mid Wales are still warned by farmers to avoid the mountains around the 'five peaks', where Glyndwr won his famous victory, for he still rides with his companions, on the lookout for alien interlopers. Such folklore tells of his enduring heroic status in Wales, a status he richly deserves, but he was also a crucial character in British history as a whole, a man worthy to stand beside Arthur, Cadwallon, Cadwaladr, Llywelyn ap Gruffydd and William Wallace. It had all been a glorious failure, at an awful cost, and it was almost the last gasp of organised Celtic resistance in the island, but the debacle had a fascinating post-script.

Glyndwr's daughter, Alys, married a country gentleman named John Scudamore who lived at Kentchurch, Herefordshire. Alex Gibbon postulates that Glyndwr, disguised as a shepherd, was given refuge for many years by the couple, spending his time between a bothy on Hergest Ridge, and Kentchurch Court itself, where a portrait said to be of him as an old man still hangs on the wall there. It is the face of a man pained beyond all imagining, the last of a line of warriors and kings stretching back into pre-Christian times. It is to be hoped he lived to see his grandchildren thrive in a prosperous, respectable household. In 2002 the Scudamore family revealed a secret they had kept for 600 long years. Disguised as a family chaplain and tutor for their children, Owain did indeed spend his final years at Kentchurch, and is buried near there under a mound at the village of Mornington Straddle in England, the last place the royal authorities would think to look. So, happily, living descendants of Glyndwr, and perhaps of Brutus 'the Trojan', first-crowned king of the Britons, survive in rural Herefordshire. Perhaps there are still other secrets, for the royal regalia of Wales, the crown, orb and sceptre, were never found. Perhaps they lie hidden, until the Son of Prophesy comes again?

There was one final gasp of organised Celtic resistance. Appropriately it came from King Arthur's old heartland – Cornwall. In 1497, Michael Joseph a smith from the Lizard Peninsula and Thomas Flamank, a lawyer from Bodmin, objected to unfair taxation levied upon Cornish folk for a war against their Scottish cousins. Fifteen thousand angry Cornishmen marched on London, initially on an unarmed 'pilgrimage'. Later, as their numbers were swelled by new recruits, Flamank thought it expedient to arm the mob. Henry VII decided to see if the Cornishmen would lose heart as they neared the capital but they came on, grimly determined to seek redress for the manifold injustices against the Cornish people. At Blackheath they encamped for the night, looking out over the immense sprawl of one of the largest cities in Europe, with a population of over 100,000, and the simple Cornishmen were astonished. None of them had ever imagined it to be a place of such size and wealth. King Henry waited for them with the royal army and the London trained bands – perhaps 20,000 men in total. Awestruck and demoralised, thousands of the Cornish crept away by night and deserted. Their leaders were quickly taken and hung, drawn and quartered. So the Celtic resistance ended in an ignominious defeat. Many may say that this was very far from the case, and this is, in a sense, true. The Highland Scots rose in 1715 and again in 1745, but these were wars of dynastic succession rather than purely nationalistic. In fact, the Cornish episode was a forerunner of the disputes and confrontations that culminated in the 'Rebecca' insurgencies, the Merthyr Rising of 1831, during which the 'Red Flag' was first used to symbolise working-class resistance, and the Newport Rising in Wales in 1839, the last full-scale armed challenge to government authority in Britain. These were essentially based on political and socio-economic grievances, and these were shared by the entire industrial working class, but with the 'Matter of Britain' and the ancient legends they had little to do, and so, despite their interest for the student of modern history, they do not fall within my purview here. The damp squib of the 1497 Cornish rebellion was, indeed, a collision between the ancient and modern eras, but there was to be one last twist in our story – an outcome so strange and incredible that not even the 'Masters of Brut' could have conceived of it in their wildest dreams, for the man who had ordered the execution of the Cornish rebels, Henry VII of England, Henry Tudor, was a Welshman, and claimed direct descent from Cadwaladr. Henry's heirs were about to take the ancient lore and transform it into the template for the greatest empire the world has ever seen.

16

The Once and Future King

Prince Hal became that iconic figure Henry V and, with the aid of his Master of Archers, Dafydd Gam, the one-time attempted assassin of Owain Glyndwr, he won the great victory of Agincourt in October 1415. Henry returned to a jubilant reception from 20,000 Londoners but died young at Meaux, leaving a baby son, another Henry – Henry VI of England. Henry's minority meant that he was not crowned King of England until 1429 and of France, more controversially, in 1431. The great French war of liberation under Jeanne d'Arc meant that 'the King's son lost all (that) his father won', according to a contemporary rhyme, and a new 'peasants' revolt' in England took place under Jack Cade. King Henry, who was a character unable to withstand intimidation, became an elective mute, and withdrew into a depressive coma. This precipitated a terrible civil war, the so-called 'War of the Roses' and unfortunately this conflict does not form a part of this history as such. Its outcome, though, proved quite another matter. Adolf Bastian, the anthropologist referred to earlier on in this history, noted a process whereby what he thought to be universal mythic themes were resolved into local variants, but the 'Matter of Britain' turned this process on its head. What had once been a recondite history/mythology of a particular folk, the Celts, recorded by an elite order of bards became, in time, an elemental and worldwide story, the mythical grounding for the 'British Empire', a term first used by the Welsh cartographer and antiquarian, Humphrey Llwyd, a contemporary of Dr John Dee. Henry VII's Welsh connections were, even being generous to him, rather specious. His putative Welsh lineage was anyway a mere sideshow; it was his ability to reconcile the bitter factionalism of the Wars of the Roses that constituted his main attraction after decades of awful conflict. However, though these recondite matters were peripheral to the English, to Henry himself they were paramount in his scheme.

Just as Cadwallon had once done, Henry returned from his Breton exile with an army around 2,000 strong. The motley force disembarked at Milford Haven and Henry unfurled the ancient banner of the Red Dragon of Cadwaladr, his putative ancestor through his grandfather, Owain Tudor. To our modern minds, these spurious connections seem like marginal issues, but to contemporary observers they contained an inherent importance because the context of the ancient Arthurian mythology had changed very radically at around this time. In the same year that Henry Tudor landed in Wales, 1485, Caxton published Thomas Malory's *Morte d'Arthur*. Now that Celtic resistance had been crushed after so many centuries, the character of Arthur presented considerable difficulties. Henry saw that he could reconcile some of these problems by utilising his alleged descent from Cadwaladr, the last of the British kings in the regnal list of Geoffrey of Monmouth. It was thought that Arthur, who was in a state of suspension between the ethereal realm and this world, would manifest in some new reincarnation, like the *bodhisattvas* of Buddhism, and that his superior qualities would mark him out. In fact, Henry could go one better, and he claimed that, via Cadwaladr, he was a direct descendant of Arthur himself and that his victory at Bosworth Field that had won him the crown had been a kind of 'second coming'. To emphasise this point, Henry deliberately named his firstborn son Arthur. His fate was similar to that of his unfortunate namesake, Arthur of Brittany, and he died aged only fifteen at Ludlow shortly after his wedding. Like his legendary namesake his body was taken by barge, this time down the Severn to Worcester Cathedral where he was buried. This necessitated a transmission of the Arthurian mythical status onto Arthur's brother, Henry, later Henry VIII. John Leland, the antiquary to the English court, hailed Henry as 'Arthur reborn' and this reawakened interest in the ancient lore meant that European scholars, among them such eminent men as Polydore Vergil, began to ask awkward questions about the historicity of Geoffrey of Monmouth's account and to denounce the melange of myth, poetry, folklore and history as nothing more than poppycock. This stimulated in its turn a response by English men of letters in an attempt to shore-up the credibility of the historical Arthur, and something more. If the Tudor royal dynasty really were the reincarnations of the heroic archetypes in the Arthurian drama, then surely that august and venerable figure 'Merlin the wizard' would reveal himself, and from his lips the future project of the Island of the Mighty would be revealed? During the reign of Elizabeth I, a man answering to the description of the expected magus became the court astrologer and magician to the Virgin Queen – Doctor John Dee.

Dee was born in London in 1527 but his people were Welsh – Dee is a corruption of the Welsh word *Du*, or 'black'. Nant-y-groes, the family home, was located at Pilleth, Radnorshire, within sight of the hill where Glyndwr had won his famous victory. Doctor Dee was one of the foremost scholars of his day: a mathematician, natural philosopher and astronomer, but also an occultist and an astrologer. He was an exceptionally devout Christian, keenly aware of the damaging religious fault lines in England following the Reformation. His magical researches led him to believe that it was possible to hold converse with angelic entities, who would reveal God's plan to reunite all Christians under the protection of a divinely ordained dynasty. This convenient revelation was well suited to the requirements of the Elizabethan regime. Pope Alexander VI had partitioned the 'New World' of the Americas by the expedient of drawing a line 370 leagues west of the Azores, apportioning the westernmost part to Spain and the rest to Portugal. The pope claimed that the Vatican had always known of the existence of these lands but had been forbidden from revealing the information. What was desperately needed was some prior claim that superseded the claims of the Iberian countries in North America. A Welsh antiquary, Humphrey Llwyd, claimed that a son of Owain Gwynedd, Madog ap Owain Gwynedd, had made landfall in North America in the twelfth century. Since Elizabeth, like Owain, was a descendant of Cadwaladr, then the North American territory belonged to her, and it was divine providence that the Native American population would now hear the English reformed gospel. Dee now developed Llwyd's theme of a 'British Empire' in his *Brytanici Imperii Limites*, which amounted to a manifesto for global imperial expansionism, in the name of opposing alleged evil forces infiltrated into the Roman Church (*Roma* was thought to be the opposite of *amor*, or 'love' – a malicious force) by means of spreading the English reformed gospel. Dee enlisted the aid of a talented scryer, Edward Kelley (or Talbot), who claimed conversation with angelic entities who communicated using a complex language called Enochian. A measure of the extent to which Dee was in Kelley's grip is that when Kelley announced that the angels had commanded that the men should swap wives, Dee obeyed despite being immensely distressed at such an immoral act. A child born to Dee's wife nine months later may well have been Kelley's. The 'language' of Enochian has been analysed by linguistic experts in more recent times and found to be consistent with a genuine language. It has been thought that the 'angels' with which the men communicated may have been malevolent, and cleverer men than Dee have been so entrapped. Dee became convinced that Arthur and before him Brutus 'the Trojan' had also led expeditions to the Americas. The Arthurian tales now became absolutely indispensable to the project of legitimating the British Empire.

The most important player in the process was Elizabeth, who was now glorified as if she were a deity and given exotic titles such as *Phoebe, Virginia,* and *Gloriana.* The cult had its basis in the notion that the young squire Arthur had served an apprenticeship in the court of a magnificent 'Faerie Queene' called Gloriana, as outlined in Edmund Spencer's poem of that name, dedicated to Elizabeth herself. Spencer was a member of the 'Society of Archers', which organised annual celebrations galas and pageants depicting the Arthurian tales. The explicit message was that the Arthurian court of Camelot has been restored in the shape of the Elizabethan court. The defeat of the Spanish Armada in 1588 came to be seen as a divine affirmation of this complex reinterpretation of history, with Elizabeth vindicated as the protector of a reformed Christianity that would unify the people of the world under a magical British dynasty. All this came about as a direct result of the 1,500-year battle for Celtic Britain but, like so many of the stories of the Celts, the British Empire was a fantasy, a pseudo-history. The fact of the British imperial project has passed away, and it is too easy to forget the complex and obscure process by which it came into being. But, although the proofs adduced for its establishment may have been spurious and obscure, there was a reality. The vicious and continual warfare against the Celts laid the foundation for the British Empire. Indeed, the Celts became an integral and important part of the worldwide imperial system. The island, which had torn itself apart in savage conflicts, now projected its dynamic energies outwards via the seaways and, although the empire is now senescent, if not extinct, it transformed the world in ways that will endure long after it has been forgotten. However, for all its achievements, this British imperial project was a distortion of the Celtic mythology. Far from being the originators of 'British' imperialism, the Celtic peoples were its first victims, as we have seen.

There were, however, other interpretations of the story of Britain, which gave rise to another rich vein in British mythic culture. On 23 September 1792 an odd meeting took place in London:

> This being the day on which the autumnal equinox occurred, some Welsh bards, resident in London, assembled in congress on Primrose Hill ... The wonted ceremonies were observed. A circle of stones [was] formed, in the middle of which was the *Maen Gorsedd*, or Altar, on which a naked sword being placed, all the Bards assisted to sheath it.

What were these mysterious bards doing in eighteenth-century Caer Lundein? The main instigator of the ceremony was Edward Williams, a stonemason, who had helpfully brought along some pebbles he had gathered to form the 'circle'. He was a Welshman and claimed descent from a family with a bardic tradition in Glamorgan. These were revolutionary times and men dreamed great dreams, including Edward, who proclaimed: 'I am giving you the patriarchal religion and theology, the Divine Revelation given to Mankind, and these have been retained in Wales until our own day.' These claims were not quite as spurious as they sound because the bardic tradition was still strong in some parts of Welsh-speaking Wales and Ireland. An *eisteddfod*, or bardic court, for the declamation of poetry, judgement and prize-giving, including a bardic 'chair', had been held three years earlier at Corwen. Perhaps as a member of the Celtic diaspora Williams felt his bardic destiny all the more keenly, for he took a bardic name 'Iolo Morganwg' (Iolo of Glamorgan), the area of Wales that, he claimed, possessed a continuous link to the ancient Druidic orders. The Druids were suddenly extremely fashionable, due in part to the speculations of antiquaries such as William Stukeley. Iolo dedicated himself to wandering around Wales, gathering poetry and folklore, to preserve it for posterity. In time he became one of the most eminent scholars of Welsh literature. Unfortunately, it has been shown that Williams fabricated some of this, or intruded his own material into the documents he had collected, and careless people dismiss him as a charlatan. But Iolo was something rather more than that, and it would be a brave scholar who would denigrate his most intriguing body of work. They would need to be a scholar of ancient Welsh, for instance, and possess the highest qualifications in the deciphering of ancient manuscripts. Within the suspect works are hidden priceless clues about the ancient Celtic philosophy that are probably correct. Iolo Morganwg did his countrymen an heroic service, for his promulgation of a Welsh patriotic consciousness centred on veneration of ancient history and culture almost certainly preserved the Welsh language, just as the ravages of industrialism were about to devastate Wales. The despoliation of nature in the name of technology and commerce had the effect of turning sensitive minds towards the fabled and mythic British past, and especially the Druidic religion. Iolo claimed that the ancient British Christianity had been 'strongly tinctured with Druidism', and there may be truth in this. The years following the French Revolution were fertile ground for strange sects, freemasonry and self-deluded and self-proclaimed prophets such as Joanna Southcott, a housemaid who had set herself up as the mother of an expected messiah named Shiloh. One of the twenty-four elders of this sect, which was at one time more influential than Methodism with over 600,000 followers, was a lexicographer named William Owen Pughe, who had been strongly influenced by Iolo's work on Druidic Cabbalism. It was probably Pughe who debated these concepts with one of the most visionary men of the time,

William Blake, but at this time Blake's significance was confined to a few close friends and his genius was unknown to the wider world. By conflating ancient British history with the outworkings of Christianity Blake effectively transfigures the Britain we are familiar with. In his *Prophetic Books*, Britain becomes the original Holy Land and the 'New Jerusalem' is the 'great wen' of London itself. 'All things Begin and End in Albion's Ancient Druid Rocky Shore', Blake claimed, but these statements are metaphors, rather than assertions of historical truth. As Blake stated himself, 'The nature of my work ... is visionary or imaginative; it is an endeavour to restore what the ancients called the Golden Age.' This 'work of the imagination' conceived of Britain as the spiritual centre of the world and his 'Golden Age' would establish the island as the centre of philosophical learning, as it had been in the days before the Romans came. Milton was also convinced that 'our ancient Druids created a cathedral of philosophy ... and God hath yet ever had this island under the special indulgent eye of his providence'.

The fate of the British Celts was neatly summed up by Geoffrey of Monmouth: 'To this day (they) suffer pain and deprivation and exile in their native land.' The agonising loss of their inheritance, the sense that they were doomed to eternal punishment for their collective sin, the awareness of a glorious quasi-historical past, all contributed to an emotional state the Welsh call *hiraeth*, a longing for a place and a time that has vanished into oblivion and so can never be reconciled or ameliorated. The poet R. S. Thomas made the sullen observation that in Wales there is no present, no future, only the past. But for the citizens of the Irish Republic there is at least the blessing that national self-determination has brought, and a pride in their ability to withstand the forces of imperialism down the ages. Thomas D'Arcy McGee wrote:

> Long, long ago, beyond the misty space
> Of twice a thousand years,
> In Erin old there dwelt a mighty race,
> Taller than Roman spears...

But the modern-day Republic of Ireland is one of the most enthusiastic members of the European Union, and this should come as no surprise. The Celtic/Irish Church had ancient links to Gaul and Egypt. Saint Patrick was said to have studied at the monastery of Lerins in the south of France, which was founded by Egyptian monks. Irishmen were still making pilgrimages to Egypt until the eighth century. The legacy of cruelty and oppression from British rule has meant that Irish relations with the United Kingdom have sometimes been less than cordial, though they are slowly improving. Scotland narrowly missed the opportunity to secede from the union in 2014, but the decision of the UK to withdraw from the EU in June 2016 means that another referendum on its status within the UK may well result in a parting of ways. In Wales, only the most Welsh-speaking areas decided in favour of the EU and an independence referendum there would seem to follow logically from a Scottish independence ballot. Even Cornwall is asking for a 'special status' and Bretons too have recently begun to agitate for more autonomy. The tensions that have lain sublimated in the island for hundreds of years seem set to re-emerge. The great Celtic diaspora means that there are more people of Celtic descent in the Americas and Australasia than the sixteen million in Europe. Only around a million of these still speak Celtic languages on a daily basis. Welsh, 'the Language of Heaven', survives in isolated pockets and the remotest of the mountain regions but there has been a genuine attempt to preserve it and nearly 600,000 people are fluent, though there are few if any Welsh monoglots. Byron Rogers remarked that 'the Welsh language, like the view, begins at 1,000 feet.' Cornish and Manx are technically extinct, but are being revived by enthusiasts. Irish survives in special reservations in the remotest regions, but over one million people speak it as a second language. Breton is spoken by a quarter of a million people in central and coastal Brittany. The latest economic cataclysm has had the effect of displacing young people from their native communities, endangering the base Celtic-speaking population, in the same way as the most talented young people are still drawn away from the West of Ireland. In the mountains of Scotland it is the same story, as the most sparsely populated area in Europe struggles to retain a viable population in the aftermath of the 'highland clearances'. Gaelic is spoken by less than 100,000 people in the increasingly confident Scotland, mainly in the Western Isles.

The Celtic diaspora includes many hundreds of thousands, if not millions, of Celts who live and work in England and, of course, many people who think of themselves as English are actually Anglo-Celts in the first place. At the 2015 Eisteddfod, the poet Benjamin Zephaniah made the interesting observation that Welsh should properly be offered as a second-language option within English schools, as French, German or Spanish are. It is, after all, the indigenous language of the island, as Tolkien said, and the idea seems so obvious that one is surprised it has not been mooted before. But the author would go further, and include an option for the study of Celtic history in the national school curriculum. At a time when many newcomers are arriving in this island, it is absolutely essential that they become familiar with the cultural traditions and history of the people who arrived before them. It seems to me that too little effort is made to acquaint them (or indeed the native population) with English history and culture, let alone the rich legacy of the Celts.

It is often said that those who do not learn from the errors of history are condemned to repeat them – but they never do. The same old mistakes are made time and again, and the bitter lessons learned, only to be forgotten, then the whole cycle is repeated. This is, it seems to me, an argument for some fundamental flaw in mankind, but these are matters for theological experts. When all is said and done, the Arthurian legends, and the religion of the ancient Celts, as well as their local interpretation of Christianity, have been a vital part of the national consciousness of the British people as a whole. At the core of those religious beliefs was the concept of the dying and reviving god common to many ancient civilisations. As a boy studying these stories I was struck by how strange it was that people preferred the Arthurian romance, the risible 'King Arthur' of Hollywood movies, to the 'reality', itself controversial but at least conceivably credible, of a Romano-Celtic resistance leader of whom we have only scant records. I was of course mistaken, because my 'historical' character was scarcely more credible than the cinematic portrayals. To find the truth of the matter, we must return to the beginning, to the mythical underpinnings of Celtic religion.

And so, as our long journey nears its end, we must now consider that great object of the Celtic quest, the mysterious vessel known as the Holy Grail. In 1891 a cauldron was discovered at Gundestrup in Jutland. It had been made in far-off Thrace and displayed typical Celtic motifs. The great god Cernunnos is depicted, the god of the hunt. Such horned gods were depicted as far back as the Stone Age, and in the Celtic pantheon they were supreme. The god assists dead warriors to immerse another in the cauldron, and a line of other warriors who have been previously sacrificed precede him to the Otherworld. This is an early depiction of a cauldron of rebirth, the ultimate source of the vessel that became known as the Holy Grail. These cauldrons were magical and mysterious. The great Celtic god the Dagda brought a huge cauldron from Murias, which could hold 80 measures each of milk, fat, and cornmeal, as well as sheep, pigs and goats, from which the mighty deity made his porridge. The god Bran has a giant cauldron too, from which no one ever leaves his table unsatisfied. In the tale of 'Culhwch and Olwen' in the *Mabinogion*, King Arthur goes on a quest in search of a cauldron belonging to a chieftain called Diwrnach; this is among the most ancient tales in all Welsh literature. The ever-replenishing cauldron is a great boon to the king and his community, but there is a price, for the cost is continual sacrifice, of the noblest, bravest exemplars of the tribe – its young and gallant warriors. The Celts were (and still are) obsessed by stories called 'sorrow tales'. As Jean Markale observed, they

> appear to delight in stories with what we would call unhappy endings, in expeditions which brought no earthly rewards but spiritual enrichment. The Quest for the Grail ends in death for Galahad and Perceval who find it; only Bohort survives. The Round Table story also ends in total disaster, with Arthur and all his knights, except Bohort being killed.

These ancient motifs were grafted onto the Christian story very early on. A story was put about that Joseph of Arimathea had brought either the dish or chalice that contained Christ's blood after the crucifixion, or alternatively the vessel containing the wine at the last supper, to Britain, where it was deposited at a simple wattle-and-daub church in Glastonbury, Somerset. The small wooden cup, much damaged by generations of pilgrims who had literally bitten chunks out of it, survived the Dissolution of the Monasteries in the care of the Powell family, who had received it from the hands of the last surviving monk from Glastonbury Abbey, to whom they had given shelter. The 'Nanteos Cup' as it is known, was recently lent out by its owners to a lady with a debilitating illness but thieves managed to steal it. An appeal on *Crimewatch* offered a reward and, on Friday 19 June 2015, the new 'Quest for the Grail' ended when an anonymous person handed the cup over to West Mercia police officers at a secret location, proving beyond any doubt the compelling power of the myth, even in our own cynical times. The Mirylees family, who inherited the cup, have now given it into the custody of the National Library of Wales in Aberystwyth.

This book has been devoted to the military and political struggles for control of the island, but ultimately the Celtic legacy to the world is spiritual, a gift of learning and peace. The Celts are individualists, even anarchists, they are rebels, and yes, they are philosophers and dreamers. They were eventually overwhelmed by more logical and rational races precisely because of these traits, as well as the fact that their resources, already constrained, were dissipated by internal conflicts. Their supposed predilection for rebelliousness is hardly surprising in view of the nature of their adversaries, but their most abiding quality is their immaterialism. The Celtic people were originally completely oblivious of the concept of judgement, or of punishment and reward, and Christian eschatology did not displace their original ideas about reincarnation and the afterlife. Of course, in our own time Celtic-descended people are as completely enmeshed in the acquisitive culture as their counterparts of any creed, race or class, but the wheels of industry and commerce turn somewhat more slowly in, say, County Mayo or Islay, Truro or St Davids, than in the great sprawls of London, Birmingham or Manchester. Here, at the westernmost fringes of Europe, a unique and ancient culture clings on, along those coastal margins that once united the Celtic peoples by facilitating a maritime highway so many centuries ago. These are the places, facing westwards towards the setting sun and the mysterious land they called 'Braesil's Island' (Portuguese sailors, when they made landfall in South America, thought they had found the mysterious island the Celts had spoken of, 'Brazil'), which exemplify all that is most sacred to these proud folk. As the

Roman Empire collapsed and the Dark Age descended, many men turned their backs on the doomed and corrupt edifice of Britannia.

One day, early in the fifth century, a young boy was taken by Irish slavers who were raiding in the area around Birdoswald Roman fort on Hadrian's Wall. His father was a magistrate and his son bore the Roman name, Patricius (Patrick). His parents were devout and respectable Christians but the sixteen-year-old was no missionary or theological expert, merely one among thousands of British slaves who were abducted to Ireland to become bond labourers; Patrick became a swineherd, perhaps in Mayo. Patrick escaped from bondage and took a ship to Gaul. He received odd intimations of a religious vocation which, by 432, resulted in him becoming a bishop, consecrated by St Germanus, who we encountered earlier in our story. He returned to Ireland and established himself at the mouth of the sacred River Boyne. The importance of his mission from Rome's perspective was that Patrick could act as a counter to the spread of the Pelagian heresy in Ireland in the same way Germanus had done in Britain. The project was designed with this limited goal in mind, principally as a ministry to the tens of thousands of British Christian captives. But God had larger plans, seemingly, because Patrick converted two Druids, Dubtach and Fiacc, the latter became the first Irish-born bishop. Patrick, though, was not a 'Celtic' Christian, he was Roman through and through. But his conversion of the Irish had extraordinary ramifications. Irish missionaries crossed to Britain where they immediately made converts of fine young men eager to become novices. The basis of Celtic Christianity was monasticism, which spread to Ireland through the still thriving contacts with Egypt. The monasteries that they founded stood in a direct line from the Druidic *bangors*, or philosophical colleges, and the transition was almost seamless. For the Celts the spiritual authority they respected most was that of the monk and the abbot, not that of the priest or the bishop. Ireland had long been an island with a reputation of being barbaric and heathen, but within a few generations it had become the spiritual hub of northern Europe, exporting its art, literature, and spiritual learning from Iceland to the Ukraine. Their way of life was mercilessly austere, and they did daily battle with demons sent to tempt them with luxury and vice. To escape the wiles of Satan they sought out remote promontories atop sea cliffs, islands off the western coasts, some of them bare of soil. Hundreds of Celtic 'saints' kept the guttering candle of Western European civilisation alive on the edge of the known world, the most famous perhaps, are St Ninian, St Iltud, St David, and St Columba but the westernmost extremities of Britain and Brittany are thickly clustered with places named in honour of more localised saints. Some say that an Irish saint, Brendan, even successfully reached North America and that the story of his adventures inspired Christopher Columbus.

There was something else about the Celtic monastic system that was remarkable: it offered a free education, and not just to its own people, but also to visitors from abroad who flocked to the famous schools of Armagh, Clonard, Clonmacnoise, Whithorn, Menevia (St Davids), Iona and Lindisfarne, for instruction. Their efforts succeeded in converting the north of Britain from heathenism before the Roman Catholic faith made inroads there. Irish monks, invariably known in Europe as 'Scots' established monastic settlements all over central and eastern Europe as far as Kiev. Their dedication and self-abnegation won the hearts of the poor rural folk, and having totally abandoned themselves to God's will, they were no longer concerned with vanity and ambition or status. They were kind, decent people, with deep stores of learning, healers and engineers, scholars and agriculturalists – and they did not always take themselves too seriously. An Irish monk, far from home, wrote a little poem to amuse himself in a cold scriptorium, dedicated to his pet cat, 'Pangur Ban', 'the fair':

> I and Pangur Ban my cat,
> 'Tis a like work we are at:
> Hunting mice is his delight,
> Hunting words I sit all night.
> 'Tis a merry thing to see
> At our tasks how glad are we,
> When at home we sit and find
> Entertainment to our mind.
> 'Gainst the wall he sets his eye,
> Full and fierce and sharp and sly;
> 'Gainst the wall of knowledge I

All my little wisdom try.
So in peace our task we ply,
Pangur Ban my cat and I;
In our arts we find our bliss,
I have mine and he has his.

Celtic 'saints' were not official like their Roman Catholic counterparts. Holy men had always been venerated and accorded a semi-divine status. The legacy of the Druids and the *gutuaters*, or 'fathers of prayer', which abounded in every Celtic community, and the stubbornness of the Celts in adhering to their own particular interpretation of the faith was what exposed them to later charges of heresy and even heathenism. It was men like the monk who wrote his rhyme in honour of his cat who saved western civilisation from extinction. They preserved the light of Christ, but also Latin literature and ancient classical philosophy for posterity, and we owe them an incalculable debt of gratitude. What is perhaps more remarkable even than these achievements, is the fact that they were accomplished in the face of the most extreme adversity, some of the most wretched times in European history. The abiding belief in the inevitable return of a semi-divine redeemer hero, an optimism not entirely predicated on Christianity, but inherent, gave them the faith in the future required to build and invent, study and explore, at a time when the rest of the world was falling apart. Jean Markale has this to say:

> For the Celts never looked back, they fed on the past solely to build the future. It was a measure of their confidence that myths like Avalon or Emain Ablach came into being. The Celts turned their eyes ever outward, above the real, towards the Land of Eternal Youth.

In Layamon's *Brut*, Arthur's final conflict is described. Constantine, the son of Cador, Earl of Cornwall and a kinsman of the great king, comes to comfort him as he lies mortally wounded. Arthur manages to speak to him:

> Constantine, thou art welcome; thou wert Cador's son, I give thee here my kingdom ... and I will fare to Avalon, to the fairest

of all maidens, to Argante the queen, and elf most fair, and she shall make my wounds all sound; make me whole with healing draughts. And afterwards I will come again to my kingdom, and dwell with the Britons with mickle joy.' Even with these words, there approached from the sea that was, a short barge, floating with the waves, and two women therein, wondrously formed; and they took Arthur anon, and bare him quickly, and laid him softly down, and forth gan depart. Then it was accomplished that Merlin whilom said, that mickle sorrow should be of Arthur's departure. The Britons believe that he is alive, and dwelleth in Avalon with the fairest of elves; and the Britons even yet expect when Arthur shall return.

Malory tells us: 'Yet some men say in many parts of England that King Arthur is not dead, but had by the will of our Lord Jesu into another place; and men say that he will come again, and he shall win the holy cross.' Arthur – in Welsh, *Arth*, or Breton, *Arz* – may derive from an ancient word for 'bear'. Bears retire from the world to hibernate, and it is just possible that this concept of a 'sleeping' god has its ultimate origins in the cult practices of Stone Age hunters. The god that had taken material form has vanished from mortal sight, and once the divine presence has left this world so begins the dissolution and chaos with which we are all too familiar.

The Celtic resistance in Britain, whether it was led by a historical king called Arthur or not, held the barbarians at bay for fifty crucial years in the fifth century. Behind the shield of the Romano-Celtic kingdoms, men like Patrick and Ninnian and Iltud and Samson and David were able to find a last desperate refuge in the far west, where they incubated the renaissance of medieval Christian culture in the remnants of the former Roman Empire. The British victory ensured that precious time was bought, and in that time the Anglo-Saxon heathens were tamed by Christianity – and this process owed just as much if not more to Celtic missionaries than to Rome. The tenacious battle to retain their land, language and religion meant that Christianity was not extinguished. Were Blake and Milton, ahead of their time in thinking that Britain would one day become 'a cathedral of philosophy'? In 1908, the Anglican Church acquired the site of the ruined Glastonbury Abbey and a vague but sincere spiritual revivalism has grown up around the town, based in large part on the Arthurian traditions. Perhaps the abbey may rise again? In 1190, the alleged skeletons of Arthur and Guinevere were exhumed in the abbey grounds. A Welsh bard had revealed the location to Henry II while he was on campaign there. They were buried deep, enclosed in a hollowed-out oak trunk and a leaden cross was unearthed. The cross was lost, but an engraving was made of it. It seems likely that it had been intruded by St Dunstan during renovation work to the abbey in the tenth century. The cult of Arthur was a highly lucrative business for the medieval abbey and it became one of the most prestigious pilgrimage centres in Europe. But, although the exhumation may have been an elaborate hoax, the evidence is not overwhelming for such a conclusion. There are ancient connections between Arthur and Somerset. The Tor itself is a possible Celtic hermitage or monastic site, occupied at about the right time. Arthur was supposed to have besieged *Aestiva Regio* 'the land of Summer' whose ruler, Melwas, had abducted his wife in *The Life of St Gildas* by Caradoc of Llancarfan. There are also strong legendary connections to Brent Knoll hill fort nearby; from the Tor, in the distance, the huge hump of South Cadbury Castle hill fort, which many people think is the most credible candidate for 'Camelot', can be seen. John Leland recorded the old legend in 1542: 'At South Cadbyri standith Camallate, sumtyme a famose toun or castelle. The people can tell nothing thar but that they have hard say Arture much resorted to Camallate.' As always, the tales say that there is a magic chamber beneath the hill, where Arthur and his knights lie sleeping, but the day will break when they awaken and the world will be transfigured once more.

Bibliography

Bartlett, W. B., *The Taming of the Dragon: Edward I and the Conquest of Wales* (Stroud, 2003).

Barton, Nicholas, *Stone Age Britain* (London, 1997).

Berresford-Ellis, *The Celts* (London, 1998).

Binchy, D. A., *Celtic and Anglo-Saxon Kingship* (Oxford, 1970).

Blake, S. & Lloyd, S., *The Keys to Avalon* (Shaftesbury, 2000).

Charles-Edwards, Thomas, *Wales and the Britons, 350–1064 AD* (Oxford, 2012).

Churchill, Sir W. L. S, *A History of the English Speaking Peoples* (London, 1956).

Davies, R. R, *The Age of Conquest: Wales 1063–1415* (Oxford, 1987).

Davis Randers-Pehrson, Justine, *Barbarians and Romans: The Birth Struggle of Europe, A.D. 400–700* (London, 1983 Edn).

Evans-Wentz, W. Y., *The Fairy-Faith in Celtic Countries* (London, 1911).

Graves, Robert, *The White Goddess* (London, 1948).

Gibbon, Alex, *The Mystery of Jack of Kent and the Fate of Owain Glyndwr* (Stroud, 2004).

Guest, Lady Charlotte (trans.), *The Mabinogion* (London, 1906).

Housman, A. E., *A Shropshire Lad* (London, 1896).

Kightly, Charles, *Folk Heroes of Britain* (London, 1982).

Markale, Jean, *The Celts: Uncovering the Mythic & Historic Origins of Western Culture* (Paris, 1976).

Moffat, Alistair, *The Sea Kingdoms: The History of Celtic Britain & Ireland* (Edinburgh, 2008 Edn).

Moore, David, *The Welsh Wars of Independence* (Stroud, 2005).

Morris, John, *The Age of Arthur: A History of the British Isles 350–650* (London, 1973).

Myers, J. N. L, *The English Settlements: Oxford History of England* (Oxford, 1986).

Piggott, Stuart, *The Druids* (London, 1968).

Sims-Williams, Patrick, *Religion and Literature in Western England: 600–800* (Cambridge, 2005).

Stenton, Sir Frank M., *Anglo-Saxon England: Oxford History of England* (Oxford, 1970 Edn).

Yeates, Stephen J., *The Tribe of Witches: The Religion of the Dobunni and Hwicce* (Oxford, 2008).

Acknowledgements

The author wishes to express his gratitude to all the kind people who have offered help and encouragement during the completion of this project, especially Tim Robbins, Dave Gardener, Al Perkins and Simon Rathbone. The author would like to thank the British Library for permission to use copyright material in this book. Individual photographers are credited alongside the captions. Every attempt has been made to seek permission for copyright material. However, if I have inadvertently used copyright material without permission/acknowledgement I apologise and will make the necessary correction at the first opportunity.

By the same author, also published by Amberley:
The Anglo-Saxon Age: The Birth of England
The Anglo-Saxons in 100 Facts

Index